Sir John Hawkwood

Sir John Hawkwood
Chivalry and the Art of War

Stephen Cooper

We talked of war. JOHNSON: 'Every man thinks meanly of himself for not having been a soldier, or not having been at sea ... were Socrates and Charles the Twelfth of Sweden both present in any company, and Socrates to say, "Follow me, and hear a lecture on philosophy;" and Charles, laying his hand on his sword, to say, "Follow me, and dethrone the Czar;" a man would be ashamed to follow Socrates ...'

James Boswell, *Life of Johnson*, Friday 10 April 1778

Pen & Sword
MILITARY

For Gaye, Izzy and Rosie

First published in Great Britain in 2008 by
Pen & Sword Military
An imprint of
Pen & Sword Books Ltd
47 Church Street
Barnsley
South Yorkshire
S70 2AS

ISBN 978 1 84415 752 5

A CIP catalogue record for this book is
available from the British Library.

Typeset in 11pt Garamond by Mac Style, Nafferton, East Yorkshire
Printed and bound in the UK
by Biddles Ltd

Pen & Sword Books Ltd incorporates the imprints of Pen & Sword Aviation,
Pen & Sword Maritime, Pen & Sword Military, Wharncliffe Local History,
Pen & Sword Select, Pen & Sword Military Classics, Leo Cooper, Remember
When, Seaforth Publishing and Frontline Publishing.

For a complete list of Pen & Sword titles please contact
PEN & SWORD BOOKS LIMITED
47 Church Street, Barnsley, South Yorkshire, S70 2AS, England
E-mail: enquiries@pen-and-sword.co.uk
Website: www.pen-and-sword.co.uk

Contents

List of Boxed Text

List of Maps and Illustrations

The Coronation of Gregory XI in Avignon is reproduced by permission of the *Bibliothèque Nationale de France*; *The Wolf of Gubbio* by permission of the National Gallery; the woodcut of Hawkwood and engraving of Sir John Temple-Leader by permission of the National Portrait Gallery, London; the illustration of Pont-Saint-Esprit with the permission of Alain Girard, *Conservateur en chef du Patrimoine* at the *Musée d'Art Sacré du Gard*.

FAMILY TREE OF SIR JOHN HAWKWOOD, c.1320–94

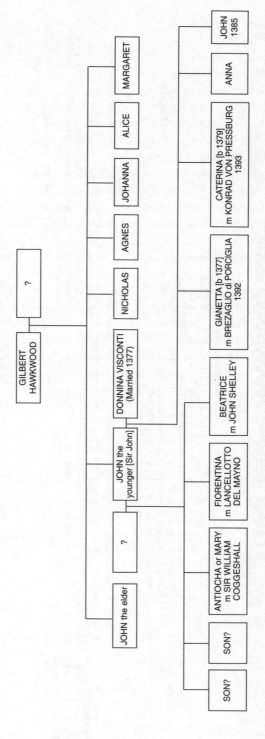

FAMILY TREE OF DONNINA VISCONTI c.1360–?

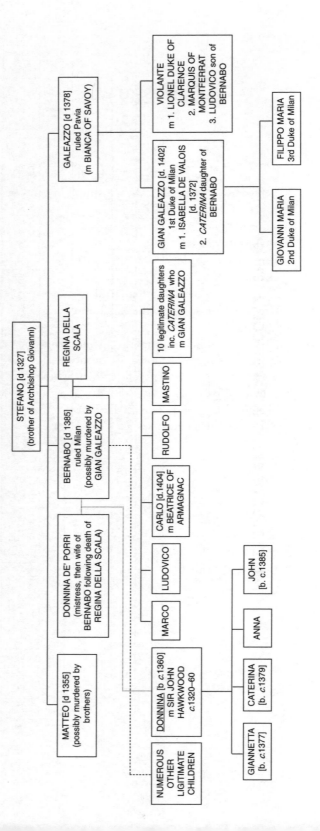

Glossary

barbute	A unit of two soldiers, typically found among German mercenaries (originally *barbuta* simply meant 'bearded man')
caporali	Junior officers
chevauchée	Mounted raid
condotta	A contract of hire
condottiere	A mercenary leader
feditori	Auxiliary troops
homage	The act acknowledging feudal allegiance
masnadieri	The common soldiers, the 'rank-and-file'
podestà	Governor
provvisionati	The locally raised militias, as distinct from mercenary troops
ribauds	A primitive form of mortar or cannon
route, routier	A band of mercenary soldiers, of which the *routier* was an individual member
Signoria	The governing body (e.g. of Florence)
vendetta	(An act of) revenge

Preface and Acknowledgements

Most people come across Sir John Hawkwood when they see his portrait in the Duomo in Florence, but I first came across him when I drove past the castle of Montecchio Vesponi, near Cortona in Tuscany. The guidebook simply said 'this was the home of the Englishman Hawkwood in the 1380s'. I found it quite extraordinary that an Englishman should have lived in Tuscany in the late Middle Ages and I wanted to know who he was. I was by no means the first to discover the castle, but when the English travel writer H V Morton did so in the 1950s, he found Montecchio in ruins, and its occupant completely uninterested in its former English owner. Fortunately for me, this is very far from being so today. Montecchio has been lovingly restored by Signora Orietta Floridi Viterbini, and I must thank her both for the ideas she has given me for this book and for her warm hospitality at the castle. I would also like to thank the people of Montecchio Vesponi and Castiglion Fiorentino in Italy and of Pont-Saint-Esprit in France for the welcome they gave me during visits in 2005 and 2007.

I emphasize the chivalric (not necessarily the chivalrous) aspects of Hawkwood's career, and for this I am profoundly grateful to Maurice Keen, Emeritus Fellow of Balliol College, Oxford, who inspired me with a love of medieval history when I was young and made many helpful comments on the typescript (without agreeing with all I had written). I also highlight Hawkwood's Englishness and his origins in Essex, for which I thank Valerie Nicholson, who also told me about the letters in Appendix 2. The emphasis on the legal side of the life of a *condottiere* is my own. Initially I relied on Temple-Leader and Marcotti's narrative and, unless otherwise stated, my source is to be found there, but in the course of writing this book I discovered that there are many more printed sources now than there were when they wrote in 1889. I consulted these in the Institute of Historical Research in London, and am very grateful to Margaret Kekewich for introducing me there, and for reading and commenting on the first three chapters in draft. I would also like to thank: Gabriele Oropallo of University College, London and Jeremy Heath for their help with translations; Paola Orrechioni and Fabio Giovannini for allowing me to read their theses about

Montecchio and for discussing their ideas with me; William Caferro and Dr Lorenzo Fabbri for the evidence relating to the presence of Hawkwood's body in the Duomo in Florence in 1405/6; Régis de Verduzan and Alain Dumont for the information they gave me about Pont-Saint-Esprit; my friend David Bostock for reading the whole text and giving me the idea of the boxed text; Brian Ditcham for his comments on Chapters 4 and 5; my colleagues Howard Connell and Adrian Barham for advice about heraldry, the High Court of Chivalry and notaries; Lieutenant Colonel Conway Seymour for his suggestion about 'ground'; Barry Dines and Nicholas Jones for their help with IT; my daughter Rosemary and Matthew Rowley for their assistance with the illustrations; and, lastly, Patrick Wormald, lifelong student of the Anglo-Saxons, whose intellect used to frighten me when we were undergraduates, but who encouraged me to write this book, shortly before his untimely death in 2004.

Stephen Cooper
Thorpe Hesley, South Yorkshire
October 2007

Introduction: The Battle near Marradi, 1358

John Hawkwood did not make the same mistake as Konrad von Landau, the German commander of the Great Company. In the summer of 1358 Landau led his men to ignominious defeat near Marradi in the central Apennines. Most surprisingly, this defeat was inflicted on professional soldiers by an amateur Italian militia, people whom Landau would undoubtedly have regarded as 'peasants' (*villani*) – the term used by the chronicler.

This Great Company was a freelance organization, several thousand strong, though composed of many smaller units. It originally came together in the 1340s and its first commander was Werner von Urslingen. Its second was a Provencal, Montreal d'Albarno, known in Italy as Fra' (Friar) Moriale. Von Landau was its third commander. In 1358, he found himself in Romagna, where he accepted an offer from Siena to attack Perugia. To get there, he needed to cross the Apennines and territories controlled by the Florentine republic. He negotiated the route he should take with the Florentines and with a deputy appointed for the purpose by the new Holy Roman Emperor, Charles IV. Eventually, terms were agreed: he and his men would travel via Marradi, Biforco, Dicomano, Isola, and descend in due course to Bibbiena. The agreement provided in detail for the way in which Landau and his men would be supplied en route.

Things did not go smoothly. At Marradi the Count's men helped themselves to the supplies they needed, without paying the agreed sums, and they committed various 'outrages', both 'by word and by deed'. The local people met to discuss how to recoup their losses and take their revenge. The men of the neighbourhood agreed to mount an attack in the mountains the following day; but word of the plot got back to Landau. He was warned that there was a plan to attack his column as it climbed the pass at the top of the Val di Lamone, but he took no notice. He arrogantly assumed that the local militias would be composed of a few amateur countryfolk, inferior in every way to his professionals, who were well armed, well trained and above all experienced. He decided to carry on and he divided his forces in the usual way – vanguard, main force and rearguard – placing himself in the middle of the column, along with some Florentine dignitaries.

He was wrong to underestimate the militias. They knew the ground and they spread out along the heights and surprised the mercenaries at a narrow defile called Le Scalelle ('the Stepladders'). They rolled boulders down from the hilltops. They threw stones from the slopes. They blocked the Count in, and cut him off from those who could assist him. Above all, they made it impossible for him to deploy his cavalry. Landau did not give up easily: he dismounted 100 of his best Hungarian archers and ordered them to chase their tormentors, but the archers were weighed down by their heavy jackets and encumbered by their weapons, and pursuit proved impossible in the face of fierce resistance from the enemy occupying the high ground. The militias wore their opponents down, until they felt bold enough to rush down and attack the centre of the column in hand-to-hand fighting. Landau defended himself with his sword but, attacked by no fewer than twelve men, he surrendered, receiving a serious head wound as he did so. It is recorded that 300 cavalrymen were killed, and a substantial number taken prisoner, including Landau himself (though he was ransomed soon afterwards). More prisoners were taken by locals who had not participated in the battle, as the mercenaries fled down the mountain. More than a thousand warhorses were captured, together with 300 hacks and quantities of valuable equipment, armour, clothing and cash. Local women, attracted by the noise of battle, rushed to help their menfolk. Others stayed to strip the corpses and help themselves to the clothing worn by the prisoners.[1]

The Battle of Le Scalelle was a highly dramatic reversal of fortune. Given the inequality of arms, it was very unusual for local men (and extraordinary for women) to resist the mercenaries. The battle must have been much talked about around the camp-fires of Italy, and in the towns and monastic *scriptoria* where the chronicles were written. Hawkwood was in France at the time; but he may have heard about the battle even there – news travelled faster than we imagine. He would certainly have heard about it three years later, when he arrived in Italy, for he fought Konrad von Landau's men several times, and in later years became acquainted with the Count's sons, who were all mercenary captains in their day. The Free Companies were fluid organizations, made up of contingents which came together, dissolved and re-formed, bringing tales of triumph and disaster with them. Hawkwood had a long and successful career in Italy, from 1361 until his death in 1394. He knew what could happen when a leader behaved arrogantly, took unnecessary risks and ignored sound advice – especially when crossing the Apennines. He was not like Konrad von Landau, whose fate was still spoken of in Venice in the 1520s. Hawkwood became famous for his prudence, as well as for his long experience.[2]

Chapter 1

'A Fine English Knight': France, 1360–2

He thought that to return to his own country would bring him no profit.

Jean Froissart, *Chronicles*

In 1314 a huge English army went down to devastating defeat at the hands of Robert the Bruce, at Bannockburn near Stirling. The Scots invaded England, occupied parts of the North and imposed peace on their terms. The English grip on Scotland was broken for a generation, some would say for ever, and the reputation of their arms reached an all-time low (though it is possible that they learned much from their defeat). By 1360, after the English victories at Halidon Hill, Crécy and Poitiers, the situation was dramatically reversed. The reputation of English soldiers rose to unprecedented heights. John Hawkwood was one of the beneficiaries, and possibly one of the agents, of this transformation.

Hawkwood's Origins and Early Life
The chronicler Jean Froissart (1337–1410) tells us that:

There was in the march of Tuscany in Italy a valiant knight who was called Sir John Hawkwood [Messire Jean Haccoude], who carried out many armed enterprises there, and who had done so before. He had come there out of the kingdom of France when the peace was made and negotiated between the two kings at Brétigny of Chartres. At that time he was a poor bachelor-knight. He thought that to return to his own country would bring him no profit; and when it was agreed in the peace treaties that all the men-at-arms had to leave the kingdom of France, he made himself leader of a band of companions, whom the people called Late Comers [Tards-Venus]. They arrived in Burgundy and in that place there assembled a great multitude of these bands of English, Bretons, Gascons, Germans and members of Companies of all nations ...

Note the obscure beginnings. Hawkwood is already a knight, but a 'poor' one, and he is a mere 'bachelor' – on the lowest rung of knighthood. In Chaucer's

Canterbury Tales, it is the squire who is described as 'a lusty bachelor', while in Marco Polo's account of his travels, Marco is presented to the Great Khan as 'a young bachelor', though he was not a knight at all; but the term does not necessarily mean that the knight was still learning the trade. Sir John Chandos was described as a bachelor at the Battle of Poitiers in 1356, and he was very far from being an apprentice.

Froissart also mentions Hawkwood in his account of an interview with a Gascon called the Bascot of Mauléon, in an inn called The Moon in the Pyrenees. This Bascot may be a creation of the chronicler's imagination, but his story has the ring of truth, and, looking back, he tells us that Sir John was both a 'fine English knight', and the captain of a company (or *route*). The veteran soldiers are described in glowing terms:

> I tell you that in that assembly there were three or four thousand really fine soldiers, as trained and skilled in war as any man could be, wonderful men at planning a battle and seizing the advantage, at scaling and assaulting towns and castles, as expert and experienced as you could ask for ...

Very little is known about Hawkwood's early life. Modern historians are not even sure when he was born, 1320 being the conventional date. Some of the Italian chroniclers tell the ridiculous story that he was born in a wood frequented by hawks,[1] but the serious point is that he was undoubtedly a commoner, in an age which attached greater importance to the circumstances of a man's birth than our own. His father Gilbert was a tanner in the village of Sible Hedingham, though he also owned land and was not a poor man. Hawkwood was a younger son, with an elder brother, also called John and referred to in later conveyancing transactions as 'John the Elder'; he had a younger brother called Nicholas and four sisters. Under the system of law which prevailed in most English counties, the eldest son inherited family land, whether or not the father made a will, and Gilbert Hawkwood's will therefore mentions only personal property: cash, furniture, animals and cereal crops. When he died in about 1340 Gilbert left our John Hawkwood only £20 and 100 *solidi* (shillings), though each of the three sons was also given five quarters of wheat, five of oats, and bed and board for a year.

Some time after the end of the year specified in Gilbert's will, Hawkwood did what countless other younger sons in England have done, and left home to become a soldier. Filippo Villani wrote that an uncle who had served in the French wars helped him, and that could well have been so. Sible Hedingham is contiguous with Castle Hedingham, which had an important castle, seat of the de Veres since the twelfth century, and it is often also assumed that Hawkwood first went to France as part of the retinue of John de Vere, 7th Earl of Oxford (1313–60). This de Vere was one of Edward III's principal commanders: he fought in Scotland and at Crécy and Poitiers in France, and was killed at the siege of Reims in 1360. There are traditions that Hawkwood fought alongside de Vere, just as there are stories that he was knighted by the King or the Black Prince, but there is no hard evidence for any of this and it is equally likely that he became a knight by other means. To understand why, we need to look at the type of warfare the English were involved in, during the first phase of what was (much later) called 'the Hundred Years' War'.

The Hundred Years' War and the Reputation of English Arms
There were several reasons for the great conflict between the English and the French kings, which (conventionally) began in 1337 and lasted until the English were finally expelled from France in 1453. French support for Scottish independence was one. Another was the English King's uneasy position as vassal of the King of France for his fiefs in Gascony in south-west France. Edward III's claim to the French throne (through his mother Isabella) became a third, though he only asserted this after the commencement of hostilities. Underlying it all was a keen desire on Edward's part to humble the Valois dynasty, whom he came to regard as usurpers.

During the reign of his father Edward II (1307–27), English armies had suffered a number of disasters, both in Scotland and Gascony, and, when Edward II was deposed and murdered, the standing of the monarchy plunged to new depths. His successor showed very quickly that he was made of sterner stuff. The young Edward III restarted the war with the Scots and defeated them at Halidon Hill, near the border, in 1333. This was a great victory, celebrated in particular by the York chronicler, who had no time at all for the Scots, but Scotland was always a sideshow and, once the continental war began in earnest, most of the fighting was done in France. The French raided Southampton, Portsmouth, Dover and Folkestone in the 1330s; they came burning all along the south coast in 1377, and they *and* the Scots ravaged the North of England in 1385; but they were never able to equal William the Conqueror's feat of launching a full-scale invasion across the Channel. By contrast the English occupied large parts of France throughout the long war and mounted long-distance armed raids (*chevauchées*) into the very heart of the Valois domains. Hawkwood was involved in the fighting along with many other Essex men.

At first the war did not go well for Edward. The Kingdom of France (though smaller than the Republic today) was twice as big as England, much more densely populated and potentially very much richer. Moreover, her Capetian monarchs had made her the leading military power in the West. Edward's early strategy was to buy alliances in the Low Countries and the Holy Roman Empire, with money borrowed in Italy. This was a failure, but he learned by his mistakes and switched to a strategy involving a number of separate strikes, at the same time exploiting wars of succession in the French provinces. The year 1346 was a 'Year of Victories': Henry of Grosmont raised the siege of Aiguillon in Gascony; the King's own campaign in Normandy and Picardy culminated at Crécy, where the English archers shattered the French cavalry; and the Archbishop of York and the northern barons defeated the Scots at Neville's Cross near Durham, capturing the King of Scots, David Bruce. In the next year, 1347, the King's forces took Calais after a siege lasting eleven months, and Sir Thomas Dagworth captured Charles of Blois, the French claimant to the Duchy of Brittany, at La Roche Derrien. In 1349 Edward founded the Order of the Garter, to commemorate his victories and assert the justice of his cause.

Because of the devastating effects of the Black Death, there was a lull in the fighting for some years, but then a new series of attacks on Valois France began. The Black Prince led two *chevauchées* in 1355 and 1356, the first from Bordeaux, across the Langue d'Oc to Narbonne and back, a second northwards across the Loire. As the Prince made his way back to Gascony after the second raid, the French caught up with him near Poitiers, where he inflicted another defeat on them, more shattering even than Crécy. The French suffered 2,500 dead, and 3,000 prisoners were taken. Among the dead was the Constable of France, Walter of Brienne, dictator of Florence for a few brief months in 1342. Among the prisoners was Jacques de Bourbon, a member of the French royal family, captured by the Captal de Buch but resold to the Prince for 25,000 *écus*. Most catastrophic of all for the French, King John II – 'John the Good' – fell into the hands of the English. It was the long list of noble prisoners which most impressed the chronicler in Montpellier who wrote the curiously named *Thalamus Parvus*. Hawkwood would have been about twenty-six at the time of Crécy and thirty-six at the time of Poitiers, but it is not known whether he fought in either of these battles. He *could* have done, but he is not recorded among those rewarded with money, annuities or offices. By one means or another, he became familiar with English strategy and tactics.

The capture of John II gave Edward III immense bargaining power and he was able to negotiate a favourable peace treaty four years later, despite the relative failure of his last campaign in 1359. At Brétigny in 1360 the French agreed to cede the town of Calais, the county of Ponthieu (near the Somme) and a vast new Duchy of Aquitaine, far larger than the old Gascony. This Duchy was ceded in full sovereignty, so that the Plantagenets would no longer have to do homage to the Valois. In return Edward agreed to give up his claim to the French Crown, evacuate his forces from those parts of France not ceded, and release King John against the promise of 3,000,000 gold *écus*, an *écu* being worth about 40p (or 8 shillings) in 1360. This was a truly enormous sum, though it was payable by instalments. It was seven times larger than the ransom set for the King of Scots three years before.[2]

In their war with the Valois, Edward III and the Black Prince restored the reputation of English arms. Jean le Bel thought that:

When the noble Edward first gained England in his youth, nobody thought much of the English ... Now ... they are the finest and most daring warriors known to man.

The Italian poet Petrarch thought much the same:

In my youth the English were regarded as the most timid of all the uncouth races; but today they are the supreme warriors; they have destroyed the reputation of the French in a succession of startling victories, and men who were once lower even than the wretched Scots have crushed the realm of France with fire and steel.

From the time they started to invade France in strength, the English aimed to inflict economic damage and show that the Valois usurper could not guarantee the security of his people. Geoffrey le Baker's chronicle of Edward III's march through Normandy in 1346 is full of images of destruction while, after the fall of Calais, Thomas Walsingham (a monk at St Albans) wrote disapprovingly that there was scarcely a woman in England who was not decked out in some of the spoils. The *chevauchées* mounted by the English were a form of attrition. The idea was to ride through those parts of France not already in the hands of the English or their allies, burning and raiding on a wide front, but avoiding pitched battles and sieges. This strategy worked well in the 1340s and 1350s, when men of the calibre of Henry of Grosmont and the Black Prince were in charge. It is generally thought to have worked less well in the 1370s and 1380s. Even then a *chevauchée*, whether led by a common soldier like Sir Robert Knollys (1370), or by a royal prince like John of Gaunt, Duke of Lancaster (1373), or Thomas of Woodstock, Duke of Gloucester (1380), still had the power to inflict widespread damage. Thomas's own account of the raid he led in 1380, as related by Froissart, was still enthusiastic:

I still remember my last campaign in France. I suppose I had two thousand lances and eight thousand archers with me. We sliced right through the kingdom of France, moving out and across from Calais, and we never found anyone who dared come out and fight us ...

These expeditions were very lucrative. The laws of war allowed the victor to take prisoners, releasing them afterwards on parole, and collecting the ransom later. It was common practice for English soldiers to pay one-third of their profits to their captain, who in turn paid a third of what he earned to the Crown, and ransoms became marketable commodities. The Black Prince sold prisoners taken at Poitiers for £20,000, but even a knight or a mere squire could win an enormous sum. Sir Thomas Dagworth was offered £4,900 for Charles of Blois, while the ransom for the Count of Denia, captured at Nájera in Spain in 1367, led to protracted litigation in the High Court of Chivalry in England in the early 1390s.

The French war presented great opportunities to men like Hawkwood, and after Poitiers these included the chance to make a profit on their own account. The French King was a prisoner, and his kingdom was in chaos. The commoner Étienne Marcel seized power in Paris, while Charles 'the Bad', King of Navarre (and lord of extensive estates in northern France) made trouble elsewhere. The lower orders rose in a terrifying revolt known as the Jacquerie. The Free Companies – bands of soldiers fighting in their own interest and including hard men from many parts of Europe – took advantage of the breakdown of law and order to mount raids of their own. The devastation lasted for years, so that when Petrarch journeyed through France (once renowned for her beauty) he found her 'a heap of ruins'.

In 1358–9 the Free Companies raided Burgundy, Brie and Champagne. A Welsh captain whom Froissart called 'Ruffin' concentrated on the area between the Seine and the Loire. Robert Knollys marched from Brittany to Auxerre, captured the town and sold it back to the inhabitants, though not before helping himself to choice items from the treasury of St Germain. The Gascon, Bernard de la Salle, in Froissart's phrase a 'strong and clever climber, just like a cat', took the town of Clermont. This man became a rival to Hawkwood in Italy.

Hawkwood became a knight at this time. Froissart tells us that the man called Ruffin 'made himself' a knight, while Robert Knollys is said to have had two of his men confer the dignity on him after he had captured Auxerre. Hawkwood may well have done much the same thing. No great ceremony was required: a simple 'accolade' – a blow or a cuff – was enough, but it did normally require a knight to make another knight, and it is unlikely that he disregarded the conventions altogether, as 'Ruffin' did. Froissart describes him as 'a poor knight, having gained nothing but his spurs', but knighthood brought important advantages. For the professional soldier, the 'Sir' lent authority. It increased the new knight's bargaining power, enabled him to make other knights (as Hawkwood later did in Italy) and meant that, if he was captured, he was more likely to be ransomed than killed out of hand. It was for this reason that Robert Knollys announced his worth to the world: his banner bore a simple message:

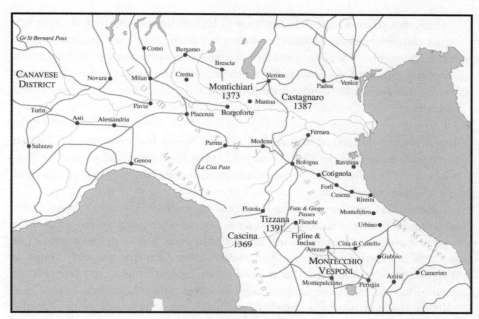

Montecchio Vesponi and Hawkwood's major battles.

> Whoever shall take Robert Knollys
> Will win 100,000 *moutons*.[3]

The Treaty of Brétigny and the Free Companies

With hindsight we can see that the Treaty of Brétigny of 1360 marked the end of a phase in the Hundred Years' War. Many now take a dim view of that war and of Edward III's achievement, but medievalists and military historians tend to be more kind, taking the view that Edward was one of our most successful commanders and rulers. There is no doubt that, for Hawkwood, the war proved a stepping-stone.

The terms agreed at Brétigny were ratified at Calais. Each side agreed to abandon the towns and fortresses in the provinces not ceded to the other, and an early date was set for evacuation. In accordance with these arrangements, most English soldiers returned home at the end of their contracts, as instructed, but, like many other members of the 'free' companies, Hawkwood stayed in France. There was no standing national army for them to join if they went home. The Bascot of Mauléon explained their dilemma well:

When this peace was concluded, one of its conditions was that all fighting-men and companions-in-arms must clear out of the forts and castles they held. So large numbers of poor companions trained in war came out and collected together. Some of the leaders held a conference about where they should go and they said that, though the kings had made peace, they had to live somehow.

A few of those who stayed 'turned French' and a very few even married French women, but most sold the castles and lands they had seized and joined the Free Companies. They continued to live off the land, as they had largely been expected to do when on *chevauchée*.

It was at this time that an organization calling itself 'the Great Company' came into being in eastern France. This was not a new phenomenon, since previous armies had used the name, both in France and in Italy. The term 'great' related to size rather than any finer quality, but size was important, for a Great Company could plan a campaign, carry out major operations and if necessary defend itself against official forces. A single *route* might be numbered in hundreds, but a Great Company could muster thousands of soldiers. Some have estimated that the Company of 1360 comprised as many as 12,000 men.

These unofficial Companies were highly organized and had constables, secretaries, treasurers and other officers. There were professional pillagers to seize supplies and loot, and booty-men (*butiners*) to share it out. The *bandes blanches* even had their own white uniforms. The Great Company of 1360 had captains of many nationalities, including English, Gascons, Spaniards, Navarrese, Germans and Scots, tough men who brought their own military traditions with them. Many of them were commoners like Hawkwood, some of them were illegitimate, some of them had *noms de guerre* – Bras de Fer ('Iron-Arm'), Tête-Noir ('Black-Head'), and Le Limousin ('the Man from Limoges'). We will meet men like these again, in Italy.

The Capture of Pont-Saint-Esprit and Hawkwood's Arrival in Italy

Having raided Burgundy, the Great Company turned on Provence. The most obvious target would have been Avignon, principal seat of the Papacy between 1309 and 1377. The Papal Palace there housed an underground Treasury which received revenues from the whole of Western Christendom, and the town of Avignon had grown rich as a result. Already on a vital trade-route between the Low Countries and Italy, it had benefited from the pontifical court's need for foodstuffs and luxury items of all kinds. It was here that Francesco di Marco Datini, Iris Origo's 'merchant of Prato' (1335–1410) first set up shop, dealing in woollen cloth, silks, spices, salt, and armour.

Unfortunately for the Great Company, Avignon was not an easy target. By 1360, successive popes had built castles in the surrounding countryside, ringed the city with new walls and machicolated towers, and turned the Papal Palace into a tremendous double keep, built on rock and invulnerable to sappers. Still impressive today, the fortress was all but impregnable then. Instead the mercenaries homed in on Pont-Saint-Esprit, a much smaller town about twenty-five miles north of Avignon. There were several reasons for doing so. Here was a fine bridge, the hub of a network of routes. The town itself was a centre for the corn and wine trades and a place where taxes and tolls were collected. A company which held the bridge could prey on the wealth of the Church by raiding the papal enclave known as the Comtat Venaissin, capturing ecclesiastical dignitaries, courtiers, merchants, bankers and travellers, and intercepting vessels on their way to the papal court. Most important, there were reports that part of the money raised to pay King John's ransom was due to arrive. All the provinces of France had been required to pay a contribution, and the levies collected in the Langue d'Oc – from Toulouse, Carcassonne and Nîmes – were coming north, escorted by an armed guard headed by Jean Souvain, the Seneschal of Beaucaire. Rumours that 40 kilos of bullion were about to arrive – or had already arrived – in Pont-Saint-Esprit triggered the assault on the town.[4]

The capture of Pont-Saint-Esprit came to the attention of the chronicler of Montpellier, in the south of France, and of Jean de Venette in the north, but each gives only a brief account. The first writer is more concerned to castigate the 'English', and the 'false French' guilty of helping them. The second damns the entire Great Company as 'miscreants' for daring to attack the Holy Church of God. Froissart gives a fuller account:

These Companies got information that at the Pont du St Esprit, seven leagues from Avignon, there was very great wealth; and that all the riches of the country thereabouts had been carried thither, as to a place of safety, trusting to the strength of its castle. They therefore consulted together and agreed that, if they could get possession of this town of St Esprit, it would be to the greatest advantage to them, for then they would be masters of the Rhône as well as Avignon. After they had well digested their plan, Guyot du Pin and Little Meschin (as I have heard it related) mounted their horses and with their companies rode one whole night to the extent of fifteen leagues. They arrived by break of day at Pont du St Esprit, which they took, and all those of both sexes therein. It was a pitiful sight, for they murdered many a discreet man and violated many a virgin. They gained immense riches and provisions sufficient to last them for a whole year. They could from this town escape easily, in an hour's time and without danger, into the kingdom of France, and in another

Holy-Spirit-Bridge

St-Saturnin-du-Port was a small town on the Rhône, about twenty-five miles north of the papal capital at Avignon, and an important centre for the trade in corn, wine and salt. It was also a place where pilgrims journeying to Santiago in Northern Spain could cross from the Holy Roman Empire (on the eastern bank of the river) to the Kingdom of France (on the west) and stay the night in a 'hospital' (hostel) provided for travellers. From about 1300 the place belonged to the Abbey of Cluny and to the King of France, who shared the profits, but, as at Avignon, there was also a religious fraternity, devoted to the Holy Spirit. The nature of that brotherhood has been much debated by French historians, but there is no doubt about the grandeur of its achievement. Between 1265 and 1309, the brothers built a tremendous bridge, so large that it gave its name to both the town and its inhabitants (still known as *Spiripontains*, or 'Spirit-bridgers'), and the building of it became shrouded in myth.

The new bridge at Pont-Saint-Esprit had twenty arches and, at 3,000 feet, it is still three times longer than Westminster Bridge. It was curved against the current of the Rhône and had corridors between each pillar, carefully constructed to relieve the force of the water. It had a bridge chapel towards the middle, and an engraving of 1620 shows how the builders of the bridge fortified their masterpiece and integrated it into the town's defences. The bridge was strengthened with towers at either end, capable of accommodating 300 guards. On the town side, a new tower was built, later made into an entire citadel, in a style we have come to associate with Vauban (Louis XIV's great engineer). The fortifications linked up with town walls which enclosed the churches and municipal buildings, but in 1358 the authorities decided to construct new walls. Unfortunately for the inhabitants of Pont-Saint-Esprit, they had only just begun these when John Hawkwood's brigade arrived from the west at the end of 1360.

The bridge at Pont-Saint-Esprit survived its sack at the hands of the Great Company; indeed it survived more or less intact until modern times. On 15 August 1944 Allied forces, which had landed on the Mediterranean coast of France some weeks after the D-Day landings in Normandy, bombarded the town and destroyed the first section of the western part of the old bridge. This has now been carefully restored and the bridge appears once more as a wonderful example of medieval architecture, far more impressive, one may think, than its more famous sister at Avignon. It is easy to see why it was regarded as something of a miracle in the late Middle Ages.

hour into the [Holy Roman] Empire. They collected the Companies together and kept advancing towards Avignon, at which the pope and the cardinals were much alarmed. These companions had chosen, at the Pont du St Esprit, a captain to command the whole of their forces, who was commonly called 'the friend of God and the enemy of all the world'.[5]

The success of the *routiers* even reached the ears of Matteo Villani in Florence, and he explained why Pont-Saint-Esprit was captured so easily:

They found the people ill-prepared, and they entered the Borgo with no resistance. The Rocca was held by a castellan from Lucca, but they captured both the place and its keeper. And, since the fact of its capture was quite incredible, because it was a strong place, many men thought that this had been brought about on the orders of the Dauphin ... The good citizens [*terrazzani*], both men and women, retreated to the church, which is a stronghold, and they waited there for help from local commanders, and also from the King of France. The noble Bridge over the Rhône was quickly occupied by the men of the Company.[6]

There are several curious features about this account, not least Villani's suggestion that the Dauphin, who later ruled France as Charles V and became known as Charles *le Sage* (the Wise, or Prudent), was somehow complicit in the sack. Equally puzzling is the reference to Pont-Saint-Esprit as having a Rocca (castle) which held out longer than the Borgo (town), for there is no castle there now. There are two possible explanations for this. Either the 'castle' referred to was a tower by the bridge – possibly on the site of the later Citadel – or the Italian chronicler simply meant to distinguish between the outer and inner (walled) parts of the town. The second is the more likely, because Matteo Villani also wrote about the Black Prince's attack on Carcassonne during the great *chevauchée* of 1355. There, he recorded that the Prince took the town and burned it, apart from the 'Rocca della Villa' 'which was a strong castle'. We know that the *rocca* referred to here was not a castle at all, but the inner town of Carcassonne, protected by walls (rather than merely by chains hung across the streets). Froissart, who wrote in French, likewise distinguished between the outer *bourg* and the inner *cité*, at both Carcassonne and Narbonne.

The idea that the outer part of Pont-Saint-Esprit fell to the Great Company in 1360 without resistance, leaving the walled town intact for the time being, fits well with what we know about the earlier history of the fortifications there. The town had walls around the innermost area as early as the eleventh century, but outgrew them, and new walls were built by 1231. Further expansion occurred (the thirteenth century being a time of economic growth) and in 1358 a third line of fortification was begun, running from the new bridge, along the line of the modern Boulevard Gambetta and round to the present day Place de la République; but the problem was that this took thirty years to complete.

We can see now why the *routiers* did not find Pont-Saint-Esprit very difficult to capture. The bridge may have been fortified at either end, and the town protected by the natural moat of the Rhône to the east; but neither of these protected the *Spiripontains* from an attack from the west or the south. The old town walls were over a hundred years old and in serious need of repair, and the townsfolk had only just begun to build their replacement. Perhaps the most critical point is that the town was garrisoned by an amateur militia, with only a sprinkling of professional soldiers, headed by an Italian sergeant from Lucca. The *routiers* were all professionals and their commanders included not only Hawkwood but a man called Bernard de Sorgues. Sorgues is both a town and a river close to Avignon, so this Bernard may well have contributed local knowledge, if his name is indeed an indication of his origins.

In the event, the *routiers* did not need to storm the old walls of Pont-Saint-Esprit, because after three days the garrison gave up the fight. This was partly because their commander Jean Souvain fell from a wooden platform on the ramparts, broke his thigh and was captured, and partly because the citizens became demoralized when they heard that contingents of the Great Company had sacked the nearby communities of Chusclan and Codolet. The terms of the surrender were that the lives of the inhabitants would be spared, provided that they paid 6,000 florins, but the agreed sum could not be raised, and the town was treated as if it had refused to yield to a lawful surrender.

During the sack, the *routiers* gained control of the bridge – there were a few papal troops on the eastern end, but these were soon chased away. They also took possession of all parts of the town apart from the quarter overlooking the Rhône, where the parish church of St Saturnin and the Cluniac priory were situated. This area acted as a kind of inner bailey, where some of the townspeople took refuge, with their valuables, but eventually even they realized that their position was hopeless, and they gave up. The men were robbed and the women and girls (including some nuns) were made to 'join the Company's service' as whores. The municipal archives, notarial registers, and many documents recording indebtedness were burned, as happened so often when law and order broke down.

The new masters of Pont-Saint-Esprit soon discovered that the treasure they had been seeking was not in any of the strongboxes in the town or buried in any inner sanctum. The tax commissioners had been delayed en route and the bullion was still in Avignon, but when the authorities heard that Pont-Saint-

Esprit had been captured, it was taken back to Nîmes. The pillagers had to be content with what they could extract from the *Spiripontains*. Hawkwood and his fellow captains had missed the jackpot, but there were other winnings to be had. Word spread that the Great Company now held Pont-Saint-Esprit and its bridge, and more and more *routiers* arrived there – like jackals round a carcass. They closed the Rhône and raided right up to the walls of Avignon. They torched the villages of Lamotte and Montaigu, and ravaged the monastic houses at Valbonne, Bagnols and Uzès. They carried on raiding throughout the winter of 1360–1.

Pope Innocent reacted very badly to the news that Pont-Saint-Esprit had been captured. The sergeant from Lucca, who had been arrested and released by the *routiers*, was re-arrested by the papal authorities. He was questioned as to how the town had been allowed to fall into enemy hands and his interrogators found the explanation hard to believe. As for the invaders, the Pope ordered them to depart, then excommunicated them, and finally preached a crusade. This meant that any soldier fighting them would have his time in Purgatory reduced when he died, in the same way as men who went to fight in the Holy Land. The Cardinal of Ostia was appointed to command the crusaders and the Pope sought the assistance of the Knights of St John. Attempts were made to raise forces in France, the Empire, Genoa, Aragon and Savoy.

It was all in vain. The Pope expected his volunteers to serve without pay, which had a chilling effect on recruitment; and the enterprise suffered a devastating setback when plague broke out in Avignon, killing no fewer than nine cardinals and seventy prelates. Innocent VI, now old and prone to depression, felt obliged to negotiate a settlement. He knew well enough that men like Hawkwood could be tempted by an offer of regular employment and he worked with the Marquis of Montferrat and Amadeus VI of Savoy to arrive at a diplomatic settlement. The negotiations lasted from the middle of February until the end of April 1361, but it was eventually agreed that Montferrat would invite the *routiers* into Italy, where they could help him with his war with the Visconti of Milan, and assist Cardinal Albornoz in restoring order in the Papal States. The Pope backed the Marquis's offer as only he, the Vicar of Christ, could do. The chronicler Jean le Bel tells us that 'he forgave them for their misdeeds and absolved them of all penalties and sin'.[7]

The monetary rewards were more tangible and the *routiers* were paid 60,000 gold florins to desist from further attacks on papal territory in France, but the Pope did not have to find the whole sum. The French King paid a contribution, and even the citizens of Pont-Saint-Esprit had to raise a further 4,000 to be rid of their tormentors. It seems that Hawkwood's *route* was paid 14,500 florins at the end of March 1361. Whatever the size of the haul, Hawkwood marched his men out of Papal territory in the spring of that year, heading down through Provence and over the Maritime Alps into Piedmont. He was to spend almost the whole of the rest of his life in the Italian states. He was on the Arno when Sir Robert Knollys and Sir Hugh Calvely fought the French at Auray in Brittany in 1364. He was in Pisan service when the Black Prince won his last victory at Nájera in Castile in 1367; and he was in the pay of the Visconti when hostilities with the French broke out again in 1369. Ostensibly, he steered a course which led him far away from the mainstream of English life.

The Battle of Brignais, 1362

According to Froissart, Hawkwood returned to France just once, to take part in the extraordinary Battle of Brignais, when the Free Companies engaged a French force led by Jacques de Bourbon.[8] There are conflicting accounts of this battle, but all are agreed that the *routiers* inflicted a humiliating defeat on the forces of the French kingdom. As usual the chronicler of Montpellier recorded the event from the official point of view:

> In the year 1362, when the enemy had occupied Brignais, the Count of Tancarville, lieutenant of our lord the king, Jacques de Bourbon, count of La Marche, the count of Forez, the lord of Beaujeu and his brothers, the Archpriest of Vélines, the *bailli* of Mâcon and many other great lords laid siege to the city until 6 April. At the ninth hour [around 3 pm] the enemy, who gathered in front of Brignais, together with others who had come from Saugues [near Le Puy], fell upon the besiegers in such a way that they defeated them, so that the counts of La Marche and Forez and the *bailli* of Mâcon were wounded and died a few days later of their wounds, and the aforesaid other great lords were taken prisoner.

The 'Archpriest' mentioned here was Arnaud de Cervole, who had once been in minor orders and captain of a company of freelances, but was now allied with the French Crown. The *routier* army included contingents led by Hawkwood and at least two other English knights, John Creswell and Robert Birkhead.

Brignais was about eighty miles north of Pont-Saint-Esprit. It had been captured in March 1362 by a Great Company lead by Hélie Meschin, sometimes referred to as 'Little Meschin' because he had once been a valet at the French court. He garrisoned Brignais with 300 men, but commanded as many as 3,000 *barbute* and 2,000 *masnadieri*, many of Italian origin. Responding to the menace he posed, the *bailli* of Mâcon arrived in Lyon and reinforced the garrison there. The governor of Dauphiné closed and fortified the river crossings on the Rhône (and its tributaries) and the French assembled a large force under de Bourbon, which included the Archpriest's men. There may have been 6,000 horsemen in the army that marched on Brignais.

Though Matteo Villani despised Little Meschin as a complete nobody – 'a man whose place of birth and parentage was almost totally obscure' – he also praised him as a 'master practitioner in warfare', whose brigade was 'spoiling for a fight, bold and really on form'. His men seem to have had a remarkable ability to communicate over long distances, and soldiers came to join him from all over France, in particular from Saugues in Auvergne, which was over eighty miles from Brignais. Perhaps no one made a longer journey than Hawkwood, who came back from Italy. His motives were probably mixed: profit may well have been uppermost, but he may also have returned to help his old companions. The *routiers* belonged to a kind of brotherhood, and some even entered into formal contracts as 'brothers-in-arms'. Word of the threat to Little Meschin's position may have reached Hawkwood in Italy relatively quickly. It is not difficult to imagine horsemen bringing news up the Ardèche and the Allier to Saugues, or through Savoy to Piedmont.

When Jacques de Bourbon approached Brignais with his thousands, the garrison consisted of only a few hundred men, since Little Meschin had gone off raiding. De Bourbon made camp and proceeded to lay siege to the town, on or about 22 March 1362. He took little trouble to guard his own positions, because he did not feel endangered, but his self-confidence proved as ill founded as Konrad von Landau's, at Marradi in 1358. Learning of the Constable's arrival, Little Meschin retraced his steps, took a shortcut, concentrated his forces, and occupied the heights surrounding the royal army. The French detected the presence of the enemy, turned their back on Brignais and prepared to attack what they took to be the main force opposing them, but, as they tried to move up the slope, both the advance guard (under the Archpriest) and the main battle-group (under de Bourbon) came under heavy fire from slingers on the higher ground. Froissart tells us that these slingers had at least 1,000 cartloads of flints ready, and made good use of them.[9] The French were driven back with heavy losses, but this was not the worst of it. As men streamed back down the hill, the French lines were attacked by a second *routier* battle-group, coming round from behind Goyet wood, surprising their right flank and attacking with newly cut lances. Meanwhile, the garrison of Brignais, small as it was, fell on the French rearguard.

Brignais was a walkover for the *routiers*. They took about a hundred important prisoners, including the Count of Tancarville, the *bailli* of Mâcon and the Archpriest, while de Bourbon was mortally wounded and died in Lyon soon afterwards. The Battle of Brignais had some points in common with Poitiers in 1356: the same judicious use of ground, the same discipline, the same use of the missile arm (though it consisted of slingers rather than archers) and the use of a reserve deployed at a critical juncture. Most impressive of all, Brignais was a victory by an army without a conventional command structure, by commoners who defeated some of the greatest aristocrats in the French kingdom.

Froissart's Bascot of Mauléon confirms that this battle 'made a great deal of profit for the companions, for they were poor – they became rich with fine prisoners, towns and fortresses that they took in the Archdiocese of Lyon and along the River Rhône.'

After such a stunning success, one may ask why Hawkwood returned to Italy. The answer may be that the risks attached to being a freelance were increasing. When there was a breakdown in discipline, a captain was sometimes murdered by his own men, as happened to the Archpriest in 1366, but there was also the possibility of punitive action by Crown forces. Edward III had agreed to evacuate English garrisons in France after the treaty of 1360, and commissioners were sent to make sure that this happened. For their part, the French were more and more inclined to prosecute those who made unofficial war in their country. Among *routier* captains who met a traitor's death was Louis Roubaut, beheaded and quartered at Villeneuve-les-Avignon in 1365, after his old friend handed him over to the authorities. In 1368 Sir Robert Birkhead (a companion of Hawkwood's at both Pont-Saint-Esprit and Brignais), was put to death by drowning, at Olivet near Orléans. In the following year Little Meschin was executed in similar fashion in the Garonne at Toulouse, for his part in an English plot against the French King's son, Louis of Anjou.

Perhaps Hawkwood saw that the writing was on the wall in France. The Battle of Brignais was a victory for the Free Companies but it had been won against the odds, and the French monarchy had immeasurably greater reserves, if it could but organize them. He may also have calculated that the risks involved in being a freelance in Italy were likely to be far less, since there was no monarchy there of equivalent strength. If that was the way he thought, it is hard to say that he was wrong. Towards the end of his life the French caught up with Mérigot Marchès and put him on trial at the Châtelet, near Notre Dame in Paris. Mérigot was one of a group of captains who had operated in France in the 1370s and 1380s. Some of them were bought out and compensated for the loss of their free-roving way of life – but Mérigot was prosecuted. In his defence, he argued that he came from the Limousin, which had been ceded to the English at Brétigny and that he

> had merely done all those things a man can and ought to do in a just war, as taking Frenchmen and putting them to ransom, living on the country and

despoiling it; and leading the company under his command about the realm of France, burning and firing places in it.[10]

The French court rejected his plea, and Marchès was beheaded. Hawkwood engaged in much the same kind of activity as Mérigot – and for far longer – but the political conditions were very different in Italy, and he was never even prosecuted.

Chapter 2

From Captain to Captain-General: Italy, 1361–77

These are free companions, and part of those pillagers who have so long harassed France: they ... seek adventures, and run the chance of gain from plundering the country ... there are among them men at arms that have five or six horses, who, if in their own country, would be constrained to go on foot like absolute paupers.

Jean Froissart, Chronicles

Hawkwood stayed in Italy for more than thirty years, long enough for him to become known by a different name there, which was Giovanni Acuto, or simply L'Acuto ('the Keen One' or 'the Sharp One'.) The basic reasons for his decision to go there, and stay away from England so long, were the wealth of Italy and the political divisions to be found there.

Italy v England

In the early nineteenth century Lord Byron compared the two countries he loved best in his poem 'Italy versus England'. The attractions of the former included the climate, the beauty of the countryside, the wine and the food, the women and the language, but Hawkwood probably went there for the money and the booty, and stayed there because both were in plentiful supply. It was particularly significant that the Italian states were prepared to pay him as the leader of a company, even though he never owned the estates required to support the status of 'banneret' in the land of his birth.

John Carrington, an English soldier who took service with Gian Galeazzo Visconti in Milan not long after Sir John's death, wrote of many Englishmen and Gascons 'and like other strange [foreign] nations that thether comen woren in hope of sallerye'.[1] Froissart says that when the Count of Armagnac wanted to enlist support for his invasion of Lombardy in 1391, some of the *routier* captains spoke up in favour of the idea:

Let us ride against these Lombards: we have a just cause and a good captain … and we will be entering the best country in the world, because Lombardy receives the wealth of the world from all directions.

The Italian expedition of 1361 was probably sold to Hawkwood's followers on much the same basis.

There were dozens of teeming cities in Lombardy, Romagna, Tuscany and Umbria, with diverse forms of government, including their own legal systems and laws. Nearly all Western Europe's trade with the East flowed through Venice and Genoa, while Milan and Florence were the workshops of the Western world and Italian merchants were the greatest of European travellers. Englishmen did visit Italy for various reasons – the Duke of Clarence was married in Milan in 1368 and his nephew Henry Bolingbroke (later Henry IV) visited both Milan and Venice in 1392–3 – but for every English knight who visited Italy, there must have been a dozen Italian merchants who made the trip to England.

The population of Italy was probably between seven and nine million – several times larger than England's, and with a much higher proportion in the towns. Milan and Florence each had around 100,000 people when the Black Death struck in 1348–9, but Milan was spared its ravages, and Florence may still have been home to 70,000 survivors. The Italians had already developed the most important features of capitalism, including joint-stock companies, banking, insurance, and double-entry book-keeping. Italian banks had branches in London. They provided much of the credit which paid for the early campaigns undertaken by Edward III in his war with the Valois. Despite the crash of the Bardi and Peruzzi banks, which was at least partly Edward's fault, Florence's currency remained the international standard. The florin, worth 3 shillings sterling in 1328, was still referred to as 'the new florin' of Florence in a bond entered into by Hawkwood in 1382. The City of London was home to an elite of Italian merchants, who imported pepper, cinnamon, ginger and other spices, as well as bankers ('Lombards') who lent money at interest. The economic miracle funded improvements in transport. The Via Francigena leading to Rome was maintained for the benefit of pilgrims, and Florence increased the number of main roads she took responsibility for, particular attention being paid to the mountain passes.[2]

The population of England and Wales was about four million in 1348 and about two and a half million in 1377. Nine out of ten people lived in the countryside. The towns, apart from London, were tiny. Only Coventry, Norwich, Lincoln, Salisbury, Lynn and Colchester had populations between 6,000 and 10,000. London, York and Bristol were bigger, but even London had only 40,000 souls after the plague. England's trade consisted almost entirely of wool and woollen cloth, and much of that was in the hands of Italian merchants. Most Italians regarded England as far away, cold and backward. Even in the mid-fifteenth century the future Pope Pius II, who was from Siena, painted a bleak picture. He recorded that the North of England was 'utterly unlike the country we inhabit, being rude, uncultivated, and unvisited by the winter sun'. The South was a little better, but only because it contained the things that appealed to the traveller: Westminster Abbey, the City of London, London Bridge and the Thames.[3]

Politically there is a very different story to tell. England was comparatively small, but remarkably united. Edward III may have spoken the French of his Norman and Angevin ancestors, but most of his people spoke English, and it was during the reign of his successor Richard II that Geoffrey Chaucer wrote his most famous works. There was a single coinage, the King's writ ran throughout the whole land, and the royal judges heard cases from all over the country. *Scrope v Grosvenor* (1385–90), a case in the High Court of Chivalry about the right to wear a coat of arms, originated in a dispute between Lord Scrope from Yorkshire and Sir Robert Grosvenor from Cheshire, but the matter was resolved in the courts. Italy, by contrast, was a political kaleidoscope, with many states and currencies. Broadly speaking, large cities dominated the North, the Papacy held the Centre, and a monarchy ruled the South; but this is to greatly oversimplify the situation on the ground, where there were in fact dozens of semi-independent fiefs and towns. Metternich's remark that Italy was 'a geographical expression' was inflammatory in the nineteenth century but was the simple truth in Hawkwood's day.

The rulers of Italy lacked legitimacy, in comparison with the monarchs of England and France, and this led to constant warfare, both between the states and within them. It was all very well for Sacchetti to praise the virtues of peace and to urge his fellow countrymen to avoid war, even if that meant putting up with a few petty humiliations, and not reacting violently when 'offence' was given. Few Italians took any notice. Medieval Italian history is full of plots, coups, assassinations, feuds and *vendetta*, of people fleeing into exile and attempting to return. At the same time, great wealth turned the country into a magnet for foreigners with a taste for fighting. During his brief tenure of power in Florence in 1342–3, the Duke of Athens used both French and Burgundian troops, but most of the early 'adventurers' were German, and when Petrarch, in his poem 'Italia Mia', complained bitterly about 'the savage beasts' with 'venal hearts' who defiled his country, he was talking about the Germans. Hanneckin von Baumgarten, who was to cross swords with Hawkwood, was fighting in Italy from 1351.

Hawkwood against Milan, 1361–3

The main cause of war in the North of Italy was Milanese wealth and ambition, for the Visconti had an income as great as that of the kings of England – estimated at 700,000 florins, compared to between 550,000 and 700,000 for Edward III. The conspicuous consumption of the Milanese, on display at weddings, was a matter for wonder throughout Western Europe, and diplomats competed to negotiate Viscontean marriages. Gian Galeazzo Visconti (1378–1402) embarked on a major building programme, including the Gothic cathedral in Milan and the Charterhouse at Pavia, which still survive, but at the time much of his wealth was spent on the military. He was among the first to pay local troops a regular wage, and he and his uncle Bernabò before him spent a good deal of their wealth on foreign mercenaries and *condottieri*.

The Visconti constantly strove to expand their domains. In Mussolini's day the British historian Dorothy Muir described the process like this: 'There was an inner circle of cities for which the Visconti always strove – Lodi, Bergamo, Como, Vercelli, Novara, Tortona, Pavia, Piacenza. Beyond these lay others more difficult of attainment – Crema, Cremona, Brescia, Alessandria, Asti. Further still – beyond the province of Lombardy – were Parma, Genoa and Bologna.' A key moment in the establishment of regional hegemony came in 1359, when Visconti forces led by Luchino dal Verme besieged Pavia, ancient capital of the Lombards. Following its capture, dal Verme began building a great castle there. From that time two Visconti brothers agreed a kind of de facto partition of their dominions, with Galeazzo ruling from Pavia and Bernabò from Milan, but neither the Pope nor the Florentines trusted either of them, and John of Legnano, professor of law in Bologna, referred to the whole tribe as 'vipers' in his *Treatise on War, Reprisals and the Duel* of 1360: the Visconti coat of arms features a viper swallowing a child.

Bologna was the most important city in Emilia, seat of the oldest law school in Europe, and the Visconti and the Pope each laid claim to it. Seized by Archbishop Giovanni Visconti, it should have passed to his nephew Bernabò on the old cleric's death, but it had actually fallen into the hands of the Archbishop's illegitimate son Oleggio. The result was civil war in the Visconti family. Oleggio allied himself with outsiders – the Gonzaga of Mantua and the Este of Ferrara; Bernabò launched an attack. Rather than surrender Bologna to his cousin, Oleggio delivered it up to Cardinal Albornoz. This provoked four years of further conflict, since Bernabò reacted with great violence to this humiliation. According to the Florentine historian Leonardo Bruni (1370–1444), the war was undertaken 'with tremendous effort on both sides'.[4]

When Hawkwood arrived in Italy, it was to fight for an anti-Visconti league, consisting of the Pope, the Marquis of Montferrat, the Republic of Genoa and the

Count of Savoy. Montferrat had a particular reason for wanting to enlist fresh support at the time, because the German *condottiere* Konrad von Landau and his Great Company had recently abandoned him. Pope Urban V, who had succeeded Innocent VI in 1362, was content to pursue his predecessor's anti-Visconti policy. Urban had personal motives for taking this line because, before his election, he had served as papal ambassador to Milan. On one such occasion, he had delivered some bad news to Bernabò, who had made him eat the papal bull containing it – parchment, lead seals and all. This sounds too good a story to be true, but there was an almost identical incident in England in 1384, when two rival bishops forced their messengers to eat a seal and a pair of shoes.[5]

Hawkwood marched into Italy at the head of a number of English *routes*, but the commander-in-chief was Albert Sterz (also known as 'Albert the German'). The *routiers* marched down the valley of the Rhône and into Provence. They set fire to the suburbs of Marseilles as they made their way through to Nice. Marching at a rate of ten to twelve miles a day, they crossed the Maritime Alps, continued on through the Genoese Republic and arrived in the Plain of Lombardy in June 1361. We have no account of their crossing of the Alps, but it cannot have been easy. Peter Spufford writes that even today 'the traveller with vertigo will still find it easier ... to travel from Avignon to Italy by sea.'

Before they could engage the Visconti, the new arrivals were forced to defend themselves, when their supposed ally the Green Count of Savoy turned against them, on account of the damage they were doing to his domains – but Sterz and Hawkwood fought back. They rode up into the Alpine foothills, where the Count probably thought he was safe, blockaded him in his castle at Lanzo, twenty miles north-west of Turin, and forced him to come to terms. The Count paid them an enormous sum, reputedly 180,000 florins, to go away. Once free of this distraction, Hawkwood fought his first war with the Visconti, the main theatre being to the west of Milan and Pavia. This has always been a cockpit, where commanders from Hannibal to Napoleon have manoeuvred, and where the Battles of Novara and Magenta were fought in the mid-nineteenth century. We read of Hawkwood's men at Castelnuovo on the Scrivia, at Tortona, and at Rivarolo Canavese, which they captured by *escalade*.

Albert Sterz signed a fresh contract with the Marquis of Montferrat in November 1361 and Sir John is recorded as being a 'constable'. The new Company was originally known to its own members as the Company of Fortune, but was re-baptized the White Company by startled Italian observers (see p. 78). It made its headquarters at Sicciano near Novara and soon confronted Konrad von Landau's Great Company, whose assistance the Visconti had been quick to enlist. In Hawkwood's absence at Brignais, it also locked horns with Luchino dal Verme. It was during this period that the Milanese annalist recorded that the

English 'killed men; committed outrages on women [*vituperabant*] in front of their husbands, and on virgins in front of their parents; and set fire to numerous lands.'

In January 1363, the White Company raided right up to the gates of Milan – surprising a group of noblemen and women who were partying outside the walls – and engaged Visconti troops who counter-attacked from a flotilla of boats on the Ticino. The 'Whites' still managed to come away with many prisoners, but this must have been a strange experience for English soldiers, who had no experience of making war on rivers. In the spring, the English sacked Briona and defeated the Great Company at the bridge of Canturino near Novara. In the hand-to-hand fighting Konrad von Landau's nosepiece was broken, and he was mortally wounded. The White Company had not only won the battle, it had decapitated the Great, by killing its commander: perhaps this explains why Canturino is the only one of Hawkwood's battles to be mentioned in the *Cambridge History of Warfare* (2005). Meanwhile, on the eastern front, the anti-Visconti league took Modena and succeeded in capturing Ambrogio Visconti, one of Bernabò's many illegitimate sons. The Milanese annalist protested that the English were bigger thieves than anyone else in Lombardy.[6]

Diplomatic relations were volatile, and Pope Urban V now decided to make peace. A treaty was negotiated which provided that the Visconti should give Bologna back to the Church in exchange for 500,000 florins. This put a temporary end to the hostilities in the North and caused the White Company to move elsewhere. The most important cities in Tuscany put in rival bids for its services. As a result, it marched out of Lombardy in the spring of 1363, having agreed to fight for Pisa against Florence, for a term of six months and at a price of 30,000 florins. Hawkwood and his Englishmen went with it and, as far as we know, he never saw France or England again.[7]

Hawkwood for Pisa, 1363–4

Tuscany had as many political divisions as Piedmont or Lombardy, despite being a home of republicanism. Florence, Pisa, Siena and Lucca were all republics, as were Volterra, Arezzo, San Gimignano and Cortona, but this did not prevent them fighting one another. Machiavelli was to write that 'in republics there is more life, more hate, more desire for revenge.' Pisa and Florence in particular were traditional enemies. Each city occupied a strategic position on the River Arno and each ruled over a country district (*contado*) containing valleys, hills and mountains: Monte Pisano near Pisa, the Mugello and the Casentino near Florence.

Pisa had once been a great port. She had enjoyed her heyday in the eleventh and twelfth centuries, when she acquired the great islands of Corsica, Sardinia and

Pisa

Nowadays Pisa lies some way from the sea, but she was once a great port. At the time of the First Crusade, she was a frontrunner in the race for wealth and power in Italy. Civic pride found expression in the Campo dei Miracoli, where the city fathers built a cathedral, baptistery, cemetery and bell-tower, which started to lean not long after it was built. These landmarks were all built long before John Hawkwood arrived in the city.

While he was still living and working in Pisa, Hawkwood helped to bring about a change of regime there, which made the merchant Giovanni Agnello ruler (or Doge) of the city. This is Filippo Villani's account of the coup d'état:

> Giovanni d'Agnello, who was acting in concert with John Hawkwood, feared that delay might be damaging to him and give time for his intentions to become clear, so, that very night, with John Hawkwood and his friends and assembled soldiers he went to the piazza and noiselessly took the entrance to the Palace of the Anziani ('Ancients') with one part of his company, leaving the rest to guard the piazza. He then entered the room where the Anziani meet, and sat in the Provost's seat. One by one he had the Anziani woken up and brought before him, and he told them – this would have been a foolish thing had it not been backed up by the force of John Hawkwood – that the Virgin Mary had revealed to him that, for the good and peace of the city, he had to take the *Signoria* and government of Pisa, with the title of doge, for one year.

Although Agnello declared that he would only rule in Pisa for one year, he soon broke his promise. He assumed the position of dictator for life and had his two young sons elevated to the same office alongside him. Hawkwood enjoyed considerable influence at his court and became godfather to one of his sons, who was called Auti – a corruption of Acuto. Agnello was a Milanese protégé – according to Bruni 'no one doubted that it was with the help of Bernabò [Visconti] that he had seized the turbulent city'. After he was overthrown in a further coup, Hawkwood schemed with Bernabò to restore him. In 1370 Sir John even attacked Pisa on Agnello's behalf, doubtless hoping to make use of his inside knowledge of the city, but the assault was repulsed without difficulty, and the Pisans even captured one of the English, hanged him and butchered him. His corpse was quartered and the pieces displayed on the walls of the city.

the Balearics. She made war on the Moslems of Spain and North Africa and sent an entire fleet in support of the First Crusade (1095–9). With the benefit of hindsight we can see that she was in relative decline by 1360, but this would not have been apparent to Hawkwood. The city had expanded into the Maremma, she periodically made attempts to gain control of Lucca, and she was holding her own against Florence. Florence was an inland city, grown rich on the profits of the textile industry. The Florentines finished woollen cloth, much of it brought from England – including Hawkwood's native Essex. The *arte della Lana* was the richest guild of all, with its own coat of arms in the form of the lamb of God. Florence had a large industrial base and a wide commercial network and she dominated the Kingdom of Naples economically. She pursued an aggressive foreign policy, taking over Pistoia in 1306 and the isolated town of Barga in mountainous Garfagnana in 1341. She purchased Prato from the Neapolitan Angevins in 1350. She repeatedly vied for control of Arezzo.

There was no love lost between the Pisans and the Florentines. Boccaccio wrote that there were few Pisan women who could avoid being mistaken for lizards, while the Florentines were known for being *dada* – hypocrites. The slyness of their merchants was proverbial:

> Florentine merchants are dealers in lies,
> To bargain with them takes a sharp pair of eyes.[8]

By tradition Pisa was Ghibelline (for the Emperor) and Florence was Guelf (for the Pope), but the war of 1362–4 was a trade war. Florence needed a port but her nearest point of access to the sea was the port of Pisa, Porto Pisano. The authorities in the two cities had come to an agreement about the use of the harbour there in 1342, but in 1356 the Pisans imposed new customs duties. Rather than submit to what many Florentines would have regarded as a 'humiliation', Florence decided to develop Talamona instead, though this in no way compared to Porto Pisano: Talamona was over 100 miles away and belonged to Siena, and Florence had tried and failed to develop the port there. Dante had described a lost cause as 'hoping from Talamona'. The affair led to war, by land and by sea.

The arrival of the White Company and the English tipped the balance of military advantage in favour of Pisa, particularly since the Florentine commander, Pietro Farnese, had recently died.[9] The Company marched down from the North via the Lunigiana and reached Lucca by July 1363, with Albert Sterz in command and Hawkwood as yet a mere captain. It joined forces with the Pisan host commanded by the Florentine exile Ghivello Ubaldini and the combined army advanced along the northern edge of the Arno to Pistoia. It made camp between

Peretola and Campi, only five or six miles from Florence. On reaching the enemy capital, the English 'ran races according to their custom' and shot arrows over the city walls, with the message 'Pisa sends you this!' They hung three donkeys, each with a placard round its neck, displaying the name of a prominent Florentine magistrate and they re-minted Florentine coins, superimposing their own Pisan motifs. This was sweet revenge (*vendetta*) for what the Florentines had done to them earlier: the Pisan fox had chased the Florentine lion back to its den, and the event was worth celebrating.

The Pisans and their English allies turned back along the Arno, pillaging and sacking Lastra, fanning out round Prato to the north and penetrating the side-valley of the Pesa to the south. The regular Pisan forces returned to their city, but the English mercenaries were made to work longer and harder, since the contract had not yet expired. The White Company was sent to raid areas rich in booty, which had not been raided by the Pisans before and were therefore taken by surprise. We read that they set out from Empoli, went between the Pesa and the Elsa, climbed over the hills and came down on the fourth day near Figline, between Florence and Arezzo.

The towns of Incisa and Figline fell into the hands of the English, in September and October 1363. The capture of Figline in particular was a devastating and humiliating blow for the Florentines, since this was the key to their security in the area and many Florentine citizens had houses there. Florence had ringed Figline with a new set of walls in 1356, yet the English took it easily. Bruni wrote that it needed 'hardly any effort' to capture the town, while Sozomeno of Pistoia says there was 'no opposition whatsoever' – which is surprising when one looks at the height of the walls today. Perhaps the explanation is the one given by Filippo Villani – 'evil men' inside the fortress surrendered it to the enemy, without a fight.[10]

The English did not just take Figline, they held onto it for two months and used it as a base for further operations, before sacking it when they left. The strategy might well have been employed by Edward III or the Black Prince. By raiding the Florentine *contado*, the White Company inflicted economic damage and undermined loyalty to Florence, just as the royal *chevauchées* aimed to do in Valois France, but not everything went well for the English. They raided far and wide from Figline, causing devastation in Chianti and even approaching the walls of Arezzo. In the mountains of Chianti they attacked Cintoia near Greve, 'Castellaccio' – possibly Castellina – and 'La Foresta' (The Forest), but they suffered a serious setback at 'Tre Vigne' (Three Vineyards) – possibly the modern Villa Vignano. At the last of these they suffered a reverse and had to retreat 'leaving several killed and wounded by stones and crossbow bolts, while the moat was full of ladders and the ground was strewn with bows and arrows.'[11] In

Florence, Sacchetti tried to make light of what the White Company had achieved. He claimed that all they got for their pains was 'three giraffes' – which presumably meant 'bugger all', giraffes being in short supply in fourteenth-century Italy:

> The Pisan cavalry was at the San Gallo gate [in Florence]
> Burning and wasting all the country round about,
> And at Figline they cut much fodder;
> Then they made peace, but all they got was three giraffes.

The Pisans, who had been blockading the Florentine enclave at Barga in Garfagnana, in the mountains north of Lucca, ordered the White Company to march up there, but most of them refused to go. This is surprising when we remember that one of the advantages of mercenaries over feudal levies was supposed to be that they would go anywhere, and it says much about the esteem in which the Company was held that their disobedience did not lead to instant dismissal.[12] Far from it: the English were kept on and when their existing contract ran out at the end of 1363, the Pisans re-engaged them on more favourable terms. Their wages were increased and the Company was expressly permitted to march where it chose. Most importantly from our point of view, Hawkwood was named as commander in place of Albert the German. The Pisans also paid for an Italian bodyguard for the new commander, consisting of two constables (assisted by two boys) and thirty-eight footsoldiers (and their six boys).[13] Sir John was referred to as 'captain-general of war for Pisa'. His lieutenants included the Englishman Andrew Belmont, but also the German, Sterz. One would not have thought that this reversal of roles would be conducive to harmony, but it was perhaps inevitable, given the numerical predominance of the English. The new treasurer of the Company was 'Gugliemo Toreton' (William Turton?), and those present included John 'Onselos' (Onslow), William 'Prestim' (Preston?) and a man called 'Dughino' (Duggan, or Duggie?). After some two and a half years in Italy Hawkwood had now reached the top, but it proved to be the top of a greasy pole. His troubles began almost immediately, with the failure of a winter campaign along the Arno. His attacks on Florence (1364), Perugia (1365) and Arezzo (1368) were all to be repulsed, sometimes with severe consequences for himself and his men.

In February 1364 the English left Pisa, together with a newly recruited band of Germans and a host of Pisans from the city and the countryside, again taking the northern route along the Arno to Pistoia and Prato.[14] The English started raiding but met unexpected resistance there from the Pistoians, surprising when one considers the inequality of arms between professional soldiers and amateur militias, let alone untrained townsmen and peasants. Froissart relates that, during the French Jacquerie of 1358, the Count of Foix and the Captal de Buch slaughtered no fewer than 7,000 'Jacks' in the course of rescuing a few high-born ladies, but local militias were not always so helpless. There were instances of successful resistance, and even of counter-attack. As we saw, local militias had defeated part of Konrad von Landau's Great Company at Le Scalelle in 1358.

In 1364, the men of Pistoia, though unused to war since they were farmers (*agricolae*), likewise determined to resist Hawkwood. According to the town's fifteenth-century historian, they ambushed the White Company in Pistoian territory, and defeated it again at the Serravalle pass, where Castruccio Castracani had vanquished a much larger Florentine force in 1324.[15] The White Company withdrew to Pisa with its tail between its legs; but, after receiving substantial German reinforcements led by Anichino Baumgarten, they resumed the offensive in April, occupying Fiesole in the hills outside Florence, where they stayed three days. They found time to mark this renewed harassment of the Florentines with a festival staged in the piazza, with processions and games, coloured lamps, music and song.

The Florentines found a remedy for their plight by digging deeper into their deep pockets. Despite the fact that the second contract made between the Pisans and the White Company still had two months to run, they offered a bribe, employing their best negotiators to offer the White Company better terms than those they currently enjoyed, and the majority took the bribe. Some of those who accepted deserted directly to the Florentine camp. Others merely agreed that they would not attack Florence for the time being. The majority of English contingents who deserted the Pisans joined a new Anglo-Hungarian White Company, commanded by the Englishman Hugh de la Zouche (Ugo della Zecca), but Hawkwood stood aside from these negotiations and remained loyal to Pisa. According to Temple-Leader only 800 others did so, though Bruni wrote that Hawkwood's 'band' (*manus*) still consisted of 1,000 knights. Whether that meant 1,000 fully equipped knights (with their attendants) or 1,000 men in all, is not clear.[16]

Hawkwood remained at his post in Pisa, to weather the crisis – for that was what he now faced. He could call on the Pisan militia, but the backbone of his White Company had been broken, and during the last month of the old contract, the situation was desperate, with the Florentines occupying most of the lower Arno. At the end of July 1364 Galeotto Malatesta of Rimini (*c.*1305–85) – an able commander – became captain-general in Florence. He occupied Cascina, a heavily fortified town next to the Arno, and only twelve miles from Pisa. Malatesta strengthened his position there by digging trenches on the western side of the town, outside the Pisan gate. He had 4,000 cavalry, 11,000 infantry and some artillery in the form of Genoese crossbowmen – men who had often shown their worth in the long war between the English and French kings.

Hawkwood was given orders to attack Cascina, but it proved too tough a nut to crack. He was heavily outnumbered, and Malatesta had longer experience of Italian conditions, though he was ill with fever at the time. On leaving Pisa, Hawkwood made camp at the abbey of San Savino, some four miles from the enemy lines. The late Roman author Vegetius, who was much read – and heavily relied on – by late medieval writers, had advised that: 'When the general is ready to draw up the line, he should attend first to three factors, sun, dust and wind.' Hawkwood kept this advice in mind, or the chronicler thought that he did. Filippo Villani noted that in the afternoon a sea wind often blows up the valley of the Arno, and Hawkwood waited for midday, thinking that the enemy would have both the sun and the dust in their faces, and then mounted three feigned attacks, so that his adversaries would not know when the real one was coming. Then he made his move in earnest, sending in a vanguard of veteran English who had learned their trade in France, keeping his cavalry in reserve, and promising the men double pay if they won. Using intelligence gathered by some unknown means, he pointed out that there were about 400 young aristocrats in the opposite camp who were ignorant of war but worth up to 2,000 florins. The prospect of these ransoms fired the vanguard with enthusiasm and, despite the heat, dust and fatigue, they charged forward.[17]

The attack was successful at first. It was hot, Malatesta was taking a siesta and his troops had disarmed and unsaddled their horses. The Florentines had both a *carroccio* and a smaller vehicle with them, with a bell for sounding the alarm, but they were taken unawares: some of them had even stripped off on the banks of the Arno: this is the moment later celebrated by Michelangelo, who showed us a group of them bathing in the river. When the English rushed the trenches, there was tremendous confusion and they broke through in some places; but the Genoese crossbowmen were keeping watch in nearby Cascina. On receiving the order, they unleashed a hail of bolts on the English. Manno Donati picked a corps of men from among the *feditori* provided by Florence and Arezzo, and some mountain-men from the Casentino, sallied out of Cascina, circled around the English line and fell on their flank.

Hawkwood's men were badly beaten at First Cascina. They retreated, leaving thirty dead and 300 wounded. Pisan doctors struggled with the casualties, though we know they had some knowledge of surgery and anaesthetics.[18] Worse was to follow. The defeat of the English vanguard created havoc in the main body of the Pisan army and the Florentines took 2,000 prisoners and captured the Pisan wine supplies. Hawkwood fell back on San Savino, where he gathered in his wounded and retreated, as best he could, to Pisa, where the chronicler records that he was greeted by men and women weeping for the husbands, fathers and brothers they had lost. Malatesta did not even bother to continue the chase. He reviewed his prisoners, disarmed the foreign troops and released them (as was customary among mercenaries) but – according to Bruni – dragged the Pisan captives back to Florence in forty-four carts 'as a spectacle for the people'. Once there, they were thrown into prison and made to do forced labour, constructing the Loggia dei Pisani on the Piazza della *Signoria*. Meanwhile, the victorious Florentines enjoyed the pleasures of the *vendetta* to the full: they paraded outside the walls of Pisa, delivering elaborate insults to those within.

Hawkwood for Milan, 1365–72

Hawkwood stayed to serve Pisa but was eventually drawn into the orbit of her larger and wealthier ally, Milan. Some say this happened as early as 1365, others as late as 1368. The explanation is probably that Sir John started working for Bernabò Visconti at an early date, but that it suited Milanese diplomacy to pretend otherwise. He was certainly in receipt of a Pisan stipend throughout 1365, but early that year he travelled north and met Bernabò for the first time. This was the start of a long but volatile relationship, which lasted until the latter's death in 1385.

The campaigns Hawkwood undertook for Milan in the late 1360s were more wide-ranging than those he had been involved in before. He led a series of expeditions in various parts of Italy, fought a variety of enemies and occasionally found unexpected allies. Temple-Leader wrote: 'the history of the mercenary companies after the Pisan War is so complicated that much of it is indecipherable.' One reason for this is that Bernabò had many enemies in Tuscany and Umbria. Another is that both Bernabò and Galeazzo Visconti were normally content to have their troops damage the target areas by burning the countryside. This was enough to frighten the country people into taking refuge in the cities and it left the marauders free to burn or loot what was left. They did not necessarily expect their mercenaries to lay siege to the enemy towns, let alone capture them. This kind of warfare was exactly what Hawkwood had learned in France, and had practised in Piedmont and the Florentine *contado*.

In June 1365 Hawkwood was sent to attack Perugia, the principal city of Umbria and an important papal stronghold. He recruited many of his troops from former members of the White Company, and advanced into the Perugino, but his opponent Cardinal Albornoz was an experienced soldier and commander, who reinforced Perugia. Hawkwood's men encountered a crack corps of German mercenaries led once by Baumgarten and Sterz (who must have learned all about English methods of warfare by now). The rival armies clashed and the English were soundly beaten, though Hawkwood escaped to fight another day.

In October Hawkwood reached an agreement with Ambrogio Visconti, one of Bernabò's many illegitimate sons, to form a new Company of St George, and they invaded Sienese territory. The Sienese attempted to buy it off with payments in kind but the Company returned in the spring of 1366, when it was paid 10,500 florins and given the right to pass through Sienese territory once a year for a period of five years, on condition it did no damage and promised not to molest the civilian population.[19]

Pope Urban V decided that enough was enough. He issued bulls condemning the mercenaries, formed a new league with Florence, Naples and various Tuscan cities to drive them from Italy, and even dreamed of sending them on a 'general passage' to the Holy Land, to assist King Peter of Cyprus's crusades. Crucially for Hawkwood, the papal league decided to concentrate on eliminating new arrivals and exempted four Free Companies which it regarded as already resident in Italy:

1. The Company of Signor Ambrogio (Visconti);
2. The Company of Signor Giovanni Acuto (Hawkwood);
3. The Company of Signor Annichino (Bongarden);
4. The Company of Signor Conte Giovanni (Johann von Hapsburg).

What put an end to the alliance between Hawkwood and Ambrogio Visconti was not the fulminations of the Papacy, or defeat in the field by the papal league, but a voluntary parting of the ways. Ambrogio took some of the men down to Naples – where he was captured and temporarily imprisoned – while Hawkwood and Belmont decided to attack Siena, yet again.

Hawkwood entered into a new contract with Bernabò Visconti in 1368, which provided for the hire of 4,000 men. His services were badly needed, because Milan was now threatened by a new papal league, organized by Urban V, who had recently gone back to Avignon. This was strengthened by the adherence of the Holy Roman Emperor, Charles IV (1316–78), who had fought with the French at Crécy. The allied forces occupied Lucca, Pisa and Siena, and the Emperor's men confronted the Visconti at Borgoforte on the River Po, but Hawkwood led the Viscontean forces which forced the Emperor to retreat. In June Bernabò's niece Violante was married to Edward III's second son, Lionel Duke of Clarence, in Milan. Some historians state that Hawkwood was present at this wedding and even that he formed part of Clarence's bodyguard, while others have him meeting Geoffrey Chaucer there. However, the evidence for Hawkwood's attendance, as for Chaucer's, is purely circumstantial. In any event, Clarence died four months later, so that the alliance between the Plantagenets and the Visconti was short-lived.[20]

In 1369 Hawkwood was taken prisoner at Arezzo by the Germans von Reischach and von Riedheim and remained in enemy hands for some months, before being ransomed for an unknown sum. Once at liberty he re-formed his brigade and moved down the Via Francigena – the pilgrim route to Rome – in pursuit of the Pope. The English raided the Papal States, causing so much damage to Bolsena that it was still noticeable 100 years later when Pope Pius II visited the place.[21] A few miles further south, they attacked the papal palace at Montefiascone, but previous Popes had fortified this and the English were ill-equipped for siege warfare, so the archers had to be content with firing insulting messages over the walls of the fortress, while others burned the Pope in effigy. Urban moved on to Viterbo, a papal city as formidable as Avignon, which had been strengthened by Albornoz and where there was a palace and thermal springs for the Pope's comfort. Hawkwood stood no chance of taking Viterbo: he burned the vineyards, stayed a few days in the suburbs, and eventually withdrew to the North, while the Pope granted indulgences to anyone who could come out and fight him.[22]

It was now Florence's turn to be the object of Visconti attentions. Bernabò wanted to put pressure on her on two fronts, by taking Livorno on the coast and persuading Pisa to make war in the Florentine *contado*. If put into effect, this strategy might have ruined Florence's commerce, but the plan was discovered and misfired. Bernabò had to be content with sending Hawkwood to relieve San Miniato al Tedesco, the hill fortress midway between Pisa and Florence. When the rival forces clashed again at Second Cascina, Hawkwood won one of his most famous victories (see Chapter 8). His men followed this up in the usual way, selling their booty in Pisa, then re-equipping and raiding around Peretola, but Hawkwood was unable to save San Miniato, which fell to the Florentines soon afterwards. Some said that his failure was due to the lack of forage, others blamed the lack of money, others again the bad weather and the state of the roads.[23] In Bruni's version 'a man of the lowest condition' called Luparello 'let the enemy in by night through a hidden and almost impassable route'. Naturally, Sacchetti celebrated Florence's success in capturing the place and denying it to the Visconti vipers:

> Neither snake nor venomous serpent, nor Hawkwood
> Will damage her, for all their efforts.[24]

Hawkwood undertook several more campaigns for the Milanese in the years 1370–2. He was unsuccessful when he fought the Florentines at Reggio in Emilia, but he beat them at Mirandola, and he and Ambrogio Visconti, newly released from prison in Naples, overcame a larger papal force commanded by Lutz von Landau at Rubiera near Modena in June 1372.

Then came the crisis in his relations with the Visconti. In the autumn of 1372 Hawkwood was sent to join their siege of Asti in Piedmont. The city had changed hands several times, in a triangular tug of war between Montferrat, Galeazzo Visconti and the Count of Savoy. Bernabò reinforced Galeazzo by sending Hawkwood, Ambrogio Visconti and 1,200 men of different nationalities. The siege was making progress but Hawkwood advised that they break off and do battle with Savoyard forces, then marching to relieve the city. Strangely, his plan was rejected, because the Visconti decided that an all-out attack would jeopardize the lives of too many of their young noblemen. The chroniclers of Piacenza and the anonymous chronicler of Milan both relate the story that Bianca, wife of Galeazzo Visconti of Pavia (and mother of Gian Galeazzo, who was then only twenty) expressly ordered that her son's life was not to be put at risk, and there was a strong feeling that, although Hawkwood commanded a formidable army of Italians, Germans and English, the outcome of a battle was always too uncertain.

One might think that Bianca Visconti's reluctance to risk her son's life was an understandable reaction on the part of a mother, but it was not calculated to appeal to Hawkwood. He was convinced that if he could engage Savoy in battle, he would win, and youth was certainly not a reason to spare one's soldiers. The English routinely used boys in their fighting units, and the testimony of the witnesses who gave evidence in *Scrope v Grosvenor* shows that fourteen or fifteen was a common age for first arming, while many witnesses in *Grey v Hastings* had been on expeditions by the time they were twelve.[25] A man could even be dubbed to knighthood at fifteen. The Black Prince was only sixteen when he fought at Crécy, and his nephew Henry Bolingbroke was the same age when he took part in his first tournament. Sir John took the Visconti veto very badly, especially because it was imposed on the advice of notaries, whom he called *escrivans* – scriveners (or 'scribblers'?). The chronicler of Piacenza uses the old French word here – it leaps off the page because he normally wrote in Latin. The entire passage shows the Englishman's disdain for men who wrote for a living but purported to advise on matters of war.[26]

A *condottiere* was not a sovereign and Hawkwood did not have the last word about strategy. All he could do, if he felt strongly, was to terminate his contract, and we are told that on this occasion he left camp when his project was turned down. It has been suggested that the real cause of the quarrel was that Bernabò Visconti suspected him of entering into negotiations with the Green Count, or else of making contact with a fellow Englishman in the opposite camp, whom he had known at Pont-Saint-Esprit.[27] However, looking at the matter from a military point of view, there is another explanation. Whatever his other qualities, Hawkwood was not an expert in siege warfare and he was unlikely to see eye to eye with his masters when it came to the best way to capture an Italian city. Whatever the reason for the misunderstanding, Sir John soon took employment with Pope Gregory XI, elected in 1370, and his relations with Bernabò remained sour for several years.

Hawkwood for the Papacy, 1372–7

Famously, Joseph Stalin once asked how many divisions the Pope had.[28] This was a rhetorical question in 1935 but in the fourteenth century, thanks to the huge income which the Popes enjoyed and stored at Avignon, they could easily afford to put large armies in the field and hire the leading *condottieri* of the day. Hawkwood's relations with the Papacy had been, to say the least, poor in the 1360s, when the Pope had forbidden anyone to give succour to the mercenaries infesting France and Italy. The election of a new Pope in 1370 presented new opportunities – including the opportunity of a lucrative contract.

Although the Papacy put down roots in Avignon, there were always strong reasons for returning to Rome. The Pope was the Bishop of Rome, St Peter had his tomb there, and the city was the most important centre of Christian pilgrimage outside the Holy Land. Many Christians who were renowned for their saintly lives, including Bridget of Sweden (*c.* 1302–73) and Catherine of Siena (1347–80) continually urged the Pope to return. Many Christians would also have agreed with Petrarch that Avignon was a

> nest of treachery in which is hatched
> all evil that today spreads through the world,
> a slave of wine, of bedrooms, and of food,
> high testing-ground for every kind of lust![29]

The Avignon Popes would not have agreed with this, but even they came to recognize the superior claims of Rome. Accordingly, from the mid-fourteenth century, a large part of the revenues enjoyed by the Papacy in Avignon was spent in Italy, with the aim of regaining control of the Papal States from rebellious Italian lords and communes. When Pope Gregory XI was elected in 1370, he accepted the argument that the papal court should transfer back to its historic home.

The Pope was a secular ruler in Italy as well as a spiritual one, as the papal coat of arms, with its triple Crown and St Peter's keys, demonstrated to the world. Pope Innocent VI had employed Gil Albornoz to pacify Lazio, Sabina, Tuscia and Umbria, but the fighting Cardinal succeeded beyond all expectations and, in 1355, brought Ancona, Urbino and Rimini to heel as well. He forced the Manfredi to surrender Faenza in 1356, Cesena fell in 1357 and Forlì the following year. By the end of his period in office, Albornoz controlled almost the whole of Romagna, and Pope Innocent's wildest dreams came true when even great Bologna was brought under papal rule. The Cardinal built or rebuilt fortresses at Viterbo, Narni and Spoleto in the south of the Pope's dominions. He published a law code for all the lands of the Church, dubbed the *Egidian*

Constitutions. The scholar who edited this in 1912 thought that Albornoz was 'the only pontifical legate who knew how to put down rebellion in the Papal States'.

Nevertheless Albornoz's success was limited. The next Pope, Urban V, did return to Rome in October 1367, but went back to Avignon just before he died in September 1370, and it was in Avignon that his successor, Gregory, was elected. Gregory was a Frenchman from Limoges, but he decided once again to return the papal court to Rome, though he waited several years before doing so. In preparation for the move, he undertook further wars against the Visconti and the cities in the Papal States. In the process, he seriously alienated Florence, though she had always been a Guelf city.

In 1374, the Pope's delegate in Bologna banned the export of corn from Romagna in order to prevent a famine in the area, and used troops to close the Apennine passes. The Florentines regarded this as a hostile act, especially since it seriously threatened their commerce as well as their food supply, and they retaliated. They took the extraordinary step of allying themselves with their traditional enemy, Visconti Milan, as did Pisa, Lucca and Genoa. At the same time, the Florentine Chancellor Coluccio Salutati stirred up rebellion in Umbria, Romagna and the Marches, and the revolt against papal rule in the Pope's own territories spread rapidly. No fewer than eighty towns and cities joined the new league, which adopted a red banner emblazoned with the motto 'Libertas' (Freedom!). Very little was left of the old Papal State: Bruni thought that 'no one could remember a collapse like this.' But worse was to come, from the Pope's point of view, when Bologna fell to the rebels:

> The city was being held by a large force of Englishmen, commanded by Hawkwood; but he had marched his troops out to recover the town of Granarolo, which had rebelled during those days. The Bolognesi, who had been worked on for a long time by the Eight [the Florentine magistrates appointed as a kind of war cabinet], took heart at the absence of Hawkwood's troops, seized arms and liberated themselves like the other peoples. Instantly, as had been agreed, the Florentine People sent help to Bologna. The English troops who had left the city, when they heard about the uprising of the Bolognese people, did not dare to return.[30]

The Pope responded in draconian fashion. He laid Florence under a general interdict, prohibited all priests from saying mass and celebrating other sacraments, and made it lawful for Christian rulers to arrest Florentine merchants, strip them of their goods and sell them into slavery.

According to Renouard, French historian of the Avignonese Papacy, Gregory XI was able to reconquer the Papal States 'without much difficulty', but in reality the 'War of Eight Saints' which now ensued (named after eight Florentine magistrates elected to deal with the emergency) was very bitter and hard-fought. Both sides called on the services of foreign mercenaries, but Florence had the more efficient propaganda machine. The Pope, like many of his representatives in Italy, was French and he resided in Avignon. This was a cause of resentment in Italy, just as it was in England; but now the Pope used foreign mercenaries, particularly Bretons, to do his bidding. The fire of Italian nationalism – not merely a nineteenth-century phenomenon – was ignited, and Florence deployed her ablest writers to fan the flames. These subjected the Pope and his servants, particularly his new vicar-general, Robert of Geneva, to withering criticism. Francesco Sacchetti was among the critics. He sought to blacken Pope Gregory's name by likening him to the worst and most tyrannical rulers in history and, just as we might compare a modern dictator to Hitler or Stalin, Sacchetti likened Gregory to the tyrants of the Old Testament:

> Which Pharaoh, which King of Egypt
> ever committed such a crime
> as when you sought to suppress Tuscany
> with that foreign people?[31]

Hawkwood's orders were to pacify the Papal States. These formed a central belt across the Italian peninsula, comprising parts of what we would call Lazio, Tuscany, Umbria, the Marches and Romagna. From the Englishman's point of view, the mission to restore law and order was an extremely difficult one, which even Albornoz had failed to achieve twenty years before. His success in recapturing some of the key rebel towns has been largely neglected, if not vilified. Most historians still fall for the Florentine propaganda, which created a myth readily adopted by later generations of Italian nationalists. The key message this conveyed was that the rebels were patriots and the Pope and his henchmen were guilty men, pursuing an anti-nationalist line. The truth was altogether more complex. The Pope told the Florentines in no uncertain terms that good government (by which he meant his government) was in everyone's interest and that punitive measures to put down the rebellion were fully justified. As for the 'nationalist' cause pursued by the rebels, Gregory thought that this was a front for Florentine expansion, and it is noteworthy that Alberigo da Barbiano – founder and paragon of the so-called 'Italian school' of mercenaries – took part in putting down the revolt, along with the hated foreigners.

Though Hawkwood remained loyal to the Pope for some years, relations were never easy, partly because Gregory XI resided in Avignon or in one of the papal palaces nearby and could not be contacted quickly, and partly because the Papacy was slow to pay. Medieval exchequers worked slowly; the Pope's systems for raising credit in Avignon were possibly not as good as those available to the Italian merchant oligarchies; and the papal bureaucracy was better at flattery than it was at securing the delivery of cash or bills of exchange. Thus, we find the Pope praising Hawkwood as a champion of Christ, an athlete of the Lord and a soldier of the Christian faith – but the surviving correspondence is also full of excuses for not sending money. On one occasion, he even promised that Hawkwood would get his reward in heaven – not something calculated to impress Sir John, or keep his men from complaining. Moreover, though Gregory wrote some letters of congratulation, he also sniped from the sidelines, complaining on one occasion that his commander had failed to recover sufficient territory from 'Bernabò, that son of Belial'. He also disapproved of his commander's private life. In June in 1373 he wrote to the Bishop of London from Pont de Sorgues, ordering him to ordain an illegitimate son of Hawkwood's in England, 'provided that he be not an imitator of his father's incontinency'.[32]

Hawkwood did not always make war according to the Pope's rules, but the Pope did not always set realistic objectives. In the summer of 1375 Gregory sent him to attack Florence itself, but Sir John could no more have captured that city than Edward III could have captured Paris in the 1340s and 1350s. In Novella 79 Sacchetti relates a conversation between an armchair strategist and a knight, during which the former boasts that he could storm Florence with 200 *barbute* (400 men). The knight, who is the voice of experience, replies that not even 500 would be enough. In reality it would have needed very substantial forces, since Florence was home to some 70,000 people, even after the plague had taken its toll, and she was ringed with walls and towers completed in 1333. The walls were forty-seven feet high and seven feet thick, the towers seventy-five feet high. We do not know how many men Hawkwood took with him when he marched south for the Arno in 1375, but it was most unlikely that he could have undertaken a siege, or that he could have taken the city by storm.

There was no attack on Florence in 1375. Although the illustrator of Giovanni Sercambi's chronicle shows Hawkwood and his men in front of the city walls, flying banners which bear the papal coat of arms as well as his own, Sir John allowed himself to be bought off for 130,000 gold florins. Following this undoubted coup, he extracted lesser sums from Arezzo, Lucca, Pisa and Siena.[33] In July, the Florentines even agreed to pay him a pension of 1,200 florins a year for life, but he did not pass into their employment. The award of the lump sum and the pension meant only that he would not attack them again.

It was at this time that Caterina di Benincasa wrote to Hawkwood. She was a holy person who was eventually made a saint in 1461. She led an ascetic way of life and campaigned vigorously for religious reformation, peace and a crusade against the Turks. She travelled to Avignon to urge Gregory XI to move back to Rome. With the help of a series of secretaries and her confessor Raymond of Capua, she also wrote hundreds of letters to prominent figures, including the King of France, Louis of Anjou, Queen Joanna of Naples and Pope Gregory. Her letter to Hawkwood urged him to go on crusade. She therefore sought to appeal to him as a fellow Christian but, at the same time, she condemned his way of life. It is clear from the terms of her letter that she was not a strategist:

> To Sir Hawkwood, *condottiere*, and head of the Company which came in the time of famine:

> Oh dearest and most gentle brother in Christ Jesus, would it really be such a great effort to look into your heart and consider the stresses and strains you have endured in serving the devil for money? Change your way of life and sign up for the crucified Christ instead, you and all your followers and companions. That way you would become a member of Christ's company, going to fight the infidel dogs who possess our holy places. You who so delight in making war and fighting, campaign no more against Christians … I am astounded that you, having promised (as I have heard) that you would go and die for Christ on the crusade, should now want to make war here …[34]

Catherine's request bore little relation to political or military reality. She ignored the fact that Hawkwood was already in the Pope's service, indeed that he fought under the banner of the 'Holy Company' (*Compagnia Santa*). Later on, when he fought for the Pope in Naples, he bore the title of 'captain-general of the Church'. Catherine was also naive in thinking that he could simply depart for the East, as if he were a pilgrim. It was never likely that Hawkwood would take up the Cross unless someone offered him a *condotta*, and a command to go with it, and this Catherine was not in a position to do.[35] Instead Hawkwood continued to work for Pope Gregory. They still bickered about money, but Gregory was able to leave Avignon, on 13 September 1376: he arrived in Rome on 17 January 1377.

Tying the Knot with Milan, 1377

Hawkwood married Donnina Visconti in March 1377, when he was in his late fifties and she was in her teens. The marriage was contracted for military and diplomatic reasons, with a large monetary consideration, though the Milanese Annals describe Donnina as being very beautiful (*pulcherrima*). Back in England the anonymous writer who continued Adam Murimuth's chronicle heard about the wedding:

> In this year Sir Hawkwood ... took to wife the daughter of Bernabò, lord of Milan, a Bastard, and with her the said lord also gave him an income – of 10,000 Florins; and from that time Hawkwood did not lead his companies against him as he had done before.[36]

Bernabò liked to spin a complex web of alliances. He had sixteen legitimate children, and many more illegitimate. He arranged for the legitimate offspring to marry into various royal and aristocratic houses of Western Europe – French, Bavarian, Cypriot, Mantuan and others, but no fewer than five illegitimate daughters were married to *condottieri*,[37] and in 1377 it was Hawkwood's turn. After a period of several years' absence from Lombardy, he now commanded a new anti-papal league, of which Florence was treasurer but Bernabò was chief executive. The German *condottiere* Lutz von Landau married Elisabetta Visconti at the same time.

The marriage was celebrated in chivalric manner, which included jousting, but there was no dancing because the Visconti were in mourning for one of the bride's half-sisters. Dancing was evidently thought disrespectful, whereas jousting was indispensable. The Mantuan ambassador described some of the magnificent wedding presents:

> After the dinner the lady Regina made a present to the bride of a thousand gold ducats in a vase. The Signor Marco gave her a necklace (*zardino*) of pearls, worth three hundred ducats, and the Signor Luigi a gift of pearls of the same value, and in like manner did many of the nobles. So much silver was offered in largesse to the Englishmen, that it is estimated at the value of a thousand ducats.

William Caferro thinks that it was at this time – as part of Donnina's dowry – that Hawkwood was given a share of Gazzuolo, a fishing village on the River Oglio, not far from Borgoforte and its confluence with the Po.

Hawkwood had almost certainly been married before, though nobody knows who his first wife was, or what became of her. However, despite its mercenary origins in a bargain struck between master and *condottiere*, and the forty years separating bride and groom, this second marriage does seem to have proved a success. The union must have rejuvenated him, for he had three children in quick succession, and it lasted until his death in 1394, though we have very little other evidence as to the nature of the relationship. There is no sign of his ever having been married in either of his memorials, in Florence or in Essex. In particular, the emblems displayed along the base of the tomb in Essex are shields, which would have carried the arms of his friends – not lozenges, as one would expect if a woman had been commemorated. On the other hand, a letter does survive, which Donnina wrote to the Gonzaga lord of Mantua in 1379, in which she proudly signs herself 'Donnina Visconti of Milan, consort of the lord Hawkwood'.[38]

Chapter 3
'The Best Commander': Italy, 1377–94

The people rejoiced because he was the best commander of men who was then in Italy.

Cronica Volgare

Reconciled to Florence

The chronicler Andrea Gataro tells us that in 1378 Hawkwood and Lutz von Landau (who seem at this time to have been brothers-in-arms as well as brothers-in-law) received an offer from the Venetians of 30,000 gold ducats to mount a *chevauchée* into Paduan territory. They discussed the proposal, but rejected it. Instead, Bernabò Visconti sent them against the Scaligers of Verona, in support of his wife's hereditary claim to that city. The English brigade established 'an entrenched camp' under the walls of the city – which implies a siege – but Verona was not destined to fall to Bernabò in 1378. She maintained her independence for a further ten years, before losing it to his nephew Gian Galeazzo.

The *condottieri* encountered stiff resistance when Hungarian troops intervened in aid of the Veronese. They managed to defeat these at the Battle of Sebeto on the Adige in March 1379, but despite this achievement and the ties of kinship, Bernabò soon lost patience with them. We are told that he stopped their pay, accused Hawkwood and Landau of being afraid of a fight, and even put a price on their heads. This sounds like an intemperate reaction, but according to Gataro the campaign against Verona was a indeed a failure, while others say that Hawkwood and Landau raided Milanese territory in retaliation for the withholding of their pay. If this was true, Bernabò may have had good cause.[1] Whatever the exact reason for the falling out, his father-in-law's reaction was the last straw so far as Hawkwood was concerned, and he now started to gravitate towards the Florentine sphere of influence. Florence had offered him employment before, and her proposals seemed more and more attractive.

The Florentines were bound to have mixed feelings about Hawkwood. The poet Sacchetti was not exactly complimentary:

Inconstant Florence, how many times unexpectedly
has the English viper taken up arms,
with many heads, always growing two more,
but you, with soft tempers,
and without any fire, have so bent him to your will,
that he has mustered under your standard.[2]

Hawkwood is being compared here, not just to a snake in the grass, but to the many-headed hydra which Hercules had laboured to kill. However, whether Sacchetti liked it or not, Sir John was now hired, and his alliance with the Florentine republic proved an enduring feature of the last fourteen years of his life.

Since Florence was at peace for most of the 1380s and Hawkwood lived by war, his new masters allowed him to fight several campaigns in other parts of Italy, until the time came when they felt compelled to confront Milan. This is why we find him engaged in other wars and other places throughout the 1380s. He did act as a kind of policeman for the Florentines, but he also mounted campaigns for Lucca, Siena, Perugia and Pisa against their exiles (1379), as well as fighting for Rimini (1383) and Bologna (1388). In the early 1380s he found time to defend his own Romagnol properties against the attacks of his enemy Astorre Manfredi, and he continued to form Free Companies and engaged in freelance activity as well, intermittently. As if all this were not enough for one man, he found time to intervene in the far South of Italy.

The War in Naples and the English Connection
Though they paid him well, the Florentines did not keep Hawkwood fully employed, and, throughout the 1380s, he found work where there were wars to be fought. The most protracted of these was the civil war in Naples, which broke out when it became clear that Queen Joanna was going to die without issue, despite having had four husbands. The main contenders for her crown were the heads of two branches of the far-flung and powerful Angevin dynasty – Louis, Duke of Anjou and senior uncle of King Charles VI of France, and Charles of Durazzo (in modern Albania), but the matter was further complicated by the Great Schism in the Papacy, which had divided Western Christendom since 1378. The French and their allies (Castile and Scotland) were staunch supporters of the 'anti-Pope' Clement VII, who took up residence back in Avignon. Charles supported Pope Urban VI in Rome, as did England and many Italian states, including Florence. Towards the end of her life, Queen Joanna proclaimed Louis of Anjou as her successor. This provoked a successful invasion of Naples by Charles of Durazzo, who entered her capital in the summer of 1382. Joanna was

either strangled or suffocated and Charles proclaimed himself king. This triggered a second invasion by Louis, blessed with the status of a crusade by Pope Clement.

What part did Hawkwood play in this maelstrom? In short, he went south to fight for the Durazzo-Angevins, in 1382–3.[3] The deal was brokered by Pope Urban and Hawkwood was commander-in-chief of the forces opposing Louis of Anjou. The mission was difficult, because Louis was regent of a resurgent France. His invasion of Naples was backed by French money and undertaken by a largely French army.[4] He forged alliances with Visconti Milan and the Count of Savoy, thereby securing his route to Italy. He raised taxes in France to finance his expedition, and when he arrived in Italy 'he had his mint with him, where he coined florins and white money, with which he made his payments through Lombardy and Tuscany.' The ability to make one's own money was something Hawkwood could only dream of.

It sounds an unequal contest; and it would be idle to pretend that Hawkwood did more than hold his own. There were some skirmishes, but no major battles, and the Durazzo-Angevin siege of Paduli (near Benevento) proved unsuccessful. Nevertheless, Louis of Anjou's expedition became thoroughly bogged down. He was forced to retreat from the city of Naples to the heel of Italy, where he died of fever in 1384, passing his ancestral claims to Naples to his son of the same name.

In comparison to his position in Florence, Hawkwood's intervention in the Neapolitan war of succession was a sideshow, but this is not how it was seen by the English court. Diplomatic records show that Hawkwood played an important role as an ambassador for Richard II (1377–99) in the early 1380s, and the fighting in Naples was part of the English war effort against the French, though it cost the English Exchequer nothing.

English diplomacy in the 1370s and 1380s was once again driven by the fact that the country was locked in a war with Valois France, but it now seemed like a war that could not be won. Since the fighting had resumed on a grand scale, the English had lost most of what they had won at Brétigny, and Louis of Anjou had played a leading role in their defeat. He had fomented rebellion against the Black Prince's government in English Aquitaine and personally led several invasions of the Principality. He was an inveterate and irreconcilable opponent, going so far as to have tapestries woven for his palace at Angers, showing Edward III and his sons as agents of the devil.[5] Seemingly powerless to stop the rot, the English considered ways of undermining French power elsewhere. John of Gaunt argued for 'the Way of Spain' – an invasion of Castile in alliance with Aragon or Portugal, but Hawkwood's war in Naples was also a kind of proxy war with England's arch-enemy.[6]

It also made sense for the English to counteract French influence diplomatically, via Pope Urban in Rome; and Hawkwood was almost uniquely qualified to help here. He was resident in Italy, experienced in Italian affairs, fluent in Italian and had many contacts. So it is that we find him appointed, in May 1381 and again in September 1385, as a royal ambassador. On the first occasion, he and his two colleagues (Walter Skirlawe, Dean of St Martin's, and Sir Nicholas Dagworth, a knight of the royal household) were authorized to 'treat with the Pope about proceedings against *schismatics*' – which meant the supporters of Pope Clement – and to negotiate with the 'dukes, counts, lords or communes' of Italy, provided these were not themselves schismatic. On the second occasion, Hawkwood was appointed with Dagworth and the King's secretary John Bacon, to negotiate for alliances with Pope Urban, Charles of Durazzo and others in Genoa.

What were Hawkwood's responsibilities? Ambassadors were used for two different purposes: to deliver messages and to negotiate, and there is clear evidence of Sir John's role as messenger. On 23 May 1382, the Crown paid ten marks 'to John Northwood valet of Sir Hawkwood coming from the parts of Lombardy as messenger to the lord king from the said Hawkwood and going back there with an answer'. However, it seems fundamentally unlikely that Hawkwood would have conducted negotiations. His fellow ambassadors were (in effect) civil servants. They knew the King's mind, they were sent out from England with detailed instructions, and they had access to writing offices, charged with drafting the complex documents the job entailed. In addition Skirlawe and Bacon would have been well versed in Latin, the language in which negotiations were conducted. It is much more likely that Hawkwood supplied his colleagues with information about the Italian scene and provided them with escorts – a very necessary service at a time when travel by road was insecure.

As a result of his military and diplomatic services in Naples and in Rome, Hawkwood's relationship with the English Crown was transformed. For much of the 1360s and 1370s, he cannot have been popular with those who wielded power at the court of King Edward III. Edward had wanted to keep control of his soldiers, and it was not in his interests that veterans should leave for Italy and stay there. Moreover, Sir John himself recognized that he had done wrong because, at the very end of Edward's reign, he petitioned for a pardon 'as the King has granted Sir Robert Knollys for God and charity'.[7] The latter had sought forgiveness for wrongs committed in France some years previously, and it seems reasonable to suppose that this was the kind of behaviour which Hawkwood had in mind:

> seditions, adherence to the king's enemies, receiving the enemies' assent, counsel and favours, castles, fortresses and prisoners surrendered without licence or sold, and all other offences against the Crown, the common law and the statutes.

The pardon was duly granted in the spring of 1377, but this did not take Hawkwood very far. The old King died soon afterwards and, when Richard succeeded later that year, he was a mere boy of ten. It was several years before he could effectively take decisions, instead of his uncles. Gradually though, the new King must have come to realize that Hawkwood could be of considerable use, and the early 1380s seem to have been the turning-point. In the letters appointing him ambassador in 1381, Richard described Sir John as a 'most dear counsellor, in whom we have full confidence'. Perhaps it is not too much of an anachronism to say that by the middle years of the decade, Hawkwood had become 'our man in Italy'.[8]

Gian Galeazzo's coup, 1385

The crisis in Hawkwood's personal life was the Milanese revolution of 1385, when Gian Galeazzo Visconti overthrew his uncle Bernabò, seized control of Milan and its vast wealth, and disinherited Bernabò's children. Philippe de Mézières likened these events to a fight to the death between two poisonous vipers, with Gian Galeazzo the more deadly. The coup d'état produced a rich harvest of dynastic disputes, but in Italian terms it was not unusual, while in Romagna, where Hawkwood had planned to make a home, the imprisonment and even murder of one's relatives was almost routine. News of Bernabò's downfall reached England. Chaucer commented on it in *The Canterbury Tales*:

Of Bernado of Lombardy:

Your ill fortune, great Bernardo, Viscount
Of Milan, O you scourge of Lombardy,
God of enjoyment, why should I not recount,
Since in the world's eyes you once climbed so high?
Your brother's son – and doubly your ally,
Being your nephew and your son-in-law,
Shut you within his prison, there to die;
And you were killed, I don't know how or why.

The monk of Westminster wrote about Bernabò's fate in more lurid terms. Though he admitted that he did not know how he had died, he was willing to speculate that it could have been 'by cold steel, by starvation, or by poison'. There were others who said that the old man died of rage.

Hawkwood learned the news when he received a letter from Carlo Visconti – Bernabò's eldest legitimate son, and his own brother-in-law:

To our magnificent, dearest, and closest friend

We are writing to tell you that today at high noon in Milan, the Lord Count of Virtue[9] has captured and imprisoned the magnificent and high Lord, his lord and our lord and father, together with our magnificent and dearest brother and Lord, Luigi Visconti. We ourselves are free, in our citadel of Crema, and the fortress of Porta Romana[10] is also holding out in our name. Accordingly, we affectionately ask you to show your worth as a brother, by coming to our aid immediately via Parma, and bringing with you any men-at-arms which you have yourself, or which you can gather together from among your friends; and we have plenty of money available, ready to be paid out in wages, according to your commands; but it is time for you to show your strength, in the way you know how, and as you always used to do. Please reply immediately.

  Given at Crema on May 6 [1385]

What had happened was that Gian Galeazzo had tricked Bernabò into meeting him without a proper escort. By capturing his uncle, he made himself lord of Milan as well as Pavia and greatly increased the extent of his domains. He now controlled all the territories the Visconti had fought so long and so hard for. Bernabò's legitimate sons became his prisoners or fled. The principal exile was Carlo, and it was he who sought Hawkwood's help, as a kinsman. Sir John soon had an additional reason for opposing Gian Galeazzo, which was that, on taking power in Milan, the latter declared that Bernabò's second marriage (to his former mistress Donnina dei Porri) was invalid. This meant that Hawkwood's own wife could no longer be regarded as legitimated by that marriage. Yet, despite these insults, Sir John made no move to help the exiles. Indeed, instead of going to Carlo's assistance, he obtained confirmation – from Gian Galeazzo – of his title to the property which had come to him as part of his wife's dowry in 1377 and, on 1 July 1385, he even signed a *condotta* with the usurper:

Be it known that Sir Hawkwood, of England, knight, has promised and sworn to Francischino de Caymis, proctor of Gian Gaeazzo Visconti, Count Virtù, of Milan, and Martin, public notaries to observe faithfully all the following matters.

  Firstly, if the said count requires his services, he promises to come, unless he is in the pay of some community or lord so that he cannot do so honourably, and even then he will be bound to serve, if the Count desires, at the expiry of his contract. On the other hand, the said proctor undertakes that if Sir John comes when required, the Count will give him a provision of 300 florins a month. Also Sir John may bring with him esquires up to thirty lances, to whom the Count will pay such wages as he is giving to the other esquires then in his service. If Sir John brings more than thirty, by the Count's order, they shall receive the same as other lances receiving wages from the Count. Moreover the Count shall not be bound to pay the 1,000 florins, which the said proctor offered to Sir John yearly, if he does not come and has not been prevented by just impediments, up to the fourth month after the request ...[11]

At this point in their narrative Temple-Leader and Marcotti, normally so admiring of Hawkwood, are moved to exclaim 'Papers will speak!' Shocked by their hero's cynicism, they confess astonishment 'that Hawkwood, who was accustomed to put quite a different price on his sword, should needlessly and for mediocre gain sell himself to one who so seriously compromised his own interests and even his family peace.' Was it really so shameful to sign a *contratto aspetto*, a contract agreeing to serve Gian Galeazzo at a future date, if called upon to do so? Was it even surprising, when one considers Bernabò's high-handed treatment of both Gian Galeazzo and Hawkwood in the late 1370s and early 1380s? Hawkwood would have understood Gian Galeazzo's reasons for wanting to supplant his uncle, so as to unify Visconti control of Lombardy. This was an obvious objective, from the strategic as well as the dynastic point of view. To achieve it involved a high degree of ruthlessness, which clearly shocked Victorian sensibility, but it would scarcely have raised an eyebrow among medieval English monarchs or the Italian *signori* of Machiavelli's day. Even within the Visconti family, the coup did not have the same impact on everyone. One of Bernabò's daughters (Caterina) was married to Gian Galeazzo – and remained so – and several of her sisters continued to live at the Milanese court. They seem to have had no difficulty in reconciling themselves to what had happened. From an English point of view, Hawkwood's refusal to help Carlo Visconti in 1385 is very understandable, since by this date he had become an important agent for the Crown, whose interests required that he should deal with whoever was in de facto control of Milan – and it rapidly became clear that this was Gian Galeazzo.

Yet, as time passed it became clear that the agreement reached between Hawkwood and Gian Galeazzo in July 1385 did not lead to a new relationship. It merely papered over the cracks in the Visconti dynasty. These grew wider as Bernabò's sons remained in exile or in prison, and became irreparable when Bernabò died at the castle of Trezzo on the Adda later that year.

Hawkwood for Padua, 1386–7

Hawkwood had by now acquired a pan-Italian reputation. Galeazzo Gataro, the senior chronicler in Padua, regarded him as 'the most famous captain in all Italy, the most expert and prudent in feats of arms', and the lords of Padua decided to hire him, together with his entire Company.[12]

Padua was ruled by the Carrara, whose coat of arms was a *carroccio* – a chariot drawn by oxen. The senior lord of Padua, Francesco Carrara, was known as Il Vecchio (the Old Man) to distinguish him from his son, Il Novello (the New Man). The city was traditionally Guelf; indeed being Guelf was thought to be an essential part of the quality of 'Patavinitas' (being Paduan), but her foreign policy was governed by the dynastic ambitions of the Carrara. Their enemies included, first and foremost, the Scaligers of Verona, though the Florentine historian Gregorio Dati thought that the war which broke out in 1385 was brought about by the machinations of Gian Galeazzo of Milan. There was certainly a great deal of animosity between the ruling houses of Padua and Verona, to judge by an incident at the start of the conflict. The Scaliger lord invited Il Vecchio to settle their differences with a duel and Francesco 'Novello' offered to be his father's champion; but the Old Man would not hear of it. He told his son:

> It's neither right nor honourable, that you and I, who are born of noble and legitimate matrimony, should fight with a most vile bastard, born from the stomach of a wretched baker woman.

Nowadays, it means little to call a man a bastard. Attitudes in Hawkwood's day were different. The Black Prince's principal reason for invading Castile in 1367 on behalf of King Pedro 'the Cruel' was that Pedro had been deposed by his half-brother, Enrique of Trastamara, who was illegitimate.[13]

In 1386 the Paduans won a decisive victory at the Battle of Brentelle, but in the following year the Veronese counter-attacked, and it was now that the Carrara called on Hawkwood to assist them. He agreed to come because the price was right, but it may have helped that the Carrara had received military assistance from Florence before. In the 1370s three Florentine knights had served on Il Vecchio's Council of War, including Manno Donati, who now lies buried in Padua. The army had been under the joint command of Novello and Ubaldini, but when Hawkwood arrived with a force of 500 lances and 600 archers, the latter renounced command in his favour, declaring: 'From this day forward I would no longer wish to hold [the baton of command] in the presence of the lord John Hawkwood.'[14] The Paduan army now consisted of 7,500 horsemen and 1,000 footsoldiers, but the Veronese were probably more numerous, having around 9,000 horse, 1,000 foot, 1,600 archers and crossbowmen and innumerable *gentaglia* ('common people'). Hawkwood laid siege to Verona nonetheless, but he was soon forced to fall back along the south bank of the Adige. He decided to stand and fight at Castagnaro. The result was his most famous victory (see Chapter 8).

Hawkwood's success was celebrated in Padua, but it did not produce any lasting benefits for the city. In Sacchetti's words, she soon became a 'sad place' when she was annexed by Milan. In 1388 Gian Galeazzo Visconti formed an alliance with the Venetians and moved against the Paduans, not long after he had conquered the Veronese. Jacopo dal Verme led the army of invasion, the military and economic pressure proved too great, and the Carrara lords were forced to abdicate. Il Vecchio was first to go, though his son fled soon afterwards. Centuries later in 1850, the British artist Eastlake recreated this incident in a typically melodramatic Victorian painting, *The Escape of Francesco Novello of Carrara, with his Wife, from the Duke of Milan.*

With the assistance of Hawkwood and the Florentine army, Francesco Novello was able to return to Padua in triumph in 1390, but fate continued to be unkind to the Carrara. Il Vecchio died at Monza in 1393, still a prisoner of Gian Galeazzo. His son enjoyed a new lease of life as ruler of Padua, but only for a decade. He might have been expected to survive longer, given that Gian Galeazzo died prematurely in 1402, but Novello overreached himself in his dealings with the Venetians. In 1405 they convicted him of treason, beat him up and strangled him in his cell. Padua was swallowed whole by Venice, and her new rulers ruthlessly suppressed any symbols of the Carrara, which were viewed as a potential focus for rebellion. They destroyed Il Vecchio's tomb in the Piazza del Duomo, and they arranged for the *carroccio* motifs both there and on the town's walls to be painted over or removed, though a few remain, high up in the Baptistery.

Hawkwood against Milan, 1389–91

Duccio Balestracci thinks that the relationship between Hawkwood and Florence grew closer in the aftermath of the Paduan war. In a new contract, the Florentines refer to him as '*sometime* captain of the English Company', which indicates a loosening of his connection with his English brigade. Whether or not that is so, the relationship with Florence was certainly cemented by the events of 1389–91. In the 1360s Hawkwood had fought the Florentines in a trade war over customs duties. Now he fought for them in a war of survival. He was now around seventy years old, but it proved to be his finest hour.

The Florentines had decided it was time to stand up to Gian Galeazzo. The Milanese dictator had gone too far in taking over both Verona and Padua, and was now seeking to project his power outside the plain of Lombardy. For Florence the struggle was also ideological. Viewed in the light of Roman history, the city on the Arno represented republican liberty, while Gian Galeazzo was the personification of imperial tyranny.

Arno

The Arno rises in the Apennines and heads south, running down through the Casentino to Arezzo, before it turns north, through Figline and Incisa, to Florence. It then takes a westerly course, picks up the waters of the Era, Elsa and Pesa and flows through a wide valley punctuated with lumpy hills, before arriving in Pisa and discharging into the sea. When Hawkwood was employed by the Pisans in 1363–4, he raided all around Florence and up into the middle Arno valley, capturing Incisa and Figline easily, and even reaching the walls of Arezzo.

He also fought two pitched battles with the Florentines at Cascina. He won the second of these, in 1369, but lost the first, in 1364. Naturally, it was First Cascina, and their victory over Hawkwood and the Pisans, that was celebrated by the Florentines, and that is now remembered by historians of art, thanks to Michelangelo. In the early sixteenth century, he was commissioned to paint a fresco about the Pisan War for the Palazzo Vecchio. He started by drawing a cartoon in the usual way, and (in Vasari's account):

> He filled it with nude men bathing during the heat in the River Arno, imagining the moment when the alarm is sounded as in the camp at the assault of the enemy, and while the soldiers emerge from the water to dress, the divinely inspired hands of Michelangelo depicted some hurrying to take up their arms to help their comrades, while others buckle on their cuirasses.

At the time, this cartoon did not appeal to the city authorities, presumably because it was not suitably triumphant, but its virtuosity 'astonished and amazed' other artists, and the road leading from the town to the river in Cascina is still called Via Michelangelo.

A few miles from Cascina lies the fortress of San Miniato al Tedesco. 'Al Tedesco' indicates that this place was – long before Hawkwood's time – a seat of deputies appointed by the German Emperors. The citadel sits on a peak and nowadays a lift has been installed to help those who arrive in the lower town to reach the top. The Milanese, led by Hawkwood, tried to break a Florentine siege here in 1368, but it fell to Florence nonetheless.

A similar fortress dominated nearby Montopoli, which the Florentines had controlled since 1349, and the village below, site of Uccello's *Battle of San Romano*, fought in 1432. Before leaving for Bologna in May 1390, Hawkwood ordered that a dyke (*fosso*) be dug here, to defend the Florentine frontier. This was said to be twenty feet wide and twenty feet deep and more than a mile long. Sir John also built a tower at San Romano and linked it to the dyke, so as to block the road between Florence and Pisa. This kind of defensive strategy had been tried before, at considerable cost and effort: the Florentine historian Leonardo Bruni tells us that his compatriots tried more than once to close off the approaches to the city. The effort was never worthwhile, since enemy columns could always bypass fixed defences, as the Germans bypassed the French Maginot line in 1940.

Hawkwood's tower at San Romano no longer exists, nor does the fortress on the hill at Montopoli. Kesselring's German troops, ordered to destroy any buildings capable of being useful to the Allies, mined and destroyed them both, as they retreated from the Arno to the Gothic line in 1944.

The Milanese and Paduan exiles living in Florence constantly stirred the brew. Exiles were a regular feature of life in many Italian cities and Hawkwood's invasion plans were co-ordinated with both Carlo Visconti and Francesco Novello Carrara. There were attempts to negotiate a diplomatic settlement of the various differences between Florence and Milan, but the exiles did not want peace – they wanted an invasion, to restore them to their native cities, and if possible punish Milan. They had everything to hope for. Conspiracies involving the disinherited had proved successful in Scotland in 1332 and in Castile in the 1360s.

Florence launched the first strike when she took Montepulciano under her protection. This caused Gian Galeazzo to declare war in April 1390, using traditional propaganda to arouse old fears. He accused the *Signoria* of being in the thrall of the 'Archguelfs' and of seeking to dominate Italy. Coluccio Salutati, who was a consummate politician as well as a distinguished writer, responded with elegant vitriol. Adopting an almost Churchillian stance, he declared that Florence would resist the 'Tyrant of Lombardy' with all her might, in the name of liberty for all. In a letter to the Count of Armagnac, the Florentines made a joke at Gian Galeazzo's expense, punning that he was not the Count of Virtue, but a slave to every vice.[15]

Gian Galeazzo laid siege to Bologna, while the Florentines recalled Hawkwood from the South. Instead of taking the traditional route home along the Via Francigena, he journeyed back through the swamps of the Maremma, laying a false trail before setting off, seeking safe-conducts from places he never intended to come by, and eventually returning through Volterra. Florence put him in charge of the entire Florentine army and now, as commander-in-chief, he fought campaign after campaign, from spring 1390 through to autumn 1391. His objectives were the relief of Bologna, the liberation of Padua and Verona, and the invasion of the province of Lombardy, but in the end he had to defend the Tuscan homeland itself.

Sir John achieved his immediate objectives. He marched north through the Apennines, linked up with Giovanni da Barbiano and relieved the siege of Bologna. He drove off the Milanese led by Jacopo dal Verme, and in June Francesco Novello succeeded in recapturing Padua, much to the delight of the Carrara loyalists.[16] Meanwhile, however, dal Verme had occupied Casalecchio di Reno, where there is nowadays an ugly intersection on the motorway, but where Temple-Leader saw an attractive river. It was here that Hawkwood tried to induce his rival to give battle. On three successive days, he sent his trumpeter Zuzzo with a bloody gauntlet, the traditional invitation to combat, but dal Verme would not accept the challenge at all and moved his army away.[17] Hawkwood advanced on Parma, to the west on the Via Emilia, but made his base in newly liberated Padua.

In October 1390 the Florentines concluded an alliance with Count Jean of Armagnac, who agreed to bring an army across the Alps, consisting in part of former members of the Free Companies. The plan was for a grand pincer movement, with Hawkwood attacking the Milanese from the east, Armagnac from the west. At the beginning of 1391 the allies assembled in Padua. The titular commander-in-chief was Francesco Novello, but the field commanders were his half-brother the Count of Carrara (for Padua), Giovanni da Barbiano (for Bologna) and Hawkwood (for Florence). Florence had contributed a force of 600 cuirassiers and there were also 1,500 archers and 3,500 infantry under Bonfazio Lupo. Among other allied captains was Astorre Manfredi of Faenza, Hawkwood's enemy from Romagna. In accordance with the advice of astrologers, the army left Padua two hours before sunrise. There was a short winter offensive, and an unsuccessful attempt to liberate Verona. It was at about this time that Astorre Manfredi left camp, having fallen under suspicion of conspiring with the Visconti and plotting to kill Hawkwood and Novello, but he walked away rather than try to face charges. It is difficult to imagine that Hawkwood was sorry to see him go.

The army was reorganized under Hawkwood's direct command, and in the spring he led out 2,200 lances (about 6,600 men) plus infantry, marching from Padua to within ten miles of Milan itself and crossing the great rivers of Lombardy, just as the Black Prince had crossed those of the Langue d'Oc, thirty years before.[18] He encountered resistance in several places, not least when he reached the Adda, but not the major battle one would have expected. It seems that the majority of Gian Galeazzo's forces – under Jacopo dal Verme – lay to the west to await Armagnac's invasion, while Taddeo dal Verme was left to pin Hawkwood down on the eastern front.

Armagnac's army failed to materialize and since the Milanese had adopted a scorched-earth policy, Sir John consulted with the Florentine and Bolognese emissaries and decided to retreat. Some writers have asserted that he withdrew because he felt he had won a moral victory, but this seems unlikely. The fact is that he had been unable to bring the enemy to battle, and he was not equipped to undertake a siege of Milan. Andrea Gataro further explains that his supplies were running short, and his troops were repeatedly harassed by enemy skirmishers.[19] Hawkwood therefore fell back towards the Adige. When he reached the river, Gian Galeazzo's pioneers used the stratagem Hawkwood had used at Borgoforte on the Po in 1368: they broke the riverbanks and let the floodwater turn the surrounding plain into a swamp. It was only by using all his skills as a general that Hawkwood was able to bring most of his men back to the safety of Padua.

The Florentines were grateful that Hawkwood had rescued their army. Predictably, Gian Galeazzo boasted that dal Verme had *routed* Hawkwood, but even the Milanese annalist did not agree. He noted laconically that 'many were wounded and killed, both on the Lord Count of Virtù's side, and on the side of the Lord John [Hawkwood]', adding that the Milanese general Facino Cane was among the wounded. The fighting retreat to Padua was also noted with great pride, and considerable exaggeration, by the Westminster chronicler:

> Hawkwood … carried out a skilful withdrawal of his forces and reached Padua in good fettle, despite the manifold harassments to which he was subjected on the march by the enemy, who, to deny him a free passage towards Padua, breached the riverbanks here and there and flooded the whole surrounding countryside; but none the less he escaped unscathed with his men, of whom he did not lose above four.[20]

Frances Stonor Saunders (writing in 2004) was much more critical. She accused Hawkwood of making 'a tactical error of mystifying proportions', in allowing his men to be inundated in the first place. She suggested that he should have sent scouts back up the Adige and that, if he had done that, they would have reported the activities of the Visconti engineers, so he could have avoided the flood altogether. This criticism is unconvincing, for it assumes that Hawkwood did not even try to obtain the intelligence he needed. He may well have done so and failed to gather any useful information, or he may have learned what was going on but been unable to do anything about it. We cannot know, but no contemporary writer made the mistake of underestimating him.

Gian Galeazzo's divided armies were now able to join forces again. When the French under Armagnac finally arrived, it was too late and dal Verme crushed them decisively at Alessandria.[21] Armagnac was captured and died from his wounds, while his army retreated into Piedmont. This was a battle of European importance, and Armagnac's death was reported in France as a great tragedy, since he was widely regarded as a fine man, from a great family, brought low by

Dame Fortune. The Montpellier chronicler was but one of those who recorded his fate:

> On 24 July [1391] Count Jean of Armagnac was defeated by the men of Gian Galeazzo Visconti lord of Milan and Pavia, through a great clash of arms inflicted on his men [*per grant elcasament de fach darmas que fazia am sa gent*].[22]

After the debacle, even Carlo Visconti deserted the allied cause. He had been a major supporter of the war, but seems to have given up hope when he learned of Armagnac's death. He fled to Venice and settled his differences with Gian Galeazzo, promising to abandon Italy forever.

Hawkwood was back in Padua when he learned that Jacopo dal Verme, having driven the invaders from Lombardy, had now been ordered to invade Tuscany. Saying a fond farewell to the Paduans,[23] he returned south to defend Florence, obstructed Jacopo's advance and decisively defeated the enemy rearguard at the Battle of Tizzana (see Chapter 8). Although this was not a pitched battle, Hawkwood's success led to a cessation of hostilities, and a peace treaty was signed between Florence and Milan in 1392. For the Florentine republic, the fighting retreat on the Adige, followed by the 'backs-to-the-wall' victory near her capital, were almost what Dunkirk and the Battle of Britain were to the British during the Second World War. The praises heaped on Hawkwood were extravagant; and Sir John was granted the equivalent of a state funeral when he died.

Hawkwood's defeat of the Milanese in 1391 must also have been a cause for celebration in England, because the French King was still an enemy, despite a three-year truce agreed in 1389, anti-French feeling still ran high among old soldiers, and Milan had allied herself with France when Gian Galeazzo had married his daughter Valentina to the Duke of Touraine. There had also been talk of Milan's obtaining French assistance in her war with Florence, from the Dukes of Touraine and Burgundy. Pope Boniface IX (Urban VI's successor in Rome) told the English court about this, and the monk of Westminster even heard wild rumours of French plots to sack Rome and transfer the shrines of the saints from Rome to Avignon, still the seat of the anti-Pope Clement.[24] The English court was powerless to intervene in Italy directly, but Hawkwood's victory at Tizzana would have been seen in London as both a blow to the Milanese cause and a setback for the French, the Clementists, and the French-Angevin attempt to dominate Naples.

The Knight's Two Bodies
Dante wrote that: 'Of all those who in this world are deserving of compassion, the most to be pitied are those who, languishing in exile, never see their country again,

save in dreams.'[25] Hawkwood was not an exile, but he missed England. He did not expect to die in Italy and he did not want to be buried in Florence. On the contrary, he planned to travel home in 1393 and wrote to enquire about a safe conduct for himself, his companion John Sampson and five horses (see Appendix 2). A Florentine document dated 11 March 1394 again records that he wanted to return because he was 'weary by reason of his great age and weighed down by infirmity'.

Hawkwood did not get his wish, because on 17 March 1394 he died suddenly at his home near Florence, possibly of a heart attack or stroke (*di un subito accidente*). The Florentines paid for a sumptuous funeral three days later. There was a display of his chivalric 'achievements' – banners and pennons decorated with his coat of arms, his great helm, his pennon with a harpy device, his sword and his shield (*targa*).[26] The authorities did not provide him with the marble tomb which had been voted on, but they did pay for Agnolo Gaddi and Giuliano Arrighi (known as 'Pesello') to paint a fresco of him in the Duomo, and forty years later their successors commissioned no less an artist than Paolo Uccello to repaint the portrait.[27] This is the masterpiece which has graced the nave ever since, and which stops the tourist in his tracks, whether or not he realizes that the subject is an Englishman.

In June 1395, over a year after the funeral, Richard II asked for Hawkwood's body to be returned to England and the *Signoria* agreed. Reburials of this kind were not uncommon. The King's uncle, Lionel Duke of Clarence, who had died so soon after his marriage to Violante Visconti in 1368, had been buried in Pavia but reburied at the House of the Austin Friars in Clare in Suffolk. It is a mystery, however, whether Hawkwood (or some part of his remains) was reburied in England. The first question we have to answer is, what was it that the Florentines agreed to send back? There is a local Essex tradition that his whole body came back, wrapped in cloth of gold, but that would have been impossible, since the Florentines said they had buried the 'ashes and bones'. Was this what they agreed to send back, as Temple-Leader thought? Parts of the Constable of France, Bertrand du Guesclin (who died in 1380), were laid to rest in no fewer than four different places in that country.

It is not certain that *any* part of Hawkwood's body was brought home to Essex: the remains may be under the floor of the Duomo in Florence still, despite Richard II's request. Confirmation of this by excavation would be difficult, because it is a vast and precious area and there have been many alterations in the intervening centuries, but William Caferro and the archivist at the Opera del Duomo, Dr Lorenzo Fabbri, have pointed out to me that there is an entry in their records for 27 January 1406, which states:

The Opera … have decided that the lord John Hawkwood, formerly our captain, be moved from the place where he is and be placed lower down under the earth in the due and customary place.

This strongly suggests that the knight's remains were placed in a sarcophagus of some kind in the cathedral in 1394, and that they were transferred to a grave in the same place twelve years later. It would also mean that they were not taken to England between 1395, when Richard made his request, and 1399, when he was deposed; and that the monument in Sible Hedingham has always been a cenotaph rather than a tomb. But again, it should be noted that the memorial chapel in Sible has never been excavated and probably never will be, since that would require a faculty from the Church, and it is difficult to discharge the burden of proof on those who seek to disturb a site of Christian burial.[28]

Why did Richard II want to retrieve the knight's body? The King's biographer Nigel Saul thought psychology was at work here and that Richard had a fascination for dead bodies, but other factors were probably important. The English had begun copying French court ceremonial, and the French buried both kings and crown servants at St Denis. Similarly, Richard II had some of his retainers buried in Westminster Abbey. Though Hawkwood clearly did not receive full royal honours, the King's intervention was an extraordinary mark of respect. It confirms in a very personal way what the Willement Roll of Arms and other documentary evidence tells us: that in the last years of his life Sir John was not an exile, but an honoured member of English society, despite his absence abroad.

Personality and politics also played a part. In 1389 Richard II had dramatically announced that he had 'reached the age of maturity' and was assuming personal control of government, but he still had many reasons for feeling insecure. He was an only child, who was himself childless and whose first wife, Anne of Bohemia, died in 1394. He had never been popular with much of the old fighting aristocracy, nor with many of the self-made men who had done well out of the French wars, and he stood in great need of friends. He compensated for this by creating a select group of favourites and courtiers, and he recruited his own retainers to match the affinities built up by other powerful lords, notably his uncle John of Gaunt. In the years 1389–97 he recruited over a hundred knights and squires to serve him personally (of whom Sir Edward Dalyngrigge of Bodiam was one). Another was Nicholas Clifton, though Clifton was second in command of a group of men who had plotted to murder the most prominent Lancastrians. Richard needed to demonstrate that he valued the friendship and loyalty of his own supporters, by promoting and favouring them in public. He had been a childhood friend of Robert de Vere of Castle Hedingham, whom he had later created Duke of Ireland. Robert was forced into exile and died in a hunting accident in Belgium, but in 1395 the King attended his reburial in Essex. Hawkwood was also regarded as a loyal servant of the Crown: he had served Richard as an ambassador in the 1380s and served the English interest in other ways. The request for the return of his body (also in 1395) was a posthumous reward and an honour designed to impress the King's friends and opponents alike. The gesture was made at the same time as Richard tried to promote Nicholas Clifton by suggesting that this knight should take Hawkwood's place as captain-general of Florence.[29]

As we shall see, Caxton was to liken Hawkwood to the heroes of the Hundred Years' War – Edward III and his sons, and the knights Chandos, Knollys and Manny. The King is commemorated in Westminster Abbey, while the Black Prince lies in state in Canterbury Cathedral. Knollys's arms are displayed in several Norfolk churches, as well as on the Postern tower at Bodiam in Sussex. Manny was buried with great ceremony in his own Carthusian foundation, the London Charterhouse. Like Chandos, Hawkwood died and was buried abroad, but a memorial was created back home. Indeed King Richard may have been responding to local demand in making his request. The parish church in Sible Hedingham was largely rebuilt in the late fourteenth century and Hawkwood may well have been a benefactor – a stone hawk can still be seen high up on the west tower of the church. It was only natural that his local community should want his last resting-place to be in Essex rather than in Tuscany.

Though the tomb at Sible was reconstructed and much altered in the seventeenth century, to make way for the benches of which Protestant preachers were so fond, what remains has a remnant of medieval decoration. Whereas the brass commemorating Hawkwood's fellow ambassador Nicholas Dagworth in Norfolk concentrates on the lion, Hawkwood's tomb has several animals commonly found in medieval bestiaries. Naturally, there is the hawk, the animal Sir John used on his seal; but there is also a partridge or pheasant, a pelican and a hare. Interestingly – in view of Villani's description of Hawkwood as *volpigna* (vulpine) – there is also a fox. All these animals stood for something: the hawk for eagerness in pursuit; the pelican for self-sacrifice; the fox for wisdom. There is also a boar, a charge used by the de Veres of Castle Hedingham which had been used to represent both Edward III and the Black Prince in the *Prophecy of the Six Kings*. Harder to explain is the (headless) harpy, an unpleasant combination of woman and bird which appears in the spandrel to the right of the hawk, and which Sir John had displayed in Italy.[30] This creature stood for ferocity and was described by Philippe de Mézières as 'cruel beyond belief', but it was also used to symbolize divine vengeance. Hawkwood may have thought this animal particularly appropriate as a symbol when he was the Pope's principal commander in the 1370s.

Many late medieval tombs are macabre, especially those commissioned after the Black Death, but neither the portrait in the Duomo nor the tomb in Sible Hedingham any longer displays any very obvious reminders of mortality. They are alike in celebrating the life of the knight, the first in a flamboyant Italian fashion, the second in what seems to be a typically understated English way; but in its day the English tomb may have been the more impressive representation of chivalry. Paolo Uccello depicted only two shields, each of them showing Sir John's own coat of arms, whereas the English masons carved six – as many as appear on the Black Prince's tomb-chest. Unfortunately, the decoration has long since worn away and we can no longer tell which of Hawkwood's companions were commemorated by these shields. Likewise, the effigy of the knight himself has long since disappeared. The curious cannot look at Hawkwood in Essex, as they can look at Edward III in Westminster, or the Black Prince and Henry Bolingbroke in Canterbury. We have to go to Florence to see him brought back to life.

Chapter 4

Mercenaries, *Condottieri* and Women

Those who make their living by commerce cannot know what war is ... They engage in their usual occupations and say 'We have beaten the enemy' – like the fly who sat on the ox's neck and, when asked 'What are you doing, fly?' replied 'We are ploughing.'

Francesco Sacchetti, Novella 36

German mercenaries arrived in numbers in Italy some decades before the English. In 1360 John of Legnano wrote of 'men who are brave because they know the arts of war, like the Germans', and parts of his legal treatise were concerned to find solutions to the problems they posed. For example:

Suppose mercenaries have been enlisted, at a fixed salary, with an engagement for six months, to come from Germany to serve an Italian, and, while they are coming, the Italian loses his status absolutely; can the mercenaries bring an action for their salary?

It has been calculated that there may have been as many as 10,000 German mercenaries in Italy between 1320 and 1360. Their early arrival was an inevitable result of geography. To take only one example, Hanneckin von Baumgarten, who fought with Hawkwood in the 1360s, was forming Free Companies in Italy years before Sir John arrived there.

Italy was a vast marketplace where men in search of adventure and reward could strike profitable bargains with an employer, and the market did not distinguish between foreign and native soldiers, any more than professional football does today. In the late fourteenth century it sometimes suited the Italian states to favour Italian captains for propaganda purposes – as Urban VI's Papacy did in the late 1370s, and as Milan did after Gian Galeazzo's coup in 1385 – but deals were in fact done with men of any nationality, provided they were Christians. Hiring professionals had the great advantage that they came equipped, trained to fight and (in many cases) battle-hardened.

Machiavelli thought that the use of mercenary forces had been the ruin of Italy, but by the late fourteenth century the Italian communes paid their own cavalry and infantry, and a contract system was widespread in the peninsula. Likewise, all English troops were paid, from the highest to the lowest; and it was normal practice for them to serve in indentured retinues. This meant that, except for the great expeditions of 1346–7 and 1359–60 (where troops were paid directly by the royal household), the Crown entered into contracts with aristocratic captains, for the provision of companies of an agreed size for a limited period of time, and the captains entered into subcontracts with the men who did the fighting.[1] As a result, though there were few standing armies, the professional soldier was nothing new. What was different about Italy was that the states there had long ago opted to pay others to do much of their fighting, rather than rely on citizen or county militias alone – and they were rich enough to attract fighters from many countries, and in large numbers.

If Hawkwood's trade seems immoral – because he was not content to 'take the King's shilling' – it should be remembered that the rewards of the 'regular' soldier were by no means confined to wages. The indenture Edward III signed with Henry of Grosmont on 13 March 1345 provided that the daily rate of pay should be 6 shillings and 8 pence for Henry (an earl), 4 shillings for each banneret, 2 shillings for each knight, 1 shilling for each squire, and 6 (old) pence for each mounted archer, while the rate for a foot archer was 2 or 3 pence. Henry's contract also stipulated that he could do what he liked with prisoners and that he was to have all profits of war, including towns, castles, lands, rents and *homage*[2]. These are precisely the kinds of reward provided for in Italian *condotte*.

Even a cursory look at Froissart's chronicle tells us that the soldiers serving the Crown in France were motivated by more than a lust for glory. War could be highly profitable for the winning side. In his hugely popular novel *The White Company* Sir Arthur Conan Doyle referred contemptuously to the lure of 'gold and ill-gotten riches', but he was anachronistic in highlighting a supposed difference between the honest soldier and the dishonest mercenary. The story of a conflict between the two groups, each with its own motives for war, makes for a good story, but the distinction was unreal.

The Contract

Notaries were very numerous in Italy and France and in Avignon, where the papal notaries had their own Chamber. They not only drafted documents but – importantly in an age when forgery was an ever-present risk – they authenticated them. The artist known as Sassetta painted *The Wolf of Gubbio* in the mid-fifteenth century. This shows an Italian notary sitting outside a city wall, carefully recording the terms of a miracle worked by St Francis of Assisi. The wolf's agreement to stop eating the citizens of Gubbio is being solemnly recorded with pen, ink and parchment.

There were relatively few notaries in England, but there was little formal difference between an English indenture of war and an Italian *condotta*. However, the bargaining power of the mercenary was perhaps greater in Italy. In England, the king had a virtual monopoly, since all soldiers ultimately served the Crown. In the Italian states, political fragmentation created a much more competitive market. When the English first left Lombardy for Tuscany, they could have chosen to fight for Pisa or for Florence. Indeed, according to both Matteo Villani and Leonardo Bruni, they would have preferred to fight for the Florentines 'because a great number of Florentine citizens did business in England and they were known to and on friendly terms with many Englishmen', but 'thanks to ill counsel' the Florentines did not take the right decisions early enough, and the White Company signed up with Pisa. Later, however, there was a re-negotiation between the Pisans and the English and some of the latter struck a better deal with Florence. This sort of thing could not happen in the royal armies serving Edward III and his sons.[3]

Foreign mercenaries in Italy were prepared to enter into formal contracts of service. In March 1369 a Pisan notary was paid a fee for preparing a *condotta*, calculated on the basis of the number of *poste* (groups of five lances) at a muster held at Cascina. Ten years later, when a company led by Hawkwood and the brothers Lutz and Eberhard von Landau entered into an agreement with the Tuscan communes, the contract provided for a payment of 500 florins to Eberhard for his registrars and proctors. Visconti notaries are specifically mentioned in a contract signed with Gian Galeazzo in 1385. By 1391 Hawkwood certainly employed his own lawyer, Giacomo di Burgo della Collina.

The contract governed the number of troops to be provided and their remuneration, including the advance and the monthly pay to follow. Sometimes active service was expected immediately, but at others the contract was said to be 'in expectancy', which meant that the *condottiere* could be called on to serve later. There were even contracts with penalty clauses. In 1375 Hawkwood and his officers entered into an agreement with representatives from Lucca, agreeing to treat the city amicably in consideration of 6,000 florins, but further agreed that, if there was a breach of contract, they would pay double damages (a familiar concept in Roman law).

There was an incident in the winter of 1377–8 (when the English Company was in winter quarters in Florentine territory) which has much to tell us. Fifty men in John Cook's brigade had ridden to Corliano, a town in friendly hands, and had gone 'foraging'. During the raid they stole clothing and other moveable items, sacked some houses, ran off with cattle and insulted and wounded some

The Po

The Po is a mighty river. It is the longest in Italy (at 405 miles) and almost twice as long as the Thames. Since it rises in the Alps and has many tributaries it also carries a far greater volume of water, and it drains a vast area – the great Plain of Lombardy. In the fourteenth century it flowed through many different states on its way to the sea and, since it was navigable for much of its length, there was plenty of scope for disputes between them over rights of passage, tolls, bridges and fords.

In 1368 Hawkwood faced a coalition of forces commanded by the Holy Roman Emperor Charles IV, at Borgoforte. Today this is an undistinguished town with two rather ugly bridges – road and rail – and is of more interest to the lorry driver than the tourist, but in the late Middle Ages, there was a fortress there of great strategic importance. The town lies on the Po just below its confluence with the Oglio, and the river here almost fills the horizon, even when it is not swollen with meltwater. On either side are the *argine* – large embankments built to hold back the floodwater, where one can drive peacefully for miles on minor roads, where sportsmen fish, and birds of all kinds nest. In Hawkwood's time these embankments had military uses, which attracted the attention of rival sappers. The surrounding countryside is as flat as the Wash, though more exotic since rice and silk can be grown, and when the river is in spate, the water-level can be higher than the plain on either side. The sappers knew that, if one could harness the force of the Po, it could be used for what the Italians called 'an offensive inundation'.

Bernabò Visconti, lord of Milan, sent Hawkwood to defend Borgoforte – which was then in Milanese hands – from the imperial forces ranged against it. The Emperor had the advantage of an alliance with the Gonzaga of Mantua and the Este of Ferrara, who had a fleet of boats from which they patrolled the Po, but he also had engineers under his command. These had the idea of breaking the *argine* to flood the Visconti camp, but their plan was frustrated when the Milanese worked through the night and broke the *argine* in another place, inundating the plain and with it the imperialist encampment. The Emperor was forced to withdraw to Mantua, where he negotiated an end to his part in the war. The men under Hawkwood's command had successfully defended Borgoforte, repelled the imperialist invasion and forced one of the leaders of Christendom to come to the conference table.

local people. Florence's reaction was to claim damages from Cook, but the *Signoria* also remonstrated with Hawkwood, reminding him that it was the captain's job to deal with breaches of contract. They wanted him to ensure that this kind of thing did not happen again.[4] Hawkwood was a kind of guarantor for the behaviour of his officers and men.

There were many opportunities for fraud. It is clear from de Mézières's *Dream of the Old Pilgrim* that French captains sometimes claimed payment for troops who were absent on the day of the muster, or did not exist in the first place, and there is no reason to think that this kind of financial irregularity was confined to France. The fear of corruption explains the elaborate precautions taken by the Florentines when engaging Hawkwood's services in 1389, just before the outbreak of war with Milan. On 8 June the Dieci di Balìa sent Andrea Vettori and Giovanni Jacobi to find his camp (thought to be near Borgo San Sepolcro or Città di Castello). They were instructed to rebuke Hawkwood for his delay in coming to see them and, subject to that, arrange for a muster to be held before the troops signed on. The Florentines wanted to check how many troops should be paid for, and ensure that no one pulled the wool over their eyes. There were detailed rules to avoid the double counting of horses and men. An owner had to warrant that each his horse was his own, and he should not try to have the same horse counted twice. Vettori and Jacobi were advised to choose a narrow place (such as a bridge, or the entrance to a river valley) to do the counting. The troops must pass through one by one, and no man should step out of line. Hawkwood should be present throughout the proceedings, to ensure good behaviour.

Pay

There were many different types of *condotte*. In 1844 Ercole Ricotti drew a distinction between those providing for 'full pay' (*soldo disteso*) and 'half pay' (*mezzo soldo*). Under the first, the *condottiere* was hired with a fixed number of men and a larger degree of control, and received a larger amount himself. Under the second, he received a reduced amount, with reduced responsibility, since the employer retained the right to reject the troops when the muster was held. Giuseppe Canestrini, who wrote in 1860, thought that this classification obscured the true complexity of the situation. He listed at least ten types of contract – *reali* (real), *apparenti* (apparent), *semplici* (simple), *miste* (mixed) and so on.[5]

Like English indentures of war, Italian contracts were normally entered into for a few months only; indeed the Florentine Code of 1337 prohibited officials from entering into contracts for longer than six months without express consent of the *Signoria*. This does not seem long, but we should bear in mind that the conventional period for feudal service in twelfth-century England had been forty days in peacetime, and only two months in time of war. Likewise, the town of Pont-Saint-Esprit owed a mere forty days' feudal service to the King of France.[6]

The insecurity arising from these short-term arrangements was sometimes mitigated by an option for the hirer to retain the *condottiere* at the end of the first period of service. In 1378, for example, the Venetians offered Hawkwood 30,000 ducats to harry Padua for fifteen days, but agreed to pay 1,000 ducats per day after that. Nevertheless, it would seem that Sir John entered into more than forty contracts during his thirty-three years in Italy, or an average of about 1.2 per year, which means that he never enjoyed any real security of tenure. There was a sense in which, like an actor or a conductor, he was only as good as his last performance.

The reason for the short duration of contracts was money, which had to be raised by means of taxes and forced loans, or by sharing the burden with allies. When Bernabò Visconti hired Hawkwood for the anti-papal league in 1378, the cost was shared between Florence, Bologna, Perugia, Siena, Arezzo, Viterbo, Urbino, Città di Castello, Ravenna, and several other communes. The Florentines were rich and could sometimes afford to be generous – they honoured him with a state funeral and a fresco in the Duomo after he died – but they drove a hard bargain with him while he was alive. In April 1377 they hired him for a year, but when they elected him captain-general in April 1380, they did so for six months only,[7] though they subsequently re-elected him several times and, after his victory at Castagnaro, gave him a contract for a year. Yet, even when confronted with the might of Visconti Milan in 1389, they were reluctant to commit themselves for longer than they had to. They sent Donato Strada to propose a contract for a mere four months and – since Hawkwood was in Naples at the time – specified that the time would not begin to run until the Englishman arrived on the Tuscan frontier.

The Florentine practice of offering short-term contracts has been contrasted with the methods of Gian Galeazzo Visconti in Milan, who provided greater security of employment for his *condottieri*. Gian Galeazzo employed Jacopo dal Verme as his captain-general for almost twenty-five years, between 1379 and 1402. He also paid Alberigo da Barbiano's ransom, when the latter was captured in the Marche, thereby procuring his services for the next ten years. The Florentines, though, may have had good reasons for being conservative in these matters. There was, after all, at least some risk that a man who held office for a long period of time, whether as *podestà*, as captain of the people, or as captain-general, might eventually seize political power for himself, as the Duke of Athens had done in Florence, within living memory.

Pay was the fundamental element in the *condotta*, both in the head-contracts entered into between the states and the *condottieri* and in the many subcontracts entered into with fighting men (*squadrieri*). Hawkwood made his living (at least in part) by negotiating favourable rates of pay in relation to both types of contract, and doubtless making a 'turn'. This was no simple task, especially given the many different types of currency in daily use, though his life must have been simpler in this respect once he was in receipt of a regular income in florins from

Florence. It is noteworthy that in 1375 he specifically insisted that he be paid 130,000 florins 'of just weight and of the Florentine mint'.

Haggling over the price was a normal part of negotiations. In debate the Florentines sometimes discussed whether they should offer a 'low price' or a 'fair stipend', and in the last resort settle 'at any price'. In February 1388 Pera Baldovinetti was sent lengthy instructions on how to negotiate with Hawkwood. The Florentines realized that the Englishman had considerable experience, so Pera was given limited powers and was told to be cautious. He should first of all find out if Sir John was interested in a new contract, and what the price might be. If a figure was mentioned, he should seek to reduce that as far as possible, then offer to *lend* that amount. Then he should ask Hawkwood not take any further action until he received confirmation from Florence. If this failed to produce an agreement, Pera could promise up to 5,000 florins, but only as a loan. If that was still not enough, he could offer 3,000 florins as a grant rather than a loan, but only on strict conditions. Pera was expressly warned to be very careful: 'before you offer him money, hear from himself what he wants and do not offer the said sum all at once.' The letter gives granny detailed instructions on how to suck eggs, but the Florentines clearly thought these were necessary because their envoys were going to deal with someone who knew how to drive a very hard bargain.

When the Florentines chose Hawkwood as captain-general for the third time in 1381, the sum agreed on was 333 florins, 6 *soldi* and 8 *danari* – apparently far less than the 1,000 florins agreed upon on the first occasion – but this was a contract of the *mezzo soldo* type, which did not involve immediate active service. However, it was expressly agreed that if the captain and his brigade were put on active service, Hawkwood's stipend would be tripled and his brigade's would be doubled. The sums agreed with other English captains at this time show us how highly the Florentines valued Sir John. We find that William Gold was hired with fifteen lances at the same initial rate as Hawkwood, but in his case the amount would merely double if he was called on for active service, not triple.

It was normal to promise more if the troops were victorious. We find Hawkwood promising double pay before First Cascina in 1364. In 1376–7 the Florentines offered unprecedented rewards – between 22 and 24 florins per lance for Hawkwood's brigade[8] – while in 1377 Bernabò Visconti agreed to pay 21 (and double this rate for the first two months of the contract). When Florence was pleased with his performance in 1382, they awarded him ten 'dead lances' (*lance morte*) – the pay due for that number of men, though he was not expected to field any troops at all. The Paduan army was awarded a bonus after its victory at Castagnaro in 1387, while at the end of 1390 the Florentines voted Sir John a Christmas gift of 1,000 florins.

The extent to which Hawkwood made a profit in Italy has been much debated. In the fourteenth century, the author of *Winner and Waster* sang of men who certainly *thought* that they stood to make a profit:

> I know it was for profit they departed from home
> Whoever lured them here must have a heavy purse ...

Hawkwood was not thought to have died poor, like Bertrand du Guesclin,[9] but it is virtually impossible to say how wealthy he in fact was, because we only have one side of the picture. In accountancy terms, there is insufficient material to draw up a profit and loss account, and a balance sheet is totally lacking. It may be possible to add up the gross amounts he received from various employers, but the figures for expenditure, on subcontracts, wages, equipment and even his own ransom in the 1360s are simply not available. *The Oxford Dictionary of National Biography* (2004) is able to state with confidence that Sir Edward Dalyngrigge was worth approximately £500 at the date of his death in 1393, but we cannot make the same kind of estimate for Hawkwood. It is certainly unfair to assume that he became a wealthy man just by looking at the large amounts he charged for his services.

As we shall see, Hawkwood accumulated land and properties in several parts of Italy. By the 1380s he was sending money home to buy property at Leadenhall in the City of London and in Essex. There is a bill of exchange (one of the first of its kind) by which he sent over 4,444 ducats (or florins) home in 1382, via a banking house with branches in Lucca, Florence, Pisa and Bologna, which is recorded in the Close Rolls kept by the royal administration in Westminster.[10] Yet, in 1387, he complained to the Florentines that he was in debt, and when his second daughter was married in 1393 the bridegroom was compelled to ask an influential citizen to buy the trousseau. This incident is often cited as evidence of meanness on the father's part – mercenary by name, mercenary by nature. But it could equally well indicate a routine pay dispute between the captain and his employers, since the Florentines had agreed to pay dowries of 2,000 florins for each of his daughters. Like many an English aristocrat in this and later centuries, Hawkwood probably complained about the shortage of funds not because his income was inadequate, but because his expenditure was so great. By most people's standards he had little to complain about, especially since he did not pay ordinary taxes to the Florentine exchequer, and sometimes obtained exemption from paying tolls on goods in transit.

'Money makes the world go round' and pay was certainly a fundamental part of military life in the Age of the *Condottieri*. But the money in circulation was mostly in coin, which is heavy. In medieval times coin and bullion had to be transported by beasts of burden, which were slow and required armed guards. It is therefore likely that Sir John's duties included the provision of armed guards for those who brought the men's wages. He knew the risks involved, since he had planned to take part of King John's ransom for himself, when this came slowly up the Rhône in 1360.

The *Condottiere*'s Obligations

In return for his pay, the soldier agreed to provide loyal service. This is often all that the contract provides for, and we do not find that the details of military objectives are spelt out, let alone the strategy or tactics to be employed. These were decided or agreed upon separately, and often later, either by the employer or the *condottiere* or both. A *condotta* is a contract of service, not a series of commands.

These services varied a good deal. Campaigns could vary in difficulty and duration, and the services did not always involve making war on an external enemy. Hawkwood's experiences in Pisa prove the point. After several campaigns against Florence, he helped Giovanni d'Agnello take control of Pisa in 1364, and continued to work for the new Doge. When Pope Urban V (1362–70) decided to leave Avignon for Rome in 1367 and sailed from Marseilles, he decided to put in at the port of Pisa, Porto Pisano. Hawkwood was sent to meet him with an escort of 3,000 horsemen. (Unfortunately, the Pope had suffered from the attentions of the *routiers* in France and did not greet the prospect of being met by Sir John's brigade at all calmly. His ship was ordered not to put in at Porto Pisano after all, but further south.[11]) After the Pisans drove Agnello from power, Sir John assisted the Visconti in an unsuccessful attempt to restore him: a force of 1,000 horse and 12,000 foot under Hawkwood's command crossed the Apennines, camped under Pisa and tried to scale the walls, but the Pisans beat them off.

It does not seem that the Visconti needed the Englishman's assistance to maintain law and order in Milan – their regime was perhaps sufficiently secure – but in the 1380s and 1390s he often acted as a kind of policeman for the Florentines. On several occasions, he helped them fend off the attentions of rival Free Companies, such as the Company of the Hook ('Uncino'). After the Battle of Tizzana in 1391, he provided an armed guard, when Gian Galeazzo tried to disrupt Florentine commerce. A large supply train of 500 animals, laden with grain and other goods, was due to arrive in Florence and Hawkwood provided an escort of over 1,000 men, led by his lieutenants John Beltoft and Hugh Montfort. The need for policing of this kind did not end when peace came, because – as after Brétigny in 1360 – soldiers who were laid off when the war ended tended to look for alternative employment as mercenaries. In addition, the Bolognese demanded help from the Florentines, and Hawkwood was sent to assist them in the work of pacification.

In the 1930s Ferdinand Schevill wrote that Hawkwood consistently took an 'anti-democratic' line in Florentine politics, and it is true that Sir John did help the city authorities to suppress the Ciompi rebellion in 1382, when he was called upon to guard the streets, while the Captain of the People and the Priors rounded up members of the smaller guilds. Schevill took exception to the fact that Hawkwood, once reputedly a tailor's apprentice, helped to strip the *tintori* (dyers) and the *farsettai* (makers of padded waistcoats) of any remaining part they had won in the government of the Florentine republic, but we should be slow to condemn him on this account. He was not to know which of the various factions in an Italian medieval republic would appeal to liberals and democrats in the twentieth century. At the time, he was criticized by the chronicler Stefani for being insufficiently firm with the Ciompi.[12]

The Nomad Military State

As we have seen, mercenary companies in Italy were composed of smaller units which joined together for temporary purposes and were to some degree self-governing. Ercole Ricotti described them as 'nomad military states', a phrase often echoed by later historians. Some companies elected their own captains and, although the latter wielded real power, it was not absolute. The views of a general council of constables and marshals could be important, and sometimes even lesser ranks had their say. Perhaps Conan Doyle conveyed an essential truth in *The White Company*, when he described English troops reaching a democratic decision to march with the Black Prince into Spain, rather than join Hawkwood's 'robbers' in Italy. The White Company may have been the most 'democratic' English army before Cromwell's New Model was formed in 1644.

When Hawkwood's Company was in Florentine service, there was a dispute about winter quarters, despite the English reputation for hardiness. The *Signoria* was told that the English intended to abandon their positions in the field. Hawkwood tried to persuade his men to stay where they were, but they would not listen, and insisted that their leader find them a place where they would be more comfortable. The Florentines eventually gave way and told Hawkwood to make arrangements for billeting, minimizing the damage that would inevitably be done and guaranteeing his men's good conduct by staying in Florence himself. The episode clearly demonstrates that Hawkwood was not a dictator, and there was a limit to the control he exercised, even over his own brigade. He did not occupy the same position as Edward III when the King commanded the royal armies in person. He was not a sovereign, nor even a feudal lord.

The self-governing nature of some companies explains another striking feature of Italian contracts, which is that the notaries sometimes arranged for a plethora of soldiers to be made parties to them. This reflected a concern to make the contract binding, by spreading responsibility, and it was also a precaution against changes in leadership. Thus, when Montferrat hired the White Company in November 1361, the contract he made was with Albert Sterz (captain), twelve constables (of whom Hawkwood was one) and five other individuals, and it was expressly stated to bind 'all others and associates of our said society of English and Germans and others who are in the said society or will be in the future'. An agreement with the Florentines in October 1365 was signed on behalf of the Company of St George by Hawkwood, Ambrogio Visconti and no fewer than forty-three other captains and constables. When Hawkwood reached his record-breaking agreement with the Florentines in 1375, he signed the *condotta* as captain-general, but two marshals, the constable and twelve other *caporali* also signed.

The companies led by Sir John had officers, the 'marshals' or 'constables' being of particular importance. As in the modern French army, the rank of 'marshal' did not necessarily imply supreme command, and the marshal could be little more than a sergeant, though Marshal John Thornbury did important work in 1376, when he handled delicate negotiations between Hawkwood's men and the Perugians. During the campaign against Verona in 1378 the Constable William Gold sometimes acted as Hawkwood's deputy. They each corresponded with Lodovico Gonzaga, lord of Mantua. There was much to correspond about, including the supply of rye for the horses, and numerous incidents of indiscipline (see Chapter 7).

Hawkwood's job was not an easy one, and the degree of independence enjoyed by his men sometimes tempted an employer to divide and rule. In January 1373 Sir John sent his constable John Brise to Avignon, to persuade Pope Gregory to do something about arrears of pay, but the Pope had various strategies for avoiding criticism (and immediate payment). On this occasion, he offered his excuses, not just to Hawkwood, but to several of the marshals and constables of the Company. In the same way, when St Catherine wrote to Hawkwood urging him to go on crusade in 1375, she addressed her appeal to 'the other officers' (*gli altri caporali*) as well. Was this done out of genuine consideration for the feelings of the officers, or to undermine Hawkwood's position?

The Pope and the Saint were not alone in trying to play the leader off against his men, but it was only natural that Hawkwood should resent this. In March 1379 he reprimanded the Sienese for trying to deal with those under his command without going through him first. Adopting an almost regal tone, he wrote to them in somewhat impatient terms:

> We have heard that you want to hire some isolated parts of our company: do not sign any contract without our order and without having reached an agreement to our mutual satisfaction.[13]

A Protection Racket?

Hawkwood and his followers have been called bandits, brigands, robbers and even assassins. His adventures have been likened to the 'capers' in *The Italian Job*. Terry Jones has condemned his way of life as 'the protection racket writ large'. To tour a country extorting large sums of money as the price for going away undoubtedly offends modern sensibilities. Yet the Italian states were in some ways to blame for their own misfortunes, because they were unwilling to finance standing armies. Indeed, very few rulers in Western Europe were willing to do that before Charles VII of France set up the *compagnies d'ordonnance* in 1445, drawing on the ranks of the Free Companies to do so.

In the chronic military emergencies generated by inter-city rivalry, it often suited the Italian states to hire a mercenary company and turn the poachers into gamekeepers. This enabled them to improve their military capability significantly and at a stroke. During the period of hire, they expected the companies to buy provisions at fair prices when they were on home territory or allied soil, but live off the land when they were not, just as the English did in France when they organized a *chevauchée*. Those in power must have known full well that this involved 'foraging' and worse, and that the mercenaries would continue to live by plunder after a *condotta* expired. Essentially each city-state expected the Free Companies to live at someone else's expense, a standing army being thought to be too expensive. In 1408, Carlo Malatesta advised Giovanni Maria Visconti (2nd Duke of Milan and Gian Galeazzo's son) that employers should always pay a proper wage, and pay it promptly,[14] but few employers in Hawkwood's time were willing or able to follow this advice.

As a loyal officer of the Florentine republic, Francesco Sacchetti was highly critical of the role played by mercenaries, both in fomenting war in Italy and in helping local tyrants to subvert free institutions, but he also thought that the Italian states were much to blame: it was their addiction to war that created the environment in which the *condottieri* flourished. Sacchetti was particularly critical of Popes Urban VI and Clement VII, who in his view set a terrible example to other rulers when they hired mercenaries to do their fighting in 1378:

> look at the great pastors,
> if you don't believe me, and how the present day
> teaches Urban and Clement
> to draw cold steel and fight.[15]

Women

Sir John Temple-Leader wrote somewhat quaintly of the women who habitually accompanied medieval armies as 'voluntary courtesans'; but the process was not always voluntary. When the Free Companies captured Pont-Saint-Esprit near Avignon in 1360, they were said to have 'recruited' some of the women there 'into the service of the company'. A papal bull of 1364 condemning the activities of the mercenaries fulminated against their 'violating wives, virgins, and nuns, and constraining gentlewomen to follow their camp to do their pleasure and carry arms and baggage'. When the Paduans defeated the Veronese at Brentelle in 1386, they captured 211 prostitutes, crowned them with flowers, gave them bouquets and conducted them in triumph to Padua, where they were invited to breakfast in the palace of the Carrara, and when the Florentines entered into a *condotta* with Hawkwood and Konrad von Landau in 1389, they expressly stipulated that the lances to be taken onto the payroll must consist of 'three men and three horses, and *no women*'. The prohibition must indicate, not that there were female soldiers among the potential recruits, but that the men were likely to try to bring women with them, whether as wives, lovers, prostitutes, or helpers, and the Florentine exchequer was not anxious to pay for these.

It was not unusual for a mercenary captain to cement his *condotta* by marrying the hirer's daughter. Filippo dei Tedici married the daughter of Castruccio Castracani, the *condottiere* who made himself lord of Lucca in the 1320s, as part of a deal which gave him 10,000 gold florins and the captaincy of Pistoia. Fifty years later Hawkwood married Donnina Visconti, illegitimate daughter of Bernabò Visconti, in much the same way. The age difference between bride and groom was enormous, though not unusual for the period. Hawkwood was about fifty-seven, Donnina about seventeen, so it seems unlikely that this was a love-match. Bernard de la Salle and the German Lutz von Landau each married one of Bernabò's illegitimate daughters at the same time, and Hawkwood and Landau campaigned together after the weddings.

People can fall in love in the most unlikely of circumstances, and a romantic tale has great appeal, even in a military context. Temple-Leader and Marcotti relate the story of how Andrew Belmont – who was a *caporale*, or officer in the Company – fell in love with an Italian woman called Monna Tancia when the English were based in Figline in 1363. Monna was already married to Guido of La Foresta – which may have been situated in the Chianti mountains – but the illicit love is said to have blossomed. We are told that Belmont served Monna with such devotion that the English garrisoned at Figline did not attack La Foresta when he went courting.[16]

The same authors also tell of a love-story involving William Gold, Hawkwood's constable during the Veronese campaign of 1378. In their dry account, Gold wrote to the lord of Mantua, Lodovico Gonzaga, pleading for the return of his servant Janet, who had left for Venice taking 500 florins with her, but this narrative is based on the Mantuan Archives, which in fact contain a much more exciting story. Frances Stonor Saunders tells it better: she refers to Janet as a 'whore', which is a little unkind, though one can see why when one reads the correspondence as a whole. Servant or whore, it is clear that this 'Janet of France' had captivated William Gold. His letters show a man who is clearly smitten, despite the theft of his money. He is at great pains to explain to Gonzaga just how deep his love is. Using military jargon, he says that if Gonzaga will restore Janet to him, he 'will serve him with 500 spears and upwards', because 'sweet love overcometh proud hearts.' Later on he increases his offer, saying that if he can have Janet back 'you shall have for the asking a thousand spears at my back', and explains that his heart is 'yearning so towards her' that he cannot rest, and he protests loud and long that 'if I should have to follow her to Avignon, I will obtain this woman.'

The amorous adventures of Belmont and Gold are truly romantic, but they show the difficulties which affairs of the heart could create for a commander. In his writings Geoffrey de Charny debated in an academic way whether it was better to abstain from sex before fighting a battle,[17] but Hawkwood was faced with the practical consequences of his colleagues' infatuations. In Gold's case, he was one of Hawkwood's senior officers, yet here he was, offering to serve the Gonzaga with hundreds of men, if only this would secure the return of his lover. We do not know if he got her back, but it is no surprise that he left for Venice in 1380 and spent the rest of his days there. Hawkwood let him go – indeed he recommended him to the Venetians – but it is difficult to imagine that he was sorry to see the back of him.[18]

Chapter 5

English Tactics and the Notion of Italian Cowardice

Their success owed more to the cowardice of our own men than their valour.

Villani, *Chronicle*

The English Company

When he arrived in Italy Hawkwood commanded a relatively small group of men, possibly a brigade of a few hundred, though it formed part of a larger Company. According to Villani about 3,500 cavalry and 2,000 infantry were recruited to serve the Marquis of Montferrat in 1361. These men were variously called 'the Great Company of English and Germans' and subsequently 'the English White Company', but many of them were not from England at all. They were Germans, Flemings, Bretons and Gascons, who had fought at one time or another for the English Crown, or in some other cases simply fought in the English way – *al'inglese*. Many of those led by Hawkwood after the break-up of the White Company may well have been Italian, though the chroniclers liked to tar them with the same foreign brush.

Filippo Villani gave a detailed description of 'the English' when they were in Pisan service in 1363–4. The Company split at that time and many Englishmen left to seek employment elsewhere. There was probably a further diaspora when Hawkwood was defeated at Perugia in 1365, and again when he was taken prisoner at Arezzo in 1368, but he does seem to have rebuilt his English brigade, and this remained part of the forces deployed by the Visconti in the late 1360s and early 1370s. The leading authority, Kenneth Fowler, believes that when Sir John took service with Pope Gregory in 1372, 'the English Company' was once more 'an amalgam of the English brigades that had previously operated under different commanders'. There are regular references to these English throughout the last two decades of Hawkwood's career. In 1375 the Florentines called him 'captain of the Company of the English fighting in Italian parts' and referred to the English Company in 1377. Hawkwood referred to his followers in the same way during the Veronese campaign of 1378 and he is said to have had 500 English horse and 600 English archers with him at Castagnaro in 1387.

The numbers given by the chroniclers fluctuate wildly. They tell us that, when Hawkwood fought for the Pisans at First Cascina in 1364, he had 800 Englishmen with him, and that when he fought for Bernabò in 1368, he had 4,000. In 1379 he is said to have had 300 lances on his lands in Romagna, and 500 in Tuscany. If all these men were English, it would indicate a total force of about 2,400 men, but it was recorded that in 1388 his brigade consisted of a mere 82 lances, or about 250 men. Azario tells us that in the early 1360s Albert the German knew the English language, which clearly indicates that many of the men under his command spoke it.[1] For later decades we have the evidence of many English names (and no Welsh), recorded in *condotte* and elsewhere. On 12 February 1383, over twenty years after Hawkwood crossed into Italy, the Florentines engaged the services of John Berwick (with thirty lances), John Beltoft (with sixty-five, three fifes and a trumpeter), Johnny Swin, Johnny Butler and Ozzie Norton. On 3 October they engaged John Gulion, John Cokum, Thomas Ball and Richard Sticklet (with 100 lances and four trumpeters), Robin Corbeck and Johnny Barry (fifty lances) and John Liverpool (ten). It is likely that some of Hawkwood's Englishmen were from his home county of Essex, but they did not all come from there. John Liverpool can surely have come from only one place.

Infantry and Armour

English soldiers made a vivid impression on those who had not seen them before. When Henry of Grosmont showed his retinue of knights to a delegation of Moors who were visiting Castile in 1342, they were taken aback by the strange sight of English helmets painted with animal devices.[2] In the same way Filippo Villani was clearly impressed when he first saw the White Company twenty years later in Italy:

> These English were all lusty young men, most of them born and brought up in the long wars between the French and English; warm, eager, and practised in slaughter and rapine, for which they were always ready to draw their swords, with very little care for their personal safety; but in matters of discipline very obedient to their commanders …
>
> The armour of almost all were cuirasses, their breasts covered with a steel coat of mail, gauntlets, and armour for the thighs and legs, daggers and broadswords; all of them had long tilting-lances, which, after dismounting from their horses, they were very dextrous in handling. Every man had one or two boys, and some of them more, according to their ability to maintain them. On taking off their armour, it was the business of the boys to keep them clean and bright, so that when they came to action their arms shone like looking-glass, and thus gave them a more terrifying appearance.

Others among them were archers, their bows long and made of yew. They were very expert and dextrous in using them, and did great service in action. Their manner of fighting in the field was almost always on foot. The horses were given in charge to the boys. The body they formed was very compact and almost round; each lance was held by two men in the same manner as the spear is handled in hunting the wild boar; and thus close embodied with their lances pointed low, and with slow steps, they marched up to the enemy with terrible outcry, and very difficult was it to break or disunite them …

They had very curious ladders in pieces, the biggest of which was of three steps, and one piece socketed into the other like so many trumpets, and with these they were able to mount the top of the highest towers.[3]

We can see why the English made such an impact in Italy. They were veterans – even if they were young and 'lusty' – and they were well organized and well equipped. They were grouped in 'lances' which, according to Villani, consisted at that date of three men – captain (*caporale* or *capo*), squire (*piatto*) and page or boy (*ragazzo*). Pausing there, it is interesting that the use of boy-soldiers – which now excites such horror – was an intrinsic part of the English system, though they were mainly used as non-combatants, in looking after the equipment and the horses.

Five 'lances' made a company (*posta*) and five companies a troop (*bandiera*). This was the 'English' system, and it is generally thought that it was new to Italy in 1361, where people were more used to seeing Germans, who fought in units of two. Three-man lances were an English legacy to Italy, remaining common there in the early fifteenth century, after most of Hawkwood's Englishmen had gone home or died. Under one contract from 1380 the *capo* was paid 9 florins a month, the squires 7, the boys 5. A constable in charge of a group of lances could earn more again.

English men-at-arms won their most famous victories in France when fighting on foot, even if they arrived at the scene on horseback. They continued to fight in this way in Italy in the 1360s, but developed a distinctive way of using the lance. Rather than cutting it down, they used its full length, with two men holding onto it so as to provide extra thrust. A compact formation of well-armed and highly trained men, bristling like a hedgehog, seems to have been able to get the better of almost any opponent, and above all withstand a charge by heavy cavalry. Villani's description of English formations is reminiscent of the irresistible Greek phalanx, and the sight of serried rows of lances clearly impressed the illustrator of Giovanni Sercambi's chronicle.

High-quality armour was essential, and plate-armour was better than chainmail, though more expensive. In England, the late fourteenth century was the 'camail and jupon period', the camail being a sort of metal hood worn over the head, neck and shoulders, the 'jupon' being a cloth surcoat worn over armour. We can still see what men dressed in this fashion would have looked like, by reference to the effigy of the Black Prince in Canterbury Cathedral and the brass of Nicholas Dagworth in Blickling Church in Norfolk, and we can be fairly sure that this is the sort of armour Hawkwood would have worn when going equipped for war. The Sercambi chronicle shows him wearing both camail and jupon. As to headgear, the Prince and Dagworth are each shown wearing a 'bascinet' (a tall pointed helmet) without a visor, so as to display the face (though their heads rest on great tilting-helms). Sercambi's illustrator was also concerned to show the commander's face, and he shows us Hawkwood wearing a helmet of the English type, again without visor, but in battle the knight would surely have protected his face (perhaps by lowering and lacing up a visor like the one on the Lyle bascinet in Leeds). Uccello's portrait of Sir John shows him wearing a Florentine cap, but that is because he was commissioned to paint his subject as though he were reviewing his troops on the parade ground.

Plate-armour did not replace chainmail all at once, and many of Hawkwood's followers wore a combination of the two. In 'The Knight's Tale', Chaucer describes how knights came to the tournament:

> ... armed with breastplate and habergeon
> With a light tunic under; others wore
> Steel plates, or else full suits of body armour;
> One carried a buckler, one a Prussian shield;
> One cased his legs in armour, and would wield
> A battleaxe; another, a steel mace;
> New weapons, but on older models based.
> Thus everyone was armed as he thought best ...

Whatever its quality, armour was among a man's most valuable possessions. When Thomas de Vere, 8th Earl of Oxford, died in 1371, appointing Hawkwood's elder brother as his executor, he left his brother Sir Alberic de Vere 'a coat of mail, a new helmet and a pair of gauntlets'.[4]

Was plate armour really new to Italy in 1361? It seems unlikely, since it was first developed around 1300 and Milan was the most important centre of manufacture. There is even a good chance that the armour worn by the White Company was Italian, although it surprised Villani. On the other hand, the brasses in English parish churches show that good plate armour was relatively common in England by the 1360s, and it may have been the *quality* of English armour that attracted the attention of the chroniclers, rather than the type. The name 'White Company' is said to derive from the bright appearance of highly polished armour in the

Mediterranean sunshine – Pope Pius II was 'delighted with the brightness of the arms' when he met some squadrons of cavalry commanded by Federigo da Montefeltre in 1461, but there are other possible explanations. One is that plate armour was sometimes known as 'white harness'. Another is that some of the English (especially those originally recruited in Cheshire and Flint?) wore white coats, and it may be significant that some of the men led by the Archpriest in France were known as *bandes blanches*, or 'white bands'. The practice of painting longbows white may also have played a part.

Filippo Villani compared the English to the doughty Carthaginians who followed Hannibal, while Azario claimed that they slept by day and stood guard by night, and campaigned in the winter as well as in the summer,[5] but such flattery should be taken with a pinch of salt: it may be poetic licence. It was always more difficult to campaign in the winter – for one thing, it was far harder to find fodder for the horses, and the truth is that we find numerous examples of the English taking up winter quarters in Italy. The English spent their first Italian winter in 1363–4 in the city of Pisa. During the invasion of Lombardy at the beginning of the 1390s, Hawkwood's army stopped fighting in the winter and took up the advance again the following spring. During the defence of Tuscany which followed, he again put his men went into winter quarters, in Val di Nievole, after winning the crucial victory near Tizzana.

Fighting in a suit of armour must have been extremely uncomfortable. Terry Jones relates that, during the filming of *Monty Python and the Holy Grail*, Graham Chapman wore an item made of genuine chainmail and found the weight of it unbearable.[6] In Montecchio Vesponi in 2005, the present writer was barely able to lift the sword presented to him by a young swordsman (*spadaccino*) belonging to the modern Mercenaries of Giovanni Acuto. Small wonder that Villani described the English as 'lusty and young'. They needed to be.

It is surprising that we do not hear more about the problems of coping with the heat in Italy, when it had been a major problem for the Crusaders in Palestine in the twelfth century, as it was for John of Gaunt in Castile in 1386–7. However, we do learn that the heat was a considerable handicap for the English when they attacked the Florentine trenches at First Cascina in 1364, and if Michelangelo's drawing and Sangallo's painting of that battle are at all realistic, it was also a problem for the Florentines, for some are shown cooling themselves in the Arno, and one wears a garland of ivy on his head, to shade it from the sun. Bruni mentions fatigue and heat, as well as Hawkwood's success in keeping his men fresh, as a reason for the Florentines' defeat at Second Cascina five years later. The anonymous Milanese says that after Montichiari in 1373 the men were 'hungry and weary and suffering from excruciating thirst'. According to at least two Italian chroniclers, the death of the Count of Armagnac after the Battle of Alessandria in

1391 was partly due to the 'suffocating' heat, and even the monk of Westminster heard that some of the Count's followers had been 'miserably snuffed out' after they had become 'overheated in the sweltering conditions inside their armour'.[7]

One way of dealing with the heat of the summer was to have two short campaigning seasons, one in the spring and another in the autumn, with a break in between. We know that this was sometimes done in the South of Italy, but a summer break suited the *condottieri* more than it suited their employers. We also know that some fifteenth-century Italian commanders provided their men with supplies of water. The English must have learned to adapt to Italian conditions somehow, for we do not hear of them falling ill in large numbers from heat or disease, 'the fatal enemy of English armies in the Iberian peninsula'.[8] Perhaps they were just lucky.

Cavalry

There is no sign that the horse went out of fashion in Italy. There was no 'infantry revolution' there, despite the victories of the Flemings at Courtrai (1302), the Swiss at Morgarten (1315) and the English at Crécy (1346). The Italians were so attached to mounted warfare that when the Florentine commander in the early 1360s, Piero Farnese, had a horse killed under him, he carried on fighting on a mule: his tomb in the Duomo at one time showed him riding such an animal.[9] The horse provided essential mobility, on the battlefield and off. It also enabled a commander to provide protection for his foragers, who went lightly armed. The lance remained a mounted unit: the man-at-arms and the squire might dismount to fight, but the boy looked after the horses. Many English archers rode to the battlefield, though they were not trained to shoot from the saddle, like the Turks. In *The Cambridge History of Warfare*, Christopher Allmand criticizes the 'myth of the mounted knight', but even he concedes that, in Italy at any rate, the knights remained attached to their horses.

Knights still displayed their prowess at the tournament by means of the mounted shock combat first developed in the High Middle Ages, and Paolo Uccello's *Battle of San Romano* memorably depicts this type of warfare. Archers may have shattered the French cavalry at Crécy and Agincourt, but these victories were defensive and had to be followed up. The *chevauchées* mounted by Edward III and the Black Prince were mounted raids, and Geoffrey le Baker's chronicle of the Langue d'Oc raid of 1355 is full of references to horses – horses swimming great rivers, horses dying on the line of march, horses given wine when there was no water to be drunk. Compensation for the loss of one's horse (*restor*) was an important term in English military contracts prior to 1360, and customary in Italy – where it was known as *menda*. According to John of Legnano, mercenaries could not generally sue their employers for pecuniary loss, but the exception to

Column at Le Scalelle,
near Marradi

Holy-Spirit-Bridge, 1620

Holy-Spirit-Bridge, 2007

The Pisan Gate at Cascina

Figline Val d'Arno

The Papal Palace at Viterbo

The Po at Borgoforte

The Citadel at San Miniato al Tedesco

The Arno at Cascina

The Chamber of Notaries, Avignon

The Hawkwood
Tower at Cotignola

Castagnaro

ADDÌ 11 MARZO 1387
IN QUESTA PIANURA
TRA L'ADIGE E IL CANALE CASTAGNARO
LE MILIZIE VERONESI DI ANTONIO DELLA SCALA
SUBIRONO DA PARTE DELL'ESERCITO CARRARESE
GUIDATO DA GIOVANNI ACUTO
UNA MEMORABILE SCONFITTA
CHE SEGNÒ LA FINE
DELLA SIGNORIA SCALIGERA

The memorial plaque
in Castagnaro

The Castle of Montecchio Vesponi, with Hawkwood's banner

The sentry walk at Montecchio

The view from Montecchio towards Badia al Pino

The keep at Montecchio

The Palazzo dei Vicari,
Scarperia

The Apennines near
Firenzuola

Monte Albano from
Tizzana

Sible Hedingham parish church

Hawkwood's tomb in
Sible Hedingham

Brass of Sir Nicholas Dagworth

A *carroccio*, chariot drawn by oxen

The Papal coat of arms, Viterbo

The Visconti viper

The Carrara coat of arms

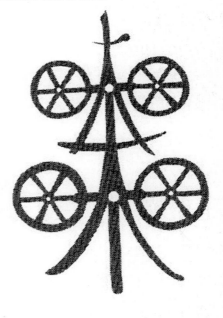

The *Palio*

Notary in Monte San Savino

The Lyle bascinet in Leeds

The banner of the 'Mercenaries
of Giovanni Acuto'

The Wolf of Gubbio by the artist known as 'Sassetta'

An engraving of Sir John Temple-Leader (1810–1903)

John Temple Leader

Paolo Uccello's portrait in the Duomo

The woodcut of Sir John Hawkwood
by Tobias Stimmer

Taking prisoners near Figline, 1363
(from Giovanni Sercambi's *Chronicle*)

CLIX. Come le genti di Firenza fenno bactere moneta
et correre pailo, & appiccarono acini,
cani & montoni.

Palio, 1364
(from Giovanni Sercambi's *Chronicle*)

CLXVII. Come messer Iohanni dell' Agnello cavalcò a
Livorna per parlare col papa, e come il papa
si tirò imfra mare.

Doge Agnello meets the Pope at Livorno,
1367 (from Giovanni Sercambi's *Chronicle*)

CCL. Come messer Iohanni Aguto cavalcò in sul terreno
e contado di Firenza.

Hawkwood outside Florence, 1375
(from Giovanni Sercambi's *Chronicle*)

this rule was 'that compensation should be given for horses lost in the service of the hirer'. Geoffrey de Charny referred to the favourable terms of military service in Lombardy, Tuscany and Apulia, where professional soldiers came to expect that they be provided with horses. There were many types of horse, and breeds from some regions of Italy were renowned in England. In 'The Squire's Tale', Chaucer refers to an animal:

> As well proportioned with regard to strength
> As any horse that's bred in Lombardy;
> And yet it was all that a horse should be,
> So quick of eye, that one could take it for
> A thoroughbred *courser* from Apulia.

The great warhorse, or *destrier*, which Hawkwood is shown riding in the Duomo was a stallion, as were all the animals depicted and sculpted by the artists who commemorated his fellow *condottieri*. These were powerful creatures, capable of carrying a man in full armour, but they were comparatively slow, expensive and rare. Knights needed other types of horse as well. A Florentine Code of 1337 required that war-horses (*cavalli*) be marked on the right leg, palfreys (*palafreni*), hacks (*ronzini*) and mules (*muli*) on the left. Florentine accounts of the 1360s refer to payments in respect of *destrieri*, but also *cursieri* (coursers), bred for speed. Horses were greatly valued, new forms of horse-armour were developed to protect them, and men doubtless grew very fond of them. We even know the names of some of Edward III's mounts – White Calais, Roan Chertsey, Griselpomyla and Peledargent. Unfortunately the great *destrier* in the Duomo, like all Hawkwood's horses, remains anonymous.

Archery and Artillery

John of Legnano wrote that 'the two chief foundations of war are arms and strength. These are divided into three parts, cavalry, infantry and fleets', but this was a lawyer's view. There was another important 'arm', which was artillery, and in the case of the English this meant archery. Villani noticed that the White Company had a new type of bow, and a Florentine Code of 1368 referred to a typical English archer as having an *archone* – not just a bow, but a *big* bow. That this was the famous longbow is clear from Azario's description:

> They carry bows on their backs ... the foot-soldiers have big and powerful bows that reach from their heads to the ground and, being drawn, shoot great long arrows.[10]

The Latin word used for 'powerful' here was *acutus*, which gives us a fascinating insight into the name by which Hawkwood was known in Italy. In the Italian imagination, he was strong and powerful, like an English longbow, as well as having a 'keen' mind.

In Hawkwood's day the longbow was the distinctive English missile weapon, but how much did he owe his success to the longbow? There are traditions that he began his own career as an archer and there were certainly contingents of archers in the forces he commanded. Archers were used when the Pisans attacked the Florentines in 1364, and in 1365 Cardinal Albornoz attempted to buy off the White Company by promising them money and 100 English bows. We read of Hawkwood having 200 archers when he was in Bernabò Visconti's service and 300 when he was in Romagna in 1376.[11] In 1379 the representatives of Lucca insisted that all the archers hired by them should be English and be 'good and valiant men well skilled in the use of the longbow', and in the same year Hawkwood reinforced his position in Romagna by calling up a force including 250 archers commanded by the English constable William Gold. When Richard II commanded his English subjects in Italy to lend their assistance to his brother-in-law the Emperor Wenceslas in 1382, he addressed them as 'men at arms and archers' (*sagittarii*).[12] A complaint about quality control provides us with further evidence of the presence of archers in 1390. The *Signoria* wrote:

> We are content to give Sir John those hundred bows which he had and will take them off his account. We will send to Lucca for the best kind of bows, for they are not good here, then we will send them at once to Padua.

There is no question that Englishmen made very good archers and that they knew how to make good longbows (and arrows), as well as use them. Christine de Pisan (1365–1430?), who was an authority on warfare and chivalry, wrote this in about 1410:

> Young Englishmen are still instructed from early youth [in archery], and for this reason they commonly surpass other archers. They can hit a target from a distance of six hundred feet ...[13]

Archery was widely practised in England: place-names containing the word 'butts' still abound in English villages and from the fourteenth century a series of statutes sought to discourage other sports. Excavation of the mass grave at Towton in Yorkshire, together with marine archaeology on Henry VIII's warship *Mary Rose* and modern scientific experiments, have confirmed that veteran bowmen were capable of great feats of arms, and their skill may well have been supplemented by the assistance of the boys, acting as helpers and carriers.

For all this, the longbow does not seem to have become a key weapon in Italy in the same way as it was when used against the French and the Scots. The reason appears to be that the number of English archers in Italy was never large, and it declined over time. The veterans who arrived in the 1360s were not replaced and they had few imitators among other nations. Hence we do not see English longbows in the works of Italian Renaissance masters, in the same way as we do in the margins of English psalters. It is the crossbow and the Turkish recursive bow which are used to martyr St Sebastian. Likewise, we see these in the illustrations to Sercambi's chronicle, but no longbows.

Hawkwood's archers were counted in hundreds, whereas thousands had fought for the Crown in France, and were to do so again. Edward III probably had 3,250 mounted archers and 7,000 foot-archers with him when he landed in Normandy in 1346. Sir Robert Knollys contracted to lead a force of 2,000 archers in 1370, and there were 5,000 with Henry V at Agincourt (three-quarters of his total force). The French historian Philippe de Commynes (1447–1511) expressed the view that archers were 'the most important thing in the world' but only if they were present in large numbers: if not, they were useless. A few hundred archers might make a difference to a campaign – they were a considerable deterrent to a would-be attacker – but they could not shatter a cavalry charge in a major battle. Professor Strickland argues that they were important at Castagnaro, but the critical moment there came when Hawkwood outflanked the Veronese and attacked them from the rear. The charge was the work of 600 mounted archers, who are unlikely to have had the chance to use their bows (see Chapter 8).

The longbow was not the only missile weapon used in Italy. A Florentine Table of Fines of 1368 also refers to a type of bow known as an ibex (*stambecco*). This was a composite or recursive bow, made from horn and similar to the weapon used by the steppe peoples who once swept across Europe. More importantly, Italy was home to the best crossbowmen available, the Genoese and the Venetians. The crossbow required less physical strength and less training than the longbow, and crossbows had a reputation for being the better weapon for attacking and defending towns. At short range, a crossbow-bolt also has more penetrative power than an arrow, so that improvements in armour were less of a problem. The English in Italy may well have used these weapons like everyone else, despite their fondness for the longbow. In 1362 the Doge of Genoa placed thirty groups of crossbowmen at the disposal of the English, so as to enable them to take the offensive against the Visconti in Lombardy.

Although Edward III had both cannon and *ribauds* at Crécy and Calais in 1346–7,[14] and though the Florentines had ordered that 'cannons of metal' be cast

Romagna

Romagna lies mostly in the plain, to the north of the Apennine mountains. In Hawkwood's time it formed part of the Papal States, though it had only been ceded to the Papacy in 1278. Bagnacavallo and Cotignola were two small settlements in the province, given to Sir John by Pope Gregory XI in 1376. Nowadays Bagnacavallo has no visible sign of its medieval connection with the English *condottiere*, and enquiries about him may well encounter a blank look. There is a road called Via Aguta a mile or so outside the town, but the knight's name is so corrupted here that few would make the link with Giovanni Acuto.

Hawkwood's connection with Cotignola is altogether more visible. Some local people even claim that his works of improvement put their town on the map. Hawkwood is supposed to have built a palace there, 'with dungeons in the manner of the strongest fortresses'. He increased the thickness of the castle walls by a factor of five, dug a deep moat, and built a number of new bulwarks, much of which remained intact until the eighteenth century. Sir John Temple-Leader, who visited the place in the following century, confirmed that this must have been so. He also climbed the Hawkwood Tower (La Torre Acuto), the last remnant of the buildings his hero had constructed, and had a photograph of the tower taken for his biography of 1889. The tower continued to serve a useful purpose long after the walls and ramparts had crumbled: as late as 1616 its bells were used to give warning of fire, flood and the approach of bandits, as well as to notify local people of the changing of the guard.

The Hawkwood Tower's continuing military potential, even in modern times, is attested by the fact that it was mined and completely destroyed by German forces at the beginning of 1945. A local history of the war has a very poignant photograph showing large lumps of masonry, including the top of the tower, sitting in the bottom of a large crater in the centre of the town. It is therefore heartening to record that the tower was faithfully and lovingly restored in the 1970s, along with the main street, the Corso Sforza, which celebrates the town's connection with a later and more famous Italian *condottiere*, who was born in the area.

Cesena (pronounced 'Say-zena') is a town of some 90,000 people, also in Romagna but at the eastern end of the Via Emilia, the long, straight road which has connected Milan with the Adriatic since Roman times. In the fourteenth century it too belonged to the Pope, though his rule always encountered resistance from powerful local families.

Hawkwood's part in the sack of Cesena in 1377 does much to explain the black legend which attaches to his name, and some people, both in Italy and in England, can never forgive him for it. However, in modern Cesena it seems, at least to the tourist, that the town remembers the cultural achievement of the Malatesta between 1379 and 1465 (especially that they founded a great library), rather than the sack that preceded it. The victims are commemorated by a small square – the Piazzetta Cesenati del 1377 – but the massacre itself is generally attributed to the Bretons rather than the English, and to Cardinal Robert of Geneva, 'the Butcher of Cesena', rather than to Giovanni Acuto.

The ruins of the old fortress which Hawkwood would have known can still be seen in Cesena, but this is a puny remnant by comparison with the forbidding walls and bastions of the Rocca Malatestiana – the fortress begun by the Malatesta *after* the city had been sacked.

as early as 1326, Hawkwood does not seem to have participated in the gunpowder revolution. When the Pisans attacked Pistoia in 1363 their English allies are said to have thrown lances, arrows and *bombarde* over the city walls, which probably refers to hand-grenades of some kind. Likewise, when Hawkwood was sent to attack Florence in 1375, he is said to have had 'bombards' with him, which on this occasion probably meant siege-guns. Whatever the precise meaning of the term, these weapons do not seem to have substantially influenced Hawkwood's methods.

At Castagnaro in 1387 the Veronese had three huge battle-wagons with three decks apiece (*tre carrette armate a tre solari*) and twelve *bombardelle* – gun-barrels fitted to the side of each deck – so that every wagon carried 144 gun-barrels, each barrel capable of firing a stone the size of a hen's egg. There were three men to each wagon, two of whom could take it in turns to fire salvoes of twelve per wagon, while a third applied the brake or wielded a hatchet. Each wagon required four large warhorses to drag it along and, since the animals were all fitted with protective harness, they were like a type of armoured car. These weapons were similar to the 'ribauds' developed by Edward III, but since each age likes to draw a contemporary analogy, Temple-Leader and Marcotti called the guns 'primitive *mitrailleuses*', after a type of machine gun developed by the French in the mid-nineteenth century. To us they sound more like the *katyusha* rockets or 'Stalin-organs' used by the Soviet army in the Second World War. The vehicles, however, seem to have suffered from the same defects as the tank in the First World War, in that they were extremely heavy, very difficult to manoeuvre and too rudimentary to be of much use, though they were doubtless very intimidating if you had to face them. As it was, the Veronese had no time to even deploy them at Castagnaro, let alone fire them, and Hawkwood's victorious Paduans captured them all after the battle was won.[15]

Sieges and Engineers

In his esteemed *War in the Middle Ages* Philippe Contamine wrote that the siege was the most usual form of warfare in the Middle Ages; but Hawkwood was not employed for his knowledge of siege-warfare. Edward III had taken Calais after a prolonged siege in 1346–7 but Sir John is not known to have been present there and, once Calais was in English hands, there was little need for the King or his sons to besiege towns of that size. In addition, English commanders found siege warfare in France difficult.[16] It was not until Henry V decided to conquer Normandy that they turned their minds to major operations of this kind once more.

Italian cities were larger than French towns (apart from Paris) and the inhabitants were used to maintaining their defences. In addition, the Italian states disliked entering into contracts for more than six months and sieges ate up money and time. This meant that Hawkwood rarely had the resources needed to capture large cities, and there are signs that he was more at home with mobile warfare. At a siege of Reggio in Emilia in 1370, the Visconti used 3,000 pioneers to construct two bastions a mile away from the town, but Hawkwood failed to make use of them. He went off on a raid to Bologna and the inhabitants of Reggio captured them while he was away. We have seen that, at Asti in 1372, the Visconti likewise wanted to carry on with a siege, while Hawkwood wanted to break the deadlock by attacking Savoy's relief force. It was this difference of opinion which led to his leaving the Visconti service. Similarly, he was ordered to lay siege to Verona in 1387 but the operation proved abortive.

The Gascons in particular were skilful climbers, and contingents of the Great Company under Hawkwood's command were able to capture Pont-Saint-Esprit in 1360, but, as we have seen, Pont-Saint-Esprit was not a fortress on the same scale as Avignon: her new walls had only just been begun, and her old walls were in disrepair. In Italy, the English Company was able to capture small towns both in Piedmont (Rivarolo and Romagnano) and in Tuscany (Incisa and Figline) and Villani was clearly impressed by the English ladders which could 'surmount the highest towers'. Even so, none of these operations seems to have involved a 'regular' siege, and the assault on Tre Vigne in the Casentino in the early 1360s failed, just as Hawkwood's attempt to storm Città di Castello did in 1375.

Engineers and pioneers were used for other purposes than siege-warfare. As we have seen, Viscontean engineers broke the banks of the Po, to defeat Charles IV at Borgoforte in 1368. According to the Paduan chronicler Gataro, Hawkwood filled in part of a ditch on his right flank before the Battle of Castagnaro in 1387, and this facilitated the final manoeuvre, which enabled him to win that battle. In August 1389 the Florentine envoy Rucellai was instructed to tell him to ravage Sienese territory. The orders included an instruction that, if Hawkwood were defeated (which 'God forbid!'), Rucellai should assist by 'hastening the work' of an engineer (*maestro*) who had gone with the army to cut off the enemy's water supply. As we have also seen in Chapter 3, Hawkwood constructed a fixed line of defence, between Montopoli and the Arno, before leaving Tuscany early in 1390. During his invasion of Lombardy he came to a dyke constructed by Antonio della Scala of Verona a few years before – and made his men fill in a large section rather than risk fording it – but two could play at this game. The army assembled by Gian Galeazzo Visconti for the conquest of Padua in 1388 included 1,500 horsemen, 1,000 infantry, 400 crossbowmen and (so we are told) no fewer than 1,000 sappers. In 1391 Jacopo dal Verme broke the banks of the Adige during the night, submerging the plains in which the retreating Florentine army was encamped, and severely impeding Hawkwood's withdrawal.

The Battle Cry
The noise made by an undisciplined mob can be terrifying. Chaucer referred to the din made by the peasants during the Great Revolt of 1381, in his 'Nun's Priest's Tale':

> Not even Jack Straw and his mob of men
> Ever let out a clamour half as shrill
> When hunting Flemings down to lynch and kill.

A battle-cry, shouted in unison by a trained army, was equally terrifying. Villani mentions the 'terrible outcry' made by the English in the early 1360s. Shakespeare's Henry V encourages his men to shout, 'God for Harry, England and St George!', but it was Edward III who had made St George the patron saint of England. At the Battle of Poitiers, the English and Gascons shouted 'St George!' and 'Guyenne!' (another term for Gascony). In Michael Prestwich's view, the battle-cry was a weapon in itself, and a crucial one in breaking French morale: 'Battle cries were important, in part as a means of recognition, in part to frighten the enemy, and perhaps also in part as a means of reinforcing a collective identity, and of supporting friends in the fight …' Maurice Keen has explained how an unauthorized cry – 'Montez!' (To horse!) or 'Havoc!' (the signal to break ranks and plunder) – could be highly dangerous for all concerned and therefore merited severe punishment, according to Richard II's Ordinances of War.[17]

When Hawkwood's troops were charged with the task of subduing Faenza in 1376, they ran through the streets shouting 'Viva la Chiesa!' (Long live the Church!). In 1387 Sir John used the terrible cry 'Carne! Carne!' (Flesh! Flesh!) as he led the decisive charge at Castagnaro. This was intended to strike fear into Veronese hearts, but it was also a play on the traditional Paduan cry of 'Carro!

Carro!' – which was short for the *carroccio*, the ox-drawn cart which was the heraldic emblem of the Carrara. In a skirmish between Hawkwood and the Sienese in 1389, the latter shouted: 'Long live the Count of Virtù, Count of Siena!' – something of a mouthful, but Sir John's men are said to have replied in kind: 'Long live the Count of Florence and Messer Carlo!'

Despite what Villani wrote, the English had little to teach the Italians in terms of bloodcurdling shouts. The poetry of Francesco Sacchetti is full of them (see Appendix 1). A common one is 'A l'arme!' (To arms!) – clearly the origin of the English word 'alarm'. The poet also has a story about Giovanni da Barbiano, who attempted to capture a fortress when he was at war with Astorre Manfredi. The cry used was 'Alla morte, alla morte!' (Unto death!). On another occasion the men shouted 'Alla terra! Alla terra!' (For the land!). The Bolognese chronicler of the sack of Bologna records several cries, including 'Popolo! Popolo!' (The people, the people!). It remains true that the yell made by the White Company when it first crossed the Alps and arrived in Piedmont must have announced to a startled Italy that the English had arrived – those same soldiers who had recently humbled the Valois King and his subjects.

The Notion of Italian Cowardice

Some writers explained the success of foreign mercenaries by reference to the cowardice of the Italians. The theory was that the native population had simply lost the martial qualities it had undoubtedly possessed in the days of the Roman Empire. Thomas Walsingham wrote that the Romans of his own time 'were well aware there had been a decline ... in military skills and expertise since the days of their ancestors'. Jean Froissart expressed the view that the inhabitants of Lombardy were 'natural cowards', and even Cola di Rienzo, dictator of Rome in 1347, asked desperately: 'Where are now these Romans? Their virtue, their justice, their power?' Filippo Villani concluded that the White Company 'succeeded rather by the cowardice of our people than because of their own valour.'[18] Italian intellectuals certainly felt that they had some explaining to do when the new model army of Charles VIII of France invaded Italy and swept all before it in 1494.

But the notion of Italian cowardice is quite absurd when we look at the late medieval record, for the Italians played their part to the full both in jousting and tournaments and in real warfare. Genoese crossbowmen were the finest in Europe and it was a largely Genoese fleet, in alliance with the French, that harried the English coast in the early years of the Hundred Years' War, and a Castilian fleet commanded by the Genoese Boccanegra, that defeated the English at the Battle of La Rochelle in 1372. There were Italian mercenaries both at the siege of Pont-Saint-Esprit and at the Battle of Brignais. Others fought in campaigns and theatres of war largely unknown to the English. In Hawkwood's own day Luchino dal Verme of

Verona was one of the captains who fought for the Visconti when the White
Company invaded Piedmont and Lombardy, but, as commander of a Venetian
expedition to Crete, he also put down a Greek uprising in 1364. Later he took
service with the Byzantines and died fighting the Turks in Syria. When Philippe de
Mézières described Western Europe in his *Dream of the Old Pilgrim*, he referred to
'the power of Lombardy, Tuscany, Apulia and Italy' as an integral part of the military
might of Christendom – and we should never forget Venice. Nobody accused the
Venetians of cowardice, in their centuries-long struggle with the Ottomans.

In Italy itself the militias raised by the city-states remained of prime importance,
despite all the publicity given to foreign *condottieri*. Even among the ranks of the
'stipendiaries', there were probably always more native soldiers than foreigners. One
of the first-ever Free Companies was a Company of St George formed by the
Milanese exile Lodrisio Visconti in the 1340s, and many more were founded by
Italians: the Company of the Star led by Astorre Manfredi; a second Company of
St George jointly led jointly by Ambrogio Visconti and Hawkwood; the Company
of the Cappelletto of Nicolò da Montefeltro; and the Company of the Rose,
commanded by Giovanni da Buscaleto and Bartolomeo Gonzaga. The Great
Company led by Werner von Urslingen in the mid-fourteenth century contained a
strong Italian element. Examination of the names of the captains present at
Castagnaro in 1387 reveals that Hawkwood was the only Englishman among them
and that there was only one German, but over sixty Italians.

In 1410 the master swordsman Fiore dei Liberi published a treatise known as
Flower of Battles (or *Flos Duellatorum*), based on his experiences in Italy and
Germany during the previous fifty years. Fiore recommends a wide range of
techniques used in hand-to-hand fighting, though it is difficult to know how well
known these were, since he did not believe in sharing his secrets with the common
herd – those 'created by God without a wit, like beasts that are born only to carry
heavy loads'. Nevertheless his work does give the lie to those who think that the
Italians lacked military virtue. *Flower of Battles* demonstrates a love of fighting
shared by all nationalities. Its Prologue refers to a number of duels which the
author witnessed or heard about. There was a notable one at Imola in Romagna
between a German and a man called Nicolo Inghileso (who must surely have been
English), but many involved Italians. Fiore also tells us how, like Bertrand du
Guesclin in Brittany, he first grew to love fighting as a boy, when he took part in
'friendly' contests in his home village of Cividale del Friuli, near Udine. A passion
for fighting infuses all his verses:

> In dagger to dagger [fighting] there is no man I fear
> Armed or disarmed I will greatly humble him
> And such is the delight I take in fighting in the ring
> That I am going to beat everyone in such a close fight.

The best proof that the Italians were not lacking in courage is that the foreign captains of the fourteenth century gave way – by and large – to native *condottieri* in the fifteenth. Temple-Leader and Marcotti studied the records of a bank which the Florentines opened for their stipendiaries in 1367, but found few English names after 1400. Likewise, although Bologna had 1,100 troops in 1397 who were classified as in some way 'English', there is no English name among the constables and *caporali* of these men present at a general review held in Mantua.[19] After Hawkwood's death the Florentines appointed an Italian as his successor, though Richard II had offered the services of Nicholas Clifton.

In Chapter XII of *The Prince* Machiavelli gives his opinion of several prominent *condottieri*, but Hawkwood is the only non-Italian, though there are many famous names – Carmagnola, Colleone, Sforza and Braccio da Montone. He deplored his countrymen's reliance on mercenaries, but thought that the answer was to raise a citizen army. He had no doubts about the valour of his own countrymen:

Now, in Italy, the opportunities are not wanting for thorough reorganization. Here we would find great prowess among those who follow, were it not lacking among the leaders. Look at the duels and the military skirmishes, how the Italians are superior in strength, skill, in inventiveness but when it is a matter of armies, they do not compare. All this is because of the weakness of the leaders.

The Italian states did not employ foreign mercenaries because their men lacked the stomach for a fight. It is true that men who were fully engaged in civilian occupations found military service burdensome, and no doubt such men did not have the same expertise as the mercenaries, but reluctance to fight on these grounds is not the same as cowardice. The fundamental reason the Italian states used professional soldiers in such numbers was because they were valuable commodities, and the Italians were the best traders in Europe.

Chapter 6
Booty, Ransoms and Rewards

Then he rideth into Tuscany, and winneth towns and castles, and wasted all in
his way that to him will not obey, and so to Spolute and Viterbe, and from
thence he rode into the Vale of the Vicecount among the vines.

Sir Thomas Malory, *Le Morte d'Arthur*

Sir Thomas Malory wrote for a fifteenth-century audience, but he wrote about a
king who – if he ever existed – lived almost 900 years before. In one of his highly
anachronistic tales, Arthur and his knights campaign in Tuscany and in 'the Vale
of the Visconti' (which must mean Lombardy). The story has no basis in anything
the real Arthur may have done, but it is just possible that it reflects the fame
which Hawkwood had won by his adventures, as well as the continuing
popularity of fantastic stories about the Round Table.

Hawkwood was the only famous Englishman to have campaigned in
Lombardy and Tuscany in the late Middle Ages, but he was more of an
entrepreneur than a knight-errant. A younger son, he left home when he was still
young, and he succeeded by using his brains as much as brawn. No one was
bound to him by feudal ties. In his day English soldiers owed allegiance to their
King, but a mere captain had to reward his followers financially if he was to
command their obedience. In addition, Hawkwood had to be a hard-headed
businessman if he was to succeed in Italy, where capitalism was king. Francesco di
Marco Datini – Iris Origo's 'merchant of Prato' – habitually began his ledger with
the words 'In the name of God and Profit', and no irony was intended.

Booty

There was more to the taking of booty than a simple lack of discipline, since
booty was one of the 'advantages of war' – a recognized supplement to basic pay.
The king in the poem *Winner and Waster*, written in about 1352, promises his
men rich rewards:

And look to me, Winner, if you want to gain wealth,
When I go to the wars to lead my men;
For in the proud palace in the rich city of Paris
I plan to have it done, and dub you to knight,
And to give great gifts, of gold and of silver,
To those who owe allegiance to me and love me in their hearts.

It was not just the lower orders who took their rewards on the battlefield or on the line of march. When soldiers won a battle, it was common practice to strip the dead, but the Black Prince took Enrique of Trastamara's charger after Nájera,[1] just as he had taken the French King's jewels and Bible after Poitiers and the King of Bohemia's ostrich-feather coat of arms after Crécy. Taking booty was not thought of as an unusual or particularly sordid thing to do; it was a matter of routine. It comes as no surprise to read, in Chaucer's 'Knight's Tale' that:

The pillagers went busily to work
After the battle and the Theban rout,
To rummage in the pile of slaughtered men
And strip the armour and the clothes from them.

The English launched large-scale mounted raids across the French provinces in 1345, 1346, 1355, 1356, 1359–60, 1370, 1373 and 1380. These *chevauchées* had strategic aims, but they were also a means of rewarding the men, for they involved plunder as well as attrition. They sapped French morale, undermined loyalty to the Valois dynasty and destroyed the tax-base of the districts affected, but they also involved material rewards. The troops were provided with enough supplies to last them a few weeks,[2] but on the march the men were expected to live off the land, carry off any moveable property they could, and destroy the rest. The Benedictine monk Honoré Bonet wrote in his *Tree of Battles* (1387) that it was for the commander to divide booty among his men – 'to each according to his valour' – but the Free Companies in France continued to behave as they had when they had served the King. Their expeditions might now be called *chevauchées à l'aventure* rather than *chevauchées de guerre*, but there was little difference in the methods employed.

The rewards to be won by fighting in Italy were potentially far greater than in poorer countries like Scotland or Ireland. Trade had made the Italian merchant classes wealthy, especially in moveable property. The Swiss historian Jacob Burckhardt wrote long ago that 'A countless number of those small things and great things which combine to make up what we mean by comfort we know to have first appeared in Italy': he described soft beds, costly carpets and bedroom furniture. There were valuables of all kinds for the taking. Raids took place so often that they were regarded as a natural hazard, like a swarm of locusts. When a company of soldiers arrived in the area, it was routine procedure for the country people to move their belongings inside the walls of the nearest town. In some districts this happened several times a year.

Booty was not limited to household goods. The Florentines were so concerned about the security of their grain supply in Romagna that they founded a number of settlements on the main roads through the Apennines and (as we have seen) built a new road over the Giogo pass to Bologna. Luca di Totto Panzano recorded how Hawkwood's men robbed him of his horses, arms, silver belt and gold rings at Incisa in 1363. In 1388 they seized a consignment of skins and animals from a party of Florentine mule-drivers. When ravaging Sienese territory in 1389, they collected 1,500 oxen, which they subsequently sold at auction. After the Battle of Tizzana in 1391, they helped themselves to horses, baggage, *bombarde* and tents which the Milanese had abandoned, though the horses were mostly lame or hamstrung.

Pillaging was all in a day's work, though it was sometimes regarded as a job for the specialist. Some Free Companies had officers known as *butiners*, who were employed to collect up the spoil, supervise an auction and divide the proceeds of sale. During the summer of 1363 the White Company deployed *un corpo di guastatori*, a specialized corps of 'wasters', to devastate Florentine territory. A letter written to the priors of Siena contains a threat made in 1374 to allow pillagers ('Sachomannos') to do the work. The language used suggests a specialist body of men: John of Legnano even defined 'saccomanni' in chapter 42 of his treatise on war as 'men who go simply in the hope of booty ... persons who seize *manu*, with the hand, and carry off in a sack'. Specialists like this were certainly found in the Visconti service in the 1390s.

Nowadays it is illegal to take booty. It must have been an unpleasant business even in the late Middle Ages, since the civilians were not always ready to hand over what they had, and strong-arm tactics were sometimes used. During the sack of Cesena in 1377, the English were said to have 'barbarously ill-treated men and women, to make them reveal where real or supposed treasures were to be found.' Santino Gallorini, the historian of Montecchio Vesponi, understandably disliked Hawkwood, because he preyed upon the Italians 'for money and booty' – *per soldi e bottino*, but in legal theory plunder was an 'incident of war' and in practice it was the foundation of many a soldier's fortune. Honoré Bonet wrote: 'If on both sides war is declared by two kings, the soldiery may take spoil from the opposing kingdom, and make war freely.' The Free Companies doubtless thought that the same principle applied to them.

There were obvious attractions to the life of a 'freebooter'. The financial rewards for members of the Free Companies could be greater than they were for more regular forces. According to Villani, Fra' Moriale had attracted large numbers of men to his Great Company because he made sure that the booty was properly auctioned and the proceeds divided fairly. We should also remember that when a man served in a free company, there was no prince or ruler demanding a third of the take, and there was no question of paying a tithe to the Church either, as Philippe de Mézières thought proper when he devised rules for a new Order of chivalry.

Prisoners
English law recognized that a soldier who took another man prisoner acquired property rights over him until a ransom was paid. Furthermore, if a man were lucky enough to capture another who had previously taken prisoners himself, he became entitled to the ransoms owing to his prisoner. Ransoms were also valuable commodities, which could be sold on at a profit; and the right to sue for the balance of what remained owing after a prisoner was released on parole was recognized by the courts.

The most lucrative kind of ransom was a king's ransom. John Coupland, previously an 'obscure northerner', captured the King of Scots at Neville's Cross in 1346. The event was celebrated in a ballad known as 'Durham Field', which portrays the King as surrendering most reluctantly, on the grounds that Coupland was 'no gentleman'. As we saw in Chapter 1, the English captured the King of France ten years later at Poitiers, the day when the English – in Professor Prestwich's phrase – 'scooped the ransom jackpot'. King John's ransom was eventually agreed at 3 million gold *écus* and, although it was never paid in full, the amounts Edward III did receive were enough to make him one of the wealthiest men in Christendom.[3]

As far as we know, Hawkwood never had the chance to win a king's ransom, but there were many other valuable opportunities in Italy, since the wealth of some Italian *signori* rivalled that of kings. During the early 1360s the English raided to within six miles of Milan and captured some 600 noblemen, whom they caught celebrating the New Year. Some of the English took as many as ten prisoners each. They lost some of these when the Visconti counter-attacked, but they still earned about 100,000 florins. In the same year the English took 400 prisoners at Ripoli near Florence. Before the first Battle of Cascina in 1364, Hawkwood encouraged his men by telling them that, if they won, as many as 400 young noblemen might fall into their hands, worth something between 1,000 and 2,000 florins. The promise was not fulfilled because the English were defeated, but after Second Cascina they took 2,000 horses and 2,000 men, including many knights and the Florentine envoy Cavicciuli.

Taking prisoners and ransoming them was again part of the routine of warfare. After Montichiari in 1373, Hawkwood took 200, including members of the Este,

Canossa and Sassuolo families, though the young Gian Galeazzo Visconti evaded him. After the sack of Cesena four years later 'all the survivors left in the city were constrained by the English to ransom themselves.' During a skirmish with the Milanese in 1390 Hawkwood captured Facino Cane (member of a notable family of *condottieri*), fifty men-at-arms and 220 horses. After Tizzana, the haul was enormous – 1,000 prisoners including Taddeo dal Verme, Gentile Varano of Camerino, Vanni d'Appiano, and 200 men-at-arms. Sometimes, of course, it was his own Englishmen who were captured. In 1378 he had to negotiate terms for the release of John Thornbury, who had taken service with the Scaliger lords of Verona and been captured near Mantua.

The *condotta* sometimes provided for the way in which the ransom money was to be divided. The contract signed with Florence in December 1381 stated that Hawkwood should receive 10 per cent of all profits earned under his command, but other terms were implied as a matter of custom. The principles at work were first expounded by teachers of law at Italian universities, but became part of the grammar used by more practical men and were sometimes incorporated in ordinances promulgated by those who did the hiring. Richard II's Ordinances of 1385 provided that the King should receive a third of all ransoms taken in Scotland, and that individual captains should keep another third,[4] but sometimes the matter was decided by decree. After the Battle of Castagnaro the officials of the Paduan army commanded by Hawkwood counted 716 dead and 846 wounded, but also 4,620 prisoners, including 2,620 mercenaries. Three days later Francesco Carrara decided that those who had fought for him were to give him the names of all the prisoners they had taken, and refrain from disposing of any without his permission. Later still, he changed his mind and said that he wanted them all for himself, though he promised compensation to those who had done the fighting.

Ransoms were not always paid willingly. In 1364 Urban V found it necessary to condemn mercenaries who tortured and maimed 'those from whom they expected to obtain ransom', and Azario gives us the names of captives who told him how they had been abused by the English.[5] It seems more than likely that they were telling the truth and that the White Company did handle its prisoners roughly, but it is very doubtful that they behaved worse than the Germans at Savignano in 1360, who were said to have dragged their captives by the nostrils, lopped off hands, feet and ears, drowned some, stretched others on beds of thorns, and held others over fires.[6] But prisoners were very often released quite quickly, if only because it was expensive to keep them in custody. There were occasions when they managed to escape first. Sacchetti tells us of a man called Bertino da Castelfafi who was taken prisoner and lay in irons in the sun near Volterra, before he was rescued by a baggage-handler whom he had befriended in happier times.[7] To release prisoners on parole and then collect the ransom afterwards (and if necessary go to court to recover the debt) was risky, but standard practice. In 1382 Hawkwood took many prisoners while campaigning against Louis of Anjou in the Kingdom of Naples. Three of these were valued at 1,000 florins each, two at 500 florins, seven at 400, twenty-one at 300, and four at 200. He released them on the security of promissory notes, but, when the notes fell due for payment, there was a deficit of 10,900 florins and he appealed to Charles of Durazzo, King of Naples. In litigation like this there was a choice of courts, but it seems as if he made the right choice here, for he obtained an order addressed to Donato d'Arezzo, judge of the Supreme Court, that the debtors should pay what they owed. He may well have recovered most of what was due because, shortly afterwards, he invested money in the purchase of a property in Poggibonsi called La Rochetta.

Not everyone thought that taking prisoners was an honourable way to fight wars. Petrarch was full of complaints against mercenaries, especially the Germans, and he railed against their unwillingness to fight to the death, which he called:

> ... the Bavarian treason
> which with hand raised makes death into a game.

John of Legnano made much the same criticism:

> Today [the mercenaries] extricate themselves more easily, because they lift a finger and pull down visors, and they surrender, and are dismissed at once, as is their custom among themselves.

But the logic of this way of looking at the matter is that it is better to kill a man than to take him prisoner. At the Battle of Crécy (1346) it was suggested to Edward III that he take prisoners, but he refused. Before Poitiers, ten years later, the French King John II ordered that no quarter be given to the English and Gascons led by the Black Prince. Both kings behaved lawfully, though harshly, but even at the time there was another point of view. John of Legnano advised that 'mercy be shown to persons captured in a lawful war ... unless by sparing them there is fear of a disturbance of the peace'.[8] It is this opinion which most appeals to modern sensibilities. Ironically, it was also in the mercenary soldier's self-interest to take prisoners, rather than kill his opponent out of hand.

Ransoming Towns and Districts

Robert the Bruce had ransomed towns and districts in the North of England in the years after Bannockburn, but the English only started to do the same on any scale when Edward III's war in France began to go well. They did this in Brittany in the 1340s and 1350s, and the practice spread after Poitiers. During the campaign of 1359 the royal army extracted 200,000 florins from the Duchy of Bar, and 200,000 *moutons* from the Duchy of Burgundy, as the price for leaving these districts alone. In areas where permanent garrisons were left in occupation, this method of financing military operations became formalized, and was called *appatis*. Some groups of soldiers became so dependant on this type of income that they demanded compensation when peace was made with the French.

Northern Italy was highly urbanized, as well as rich, and much of the wealth was owned by the urban elites. The Florentines had a strong currency and in 1363 they even set up a special bank to provide loans to mercenary companies. But there was a heavy price to pay when these 'stipendiaries' turned against their former masters, or simply decided to act independently. Hawkwood and his English were not the first to hold the towns of Italy to ransom: in 1353 Fra' Moriale had led an Italian Great Company on a kind of grand tour of Central Italy. He extracted 16,000 florins from Pisa and the same from Siena, 25,000 from Florence and no less than 50,000 from Rimini.

One of the first operations undertaken by the White Company was the harrying of the Green Count of Savoy, in 1362. The Company pursued him as far as Lanzo Canavese, which they captured. After that they blockaded him in his castle and the Count paid them 180,000 florins to go away. By 1374 this kind of transaction had become commonplace, and Hawkwood's secretaries and notaries had developed diplomatic language to express his demands. A joint letter written to the Priors of Siena on 8 August 1374 tells us about his modus operandi:

Magnificent and powerful lords, and dearest friends. [9]

So that your magnificences should not be surprised, we are letting you know that we had heard that a large company of men-at-arms was gathering outside the boundaries of your territory in order to fight with us, and for that reason we came here to find out if the facts corresponded with reports. As a result, if it pleases your lordships to spend a certain sum of money on this company, as customarily ought to be spent on men-at-arms, we will abstain from damage and, so far as we can, we will keep your territory free from harm: but if not, we will allow Pillagers from that company to do whatever they wish. Let us know your disposition in regard to these matters.

Hawkwood and Konrad Count Hechilberg
Captains

In 1375 Hawkwood equalled and then outdid Fra' Moriale's spectacular 'grand tour' of extortion, by entering into 'non-aggression pacts' with Florence (which agreed to pay 130,000 florins) and with Siena, Arezzo, Pisa and Lucca (which forked out another 95,000). Temple-Leader and Marcotti calculated that the total amount extracted from the cities in question, in only three months, was two and a half million francs, but it has to be said that, by any measure, a coup like this was extraordinary. It was much more usual for agreements to be made with one city at a time. In 1376, after he had sacked Faenza, Hawkwood sold it again. Some say the price paid was 60,000 ducats, others 40,000 and others again say 24,000 florins. Likewise, he and others in the Company of the Rose sacked Ravenna and sold it back to the Malatesta in 1384.

Italian cities sometimes banded together by way of self-defence, but the *condottieri* were also capable of forming alliances. In 1379 Hawkwood and Lutz von Landau invaded the district of Bologna and obtained 2,500 ducats before they moved on. In the same year, they led a mixed band of English and Germans towards Florence. A previous contract, dating from 1375, obliged each of them to refrain from damaging her territory, but they explained that the agreement did not bind Lutz's brother Eberhard, so that there was nothing unlawful in *his* threatening to attack the city. This argument seems weak, but Florence's response was not to reject it totally, but to send a notary to open negotiations, while taking the prudent measure of evacuating the countryside and telling the local inhabitants to take refuge behind town walls. Eventually an agreement was reached, not just with Florence but also with Perugia, Siena, Arezzo and Città di Castello.

Perks

In the early 1360s the Pisans agreed that 2,500 soldiers could have access to their city during the hours of daylight, provided that they came armed with a sword and a knife only, and left town in the evening. A contract which Hawkwood signed with Florence in 1375 includes a clause stipulating that his Company be allowed to cross Florentine territory and that both 'knights and men may enter Florence so long as not more than one hundred are within the walls at the same time'. It was a privilege for common soldiers to be allowed inside the walls of either of these two great republics, and even Hawkwood did not enter Florence himself until the winter of 1377, when his Company went into winter quarters nearby. On this occasion he made the kind of *joyeuse entrée* which we associate with visits made by the French kings to their provinces:

> 7/12/77 Today Sir Hawkwood entered Florence with his Company at the twenty-third hour (hour before sunset) and dismounted at the Palace of the Archbishop of Florence, and great honour was paid him by our *Signoria* and other councils, and a great deal of wax and sweetmeats and draperies of silk

and wool were presented to him. They made a great feast for him and his Company in the Palace of the *Signoria*, and he was much honoured. God give him grace never to injure us, either in goods or person, Amen!

Hawkwood's entry into Padua after his victory at Castagnaro in 1387 was equally magnificent. The Carrara lord, Francesco Il Vecchio, went to the city gate to embrace him and the triumph was followed by a feast for all on the Prato della Valle, a grand supper at court, 'fires of joy' and martial music, which played throughout the night.

Once established in Florence, Hawkwood was showered with favours. The city fathers helped him with the litigation he was enmeshed in (as a result of his ownership of land in Romagna) and even tried to settle his disputes with Astorre Manfredi. In 1382 they granted him ten 'dead lances', for so long as the price of a house which he had been promised remained unpaid. In 1383 a question arose as to his status for tax purposes: was he liable to pay the property tax payable by citizens of Florence, the *estimo*? The decision was that if he were *not* a Florentine citizen (and of course he was English by birth, and his wife Milanese) he would be exempt from taxation in any event, but even if he *were* a citizen (on account of his purchase of land in Florentine territory) he would still be exempt. The result was that Hawkwood paid no tax. Two years later he fell into arrears with payment of a forced loan (*prestanza*) payable by citizens and non-citizens alike, but, even then, the Florentines allowed him fifteen days' grace and agreed that there should be no penalty. When Sir John and Donnina pleaded poverty in 1387, wanting to release capital by selling their properties at San Donato and La Rochetta, the Florentines again offered to help. In English terms, they were willing to provide covenants for title to facilitate the conveyancing process, though the sales never in fact took place.

At the end of his life Hawkwood was given a seat on Florence's Council of War. He was awarded a pension of 2,000 gold florins a year (a substantial improvement on the original 1,200), and he was given wedding portions for his daughters, a pension for his wife of 1,000 gold florins a year, the promise of a state funeral and a tomb in the Duomo. The Florentines considered requests which he made, in 1387 and again in 1393, for assistance with his debts. In 1392 they made him a citizen of the republic. Their favours did not even end with his death, because they paid part of his salary to the end of March 1394, though he died on the 17th of the month, they continued to pay Donnina what amounted to a widow's pension and they granted his children immunity from lawsuits in relation to any obligations contracted by him during his lifetime. A year later, they even engaged Hawkwood junior with two 'dead' lances, from January to the end of March 1395.[10]

Land and the Struggle with Manfredi

In 1369 Edward III sought the backing of Parliament for the renewal of his war with the Valois. He promised land to those who would follow him, and indentures of war drawn up in the 1370s sometimes specified the towns, castles and territories to be awarded in the event of success. Unlike Edward, Hawkwood was not in a position to give his followers good title to land, but he did become a landowner himself, both in the Italian states and in England. The village of Carinaro in Aversa and other properties in the Kingdom of Naples were given to him by Pope Urban VI in the 1380s, in consideration of his support for Charles of Durazzo. He acquired properties in Tuscany as a result of his services to the Florentines, including San Donato near Florence itself and La Rochetta near Poggibonsi in the Val d'Era. He had a mansion with a cloister in Perugia and was co-owner of Gazzuolo, on the Oglio, not far from the scene of his triumph at Borgoforte in 1368, and he invested in the purchase of land in the Leadenhall, not far from the Guildhall in the City of London, apparently arranging for the deeds to be kept in a strongbox in St Paul's Cathedral.[11]

Pope Gregory XI intended to be particularly generous with gifts of land. In 1373 he wrote from Pont de Sorgues near Avignon, assigning his commander a hospice in Bologna, and two years later he repeatedly gave orders that Hawkwood be enfeoffed with the castle of Montefortino in the March of Ancona, but there seems to be a doubt as to whether the fief was ever transferred.[12] There is no such doubt about the towns of Bagnacavallo and Cotignola in Romagna, which Gregory gave to Sir John in 1376. These were in a fertile area and Hawkwood was doubtless pleased to receive them, but the Pope's motives for making the gift may have been mixed. It is likely that arrears of pay were due – one source says the debt amounted to 60,000 *scudi* – and Temple-Leader and Marcotti relate that the English had threatened to take reprisals, but it is also relevant that Romagna was in the north of the Papal States, in a notoriously unstable area. The Papacy feared invasion, and revolt, and wanted to build islands of stability in its northern domains. It had tried to do so before, by appointing the Count of Cunio as rector of Bagnacavallo in 1330.[13] The gift to Hawkwood may have been another attempt to pacify a troublesome area.

Romagna was where Hawkwood might have hoped to found both a dynasty and a patrimony. In the following year, he married Donnina Visconti and, in the space of just a few years, had three children by her, possibly all born in that area. We know that he spent considerable sums in re-fortifying Cotignola and building a watchtower there, but any ambitions he may have had to settle down here were soon thwarted, because he fell out with the Pope soon after these estates were conferred on him, and in any event Gregory XI died soon afterwards. Without the active support of the Papacy, it was difficult to establish a base in the Papal

State. Even more unsettling was the attitude of the local aristocracy: the Alidosi of Imola, the Ordelaffi of Forli, the Malatesta of Rimini, the da Polenta of Ravenna and the Manfredi of Imola and Faenza. These families were traditionally Ghibelline, they opposed papal rule when it became too intrusive, and they were never likely to welcome an English cuckoo in the nest.

Francesco Sacchetti's writings confirm that Hawkwood's face did not fit in Romagna. Sacchetti was a proud Florentine, a loyal servant of his city all his life, and he served her long before Hawkwood did, and for some years after his death. He was *podestà*, charged with maintaining law and order, in several Florentine dependencies, including San Miniato in the lower Arno valley, Bibbiena in the Casentino and Faenza in Romagna, and he ended his career as captain-general of Florentine Romagna, where he made friends with the local aristocrats. Some of these were educated men, who exchanged poems with him. A particular friend was Astorre Manfredi, who once sent the *podestà* some apples from Florence and from Faenza, to taste and compare. Sacchetti's attitude to Hawkwood probably reflected the views of his friends. It is therefore highly relevant that, although he admired the Englishman in some ways, Sacchetti also disliked him, just as he disliked all foreigners who meddled in Italian affairs. Marriage to a Visconti was not a mitigating circumstance, since that family had caused no end of trouble for Florence, especially in Romagna. The contrast is with Italian *condottieri* (Manfredi himself, but also Ridolfo from Camerino), whom the poet both liked and admired.

Hawkwood must have been resented as a parvenu as well as a foreigner. Many members of the local aristocracy had grandiose coats of arms and mottoes, and they could trace their genealogies back through many generations. The Alidosi claimed descent from a Roman general, the Ordelaffi from a daughter of Berengarius, King of Italy in the tenth century. The Manfredi traced their line back to the Roman emperors, while the Malatesta claimed descent from Noah. These families were often interrelated and the men sometimes met to play chess. Sir John was not a local man, and the title to his estates in Romagna was of very recent origin and dubious authenticity. Sacchetti had criticized Gregory XI for selling the lands of the Holy Church to pay for his Breton mercenaries:

> The second iniquitous, unjust and evil thing,
> Was when without love or charity,
> You sold your lands around Piacenza
> To tyrannical lordship …

How much more objectionable was it for the successor of St Peter to give Bagnacavallo and Cotignola to a mere bachelor knight from England?

Val di Chiana

The Val di Chiana is a large alluvial plain, north of Lake Trasimene, where Hannibal defeated the Romans in 217 BC. Hawkwood's castle at Montecchio Vesponi lies on the eastern edge of this plain, on an outlying spur of the Apennines, with a commanding view of the road from Florence to Perugia, especially from the castle watchtower, which gave the guards an opportunity to sound the alarm and pass on a signal over a great distance.

The plain is now fertile, but it was an insalubrious place in the late Middle Ages. Hawkwood's native Essex had its marshes, but the Val di Chiana was a malarial swamp. In Book 29 of his *Inferno* Dante had compared it to Hell:

> How miserable would it be, if the diseased from the hospitals
> Of Valdichiana between July and September
> And of the Maremma and Sardinia
> Were to lie together in one ditch?
> Such was it there, and such stench issued from it
> As can only come from festered limbs.

The chronicler Villani and the poet Boccaccio each used the word 'chiana' to describe any unhealthy place, and, when Pope Pius II travelled north from Rome in 1459, he noted that he came to 'the river or swamp called Chiana'. Doubtless it was best to keep to the high ground and avoid the plain when travelling near Cortona and Arezzo. The Medici made plans to drain the swamp, and Leonardo da Vinci did a drawing for the project which shows Montecchio Vesponi on the edge of the area to be drained, but the serious business of reclaiming the land only began in the late eighteenth century. This was when the men and women living inside the walls of Hawkwood's old castle began to move down into the plain, where their descendants live today. The castle fell into serious decay.

Montecchio was rescued and partially restored after 1872 by the banker Giacomo Servadio, but he does not seem to have lived there, or if he did it was not for long. Temple-Leader referred to the 'almost sepulchral loneliness' of the castle when he did the field research for his biography of Hawkwood, published in 1889. The castle fell into ruin again in the early twentieth century, until rescued by its current owner. Nowadays, it is no longer the abandoned ruin, inhabited by the rooks and bats, which is mentioned in old guide books. Restoration has brought the medieval occupation vividly to mind, from the sentry walk on the battlements facing Castiglion Fiorentino to the *cambio di guardia* halfway up the watchtower – where the guards supposedly changed places while keeping watch over the Val di Chiana.

Some say that Hawkwood's father-in-law, Bernabò Visconti, still haunts the castle of Trezzo on the Adda near Milan (where he died in mysterious circumstances), others that his daughter Agnese is seen from time to time in the great Ducal Palace at Mantua (where she was executed). Hawkwood did not die at Montecchio, but at his villa of San Donato near Florence, and he died a natural death. There are no ghost stories about him at Montecchio Vesponi, though his spirit does seem to possess the place, especially when his standard flies from the watchtower and they run the *palio* in Castiglion Fiorentino.

Hawkwood had a particular feud with Astorre Manfredi. This *condottiere*, born in 1345, had ambitions to re-establish his family's position. In Rendina's phrase he was 'the archetypal wronged lord who seeks a way of winning back his inheritance by becoming a soldier of fortune', and he had every reason to resist the Englishman's attempts to make a new home for himself in Romagna. Manfredi's family had been driven from their estates by the Papacy, backed with the full force of its earthly and spiritual weapons. Astorre's father had lost Faenza in Cardinal Albornoz's time and Bagnacavallo was taken from them later. Renewed fighting took place during the War of Eight Saints, when Manfredi suffered the double indignity of having Hawkwood sack Faenza *and* take possession of Bagnacavallo with the Pope's blessing.

Hawkwood might gain a temporary advantage over Manfredi, and defeat him in local skirmishing; but the local man was always likely to be in a stronger position. He could draw on traditional loyalties and offer local people a greater degree of protection. When the village of Laderchio switched allegiance from Imola to Faenza in 1376, it submitted to Manfredi in the piazza of Bagnacavallo, declaring that it did so in view of 'the immense dangers and perils arising from the wars that have sprung up in the vicinity'. The need for good lordship – as an antidote to anarchy – must have been widely felt; but an outsider like Hawkwood could not provide it: he was part of the problem, not the solution. Eventually, the Englishman's position became untenable. In 1381 he sold his estates in Romagna to the Este of Ferrara, but Astorre Manfredi recovered them not long afterwards. The Manfredi were still lords of Romagna in Machiavelli's day, 100 years after Hawkwood's death.[14]

The Castle of Montecchio Vesponi

Hawkwood owned, or at least possessed, two castles or fortified towns in the 1370s and 1380s – Cotignola in Romagna and Montecchio Vesponi in Tuscany. Nothing remains of the former, apart from the bell-tower now known as the

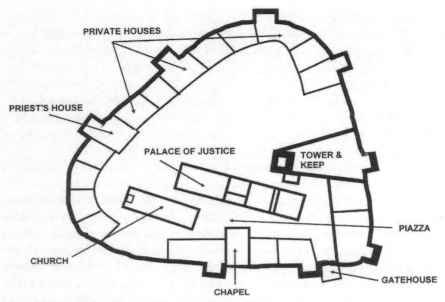

Plan of the Castle of Montecchio Vesponi from the Cabreo *of 1608.*

'Hawkwood Tower', but the latter is almost all still there, and is now once again a home, after many decades as a ruin. 'Montecchio' is a common enough name in Italy – it means 'hillock' – but Montecchio Vesponi is a quite spectacular sight, both from a distance and close up. It is not constructed on the same scale as the great fortresses of the Gonzaga in Mantua or the Malatesta in Cesena, but it is much more than a fortified manor house, such as Hawkwood – a mere 'bachelor knight' in England – would probably have had to be content with if he had stayed at home. He was lord of Montecchio for ten years.

We cannot be sure how Sir John came by this castle. Like the nearby town of Castiglion Fiorentino, it had changed hands many times in the fourteenth century, passing back and forth between Florence, Perugia and Arezzo, and we know that the Emperor Charles IV confirmed Arezzo's title to the fortress in 1355, but there is no documentary evidence that any of these three communes granted or sold it to the English captain. The most likely scenario is that he simply seized it, on his way back from Naples in 1384, just as many of his former companions had seized castles in France prior to 1360. There is evidence that, as early as 1381, two men from Montecchio presented themselves in Florence, explaining that:

> the commune of Montecchio no longer obeyed the commune of Arezzo and had come into the obeisance of the commune of Florence by virtue of an agreement with Hawkwood, who had owned the castle *for some time.*

But if Hawkwood had really owned the place for some years before 1384, one would have expected that the Tarlati, who were lords of Arezzo and Cortona would have mentioned this, when they filed a return of their properties in that year, and in fact they said nothing about it.[15]

If Hawkwood had built a manor house or castle in England, he would have needed a licence to 'crenellate' from the King, like the one granted to Sir Edward Dalyngrigge for Bodiam in 1385. The English monarchs had long wished to control the building of castles, and they generally had the power to do so, but there was no strong monarchy in Tuscany. Nevertheless, Hawkwood's presence at Montecchio would undoubtedly have interested the Florentine republic. The city authorities were very conscious of the dangers posed by unruly families in outlying districts – for example the Ubaldini, who owned fourteen castles 'scattered in the fastnesses of the Apennines' and caused a great deal of trouble there, before they were finally brought under control in 1373.[16] Moreover, in 1384 Enguerrand de Coucy – that son-in-law of Edward III who had fought alongside Hawkwood in 1373 – captured Arezzo, and held it for some months before selling it to the Florentines. Soon afterwards the Florentines instituted an enquiry to ascertain whether castles in Tuscany were being held 'contrary to right'.[17] Sir John's occupation of Montecchio would have been of intense interest to Florence, though she may have found him no more difficult to deal with than the indigenous Tarlati lords.

Why did Hawkwood want this place? Montecchio occupies a strong position on a summit 1,000 feet above sea level, close to the border between Tuscany and the Papal States. It has its own water supply and at the time had its own dependant territories which could provide a reliable supply of food. In the mid 1380s Sir John was a married man with three young children, and stood in need of a home and a base. He had sold his estates at Cotignola and Bagnacavallo, and Montecchio was perhaps more attractive than these, since Romagna was exceptionally turbulent. Montecchio was also a place Hawkwood would have come across many times while on campaign. In addition, it was only fifty miles from Florence, which paid him a regular pension and offered prospects of further work. The terms of his engagement with the Florentines required that he should not absent himself more than eighty miles from the city without their permission. In Montecchio he was well within this limit but far enough away to enjoy considerable independence.

The greatest knights in England sometimes built castles for show as well as for defence. The classic case is Dalyngrigge's lake-fortress at Bodiam in Sussex. This was built as a private residence, with profits earned from the Hundred Years' War (and Dalyngrigge may also have fought in Italy), but Montecchio is different from any castle Sir John could have acquired, or would have built, in England. The earliest known drawing of it – from 1608 – shows it more or less as it would have been in the late Middle Ages, and it was clearly more than a private residence. It was a small fortified town, with a church and a chapel, a magistrate's house and many small dwellings. Moreover, while many English castles built at this time were rectangular and dispensed with a central keep in favour of a gatehouse and towers at regular intervals along the walls, Montecchio is built in an old-fashioned way. It clings to the summit and its curtain wall follows the natural contour, with eight (surviving) towers and a sentry walk on the north side. There is a tower to one side of the main gate, but no barbican, though there may once have been a small gatehouse. There is a spectacular lookout tower, with an entrance at first floor level, which has been joined to the curtain walls so as to form a keep (or *cassero*). The walls are still over forty feet high in some places, and there is still a *fosso* or dry moat, which would have been filled with thorn bushes (rather than water) as an extra line of defence.

The central tower at Montecchio is the most surprising feature. At approximately 100 feet, it is as tall as the Norman keep at Castle Hedingham in Hawkwood's native Essex, which is one of the biggest in England, but it looks even bigger and dominates the skyline because of its position on the hill and its narrow construction. Towers like this were virtually non-existent in England, but they were very numerous in Italy – for example in San Gimignano, Pavia, Bologna and Viterbo, where some forty remain. However, they were usually built as fortified dwellings and fighting platforms, whereas the tower at Montecchio was a watchtower – a *torre d'avvistamento*, which was also used for signalling, using fire at night and smoke or mirrors by day. Indeed it may well have been part of a network of signalling posts. On a clear day one can still see across to the old abbey town of Badia al Pino to the north-west, which Hawkwood also owned.

Sir John made good use of this place. He was in residence here when the two Franciscan friars mentioned by Sacchetti in Novella 181 walked over from Castiglion Fiorentino to ask for alms and pass the time of day. He was here in 1386, when he mounted expeditions into territory belonging to Cortona, and again the following year, when the *Signoria* wrote to the local *podestà* about arms and equipment which he wanted to send on without paying the usual toll. He was here too in April 1389, when he paid his respects to the Carrara, who were living in exile at Cortona. After his death the Florentines wrote to his castellan, Riccardo Chel (or was he Richard Kell, an Englishman?), calling for the peaceful surrender of:

> the fortress of Montecchio, with its guard and garrison. We therefore require that you consign the same, with all the munitions of war which it contains, to Antonio Materio, our well-beloved familiar, whom we send for this purpose, and who will receive it in the name of our Commune by public act of notary.[18]

Hawkwood was probably also at Montecchio when Pope Urban VI wrote to him in June 1389, asking that he refrain from damaging the territory of Perugia:

Bishop Urban, Servant of the Servants of God

To our dear Son, the noble John Kavkendwod, called ACUT, knight, Captain of numerous men at Arms, greetings and Apostolic blessing.

We diligently request and exhort your Nobleness, seeing that we made a request (by messengers with letters) against your next return, and asked that you write back to Us to confirm your agreement, namely that you and your people would not enter the lands of the Roman Church owing allegiance to us, and especially not the territory of our City of Perugia, and that you would not damage them, nor (in so far as you were able) allow them to be damaged, in any way whatsoever. Even so, you should now see to it that this state of affairs is brought about, as befits your promise, and as would also be highly pleasing to us.

Given at Rome at St Peter's on the 4th day of the Nones of June in the 12th year of our Pontificate [2 June 1389].[19]

Frances Mayes writes in her book *In Tuscany* (2000) that Hawkwood *built* the castle of Montecchio Vesponi, but this is not the case. It was already old when he took possession, but there is some evidence that he may have built, or rebuilt, the keep. When one looks at it, it is very obvious that this has been constructed quickly and roughly, by joining the tower to the curtain wall at two points, to make a triangular space with several levels of occupation. The work has been done on the cheap, for in some places the walls of the keep are not keyed into the existing structure, and a gap is plainly visible. It looks like the work of someone in a hurry, a new owner who wanted to display his power and status to the world in as short a time as possible, without incurring excessive cost. Sir John fits this description, since, by the late 1380s, he was approaching seventy and had complained several times that he was in debt. Recent investigations, using specialized photographic techniques and computer analysis, show that the present keep was undoubtedly built some time in the fourteenth century, and the archaeologists involved, Paola Orecchioni and Fabio Giovannini, think it is not impossible that Hawkwood built the keep.[20] However, they also point out that the keep could equally well have been the work of the Tarlati, who owned Montecchio before Sir John and are known to have built a similar structure in Castiglion Fiorentino, in a similarly cheap and hurried fashion.

What we can say, with some certainty, is that the architecture at Montecchio was somewhat old-fashioned in Hawkwood's day, and he did nothing to change this. Elsewhere, alterations were being made to counter the threat posed, from around 1350, by siege engines and guns. Knighton's English chronicle tells us that when the Bishop of Norwich laid siege to Ypres, during his ill-fated 'crusade' in Flanders in 1383, 'he installed a great siege-tower with a *trebuchet* and a heavy gun called the Canterbury gun, against a tower by one of the gates'. In response to the development of this new technology, the towers of many castles were lowered and strengthened to act as gun platforms, arrow-loops were widened to accommodate firearms, and bulwarks – and eventually full bastions – were built, some of enormous size. As early as 1381 the authorities in Bologna placed thirty-five pieces of artillery on the walls of their city, and there is a fine example of this new look in the Rocca Malatestiana at Cesena, ironically begun *after* the sack of 1377, in which Hawkwood participated. But there is no sign of the gunpowder revolution, and its effects on castle design, at Montecchio.

Chapter 7

Leadership and Chivalry

Dal Verme and Hawkwood ... seem to have moulded some of their actions
according to the ancient code of chivalry.
> Duccio Balestracci, in S Zucchini (ed.), *Condottieri* (2006)

In 1955, in the last case heard by the High Court of Chivalry, *Manchester Corporation v Manchester Palace of Varieties*, Lord Goddard referred to the widespread popularity of heraldic symbols in twentieth-century Britain. He mentioned 'inns and licensed premises, universities, colleges, dioceses, tobacco jars, ash trays and teapots'. Coats of arms are still widely used today for civic and commercial purposes of all kinds, both in England and in Italy. The Visconti viper can be seen on every Alfa Romeo car, and St George and his dragon appear on pub signs in every English county. The Oriflamme, sacred banner of the Kings of France, gave its name to a line of cosmetics.

Yet heraldry is of medieval origin and coats of arms had a very different purpose in Hawkwood's day – to identify the owner, recognize his martial achievements and boost morale. Anyone who was anyone in Italy – including the main families and the towns, the military orders, the Papacy and the *condottieri* – had their own emblems and heraldic beasts. Florence's arms featured the lily, while her beast was the Marzocco or lion. Pisa was associated with the fox, but also with the eagle: the Pisan army was said to have brought a live bird with it to First Cascina in 1364. The arms of the della Scala included a mastiff climbing a ladder, the Carrara had their chariot, the Ubaldini a silver stag on a blue shield. The arms of the 'Honeycat' Gattamelata naturally contained a cat, while Colleoni's consisted of three pairs of testicles.

Character and Education

We can still see what Hawkwood must have looked like: although his portrait in the Duomo was painted in the 1430s, it was based on a likeness painted shortly after his death. By contrast, there is no portrait of the English knights whom Caxton later compared him to – Chandos, Knollys and Manny. If they were commemorated at all, it was by English masons in cold stone, while Hawkwood's fellow ambassador in the 1380s, Sir Nicholas Dagworth, was remembered with a brass. Hawkwood is unique among Englishmen in being depicted in vivid colours by a great Renaissance artist. Uccello shows us a lean and well-preserved (if gaunt) septuagenarian, of above medium height. The features are regular and the face is clean-shaven. The portrait is a profile, and not a close-up, and we cannot see much of the face. This is a stark contrast with Verrocchio's statue of Colleoni in Venice, which glowers down on us in three dimensions.

There are some clues as to Hawkwood's character, above all Francesco Sacchetti's Novella 181 (see Appendix 1). This is the tale of two Franciscans from Castiglion Fiorentino, who seek alms from Sir John as he is passing through the gates of his castle at Montecchio Vesponi. The friars greet him in their usual way: 'God give you peace', but he upsets them with a cutting remark – 'May the Lord take away your alms.' The friars protest that they 'mean only to be kind', but then Sir John delivers the punch-line: 'How, when you come to me and pray that God would make me die of hunger? Do you not know that I live by war, and that peace would be my undoing?' This story has been told many times and is thought by some to indicate a dry sense of humour. Sacchetti thought so himself and tells us that the friars repeated the tale in Castiglion Fiorentino, where the joke was much appreciated. But, when we read to the end of Novella 181, we discover a much less charitable view of Hawkwood.

A less well-known, but equally revealing, incident took place when Hawkwood left the Visconti service during the siege of Asti in 1372 (see Chapter 2). His plan to break the deadlock had been rejected on the advice of a notary, and he is supposed to have remarked that he 'did not choose to regulate himself in military matters according to the counsel of scriveners'. Here we detect a typically military attitude towards clerks and armchair-strategists. (At the time of the Franco-Prussian War of 1870–1, a Prussian commander thought that the Germans were bound to win if the French chose to follow 'lawyer's orders'.) In the same way, the Florentine cloth merchant Andrea Vettori offered Hawkwood some advice in 1377 and was told 'go and make your cloth, and leave me to lead the troops.' This is the voice of the professional soldier, who does not suffer fools gladly and has little time for the men who wield the pen rather than the sword. Ridolfo of Camerino is said to have expressed himself in very similar terms when two Florentine merchants advised him to move his camp in 1362.[1] Hawkwood could be a difficult man to deal with. In 1375 the Florentines wrote to Bernabò Visconti, asking that Ruggiero Cane be sent to conduct negotiations with Sir John, because 'He is the only one to whom Hawkwood is accustomed to confide his most secret designs, and who knows his weaknesses and his good moments.' This clearly implies that there were often bad moments too.

Did Hawkwood feel pity for the victims of war, or regret his way of life in later years? There is no sign of this, though he clearly wanted prayers said for the souls of fallen comrades in Purgatory. In any event, he did not let emotion stand in his way. When King Peter of Aragon listed the qualities he looked for in a knight, he said 'they should be cruel, so as not to have pity in pillaging their enemies nor in wounding nor in killing them.' For knights like these the end justified the means, and Hawkwood was the quintessential knight, despite the 'mercenary' label habitually attached to his name. In *Vows of the Heron*, when Jean de Fauquemont is asked what adventure he wants to undertake, he replies that he will go with Edward III to set a part of France ablaze and declares:

> I would not spare church or altar, or any pregnant woman I might find, or any relative or friend, however much he loved me, should he stand in the way of King Edward.

There is little doubt that Hawkwood was capable of a high degree of ruthlessness in pursuit of his objectives.

There is no evidence that Hawkwood was a patron of the arts like John of Gaunt, or a patron of learning like Henry of Grosmont, or a lover of music like Henry Bolingbroke, or a collector of books like Thomas of Gloucester and Federigo da Montefeltre, but he was probably not illiterate. It is clear from the terms of the contract signed with Gian Galeazzo on 1 July 1385 (which had to be read over and explained to him) that he did not know diplomatic Latin, and this in turn confirms what we would expect – that much of his correspondence was written for him by secretaries or notaries. However, this does not prove that he was unable to read or even write in English. He may have written the originals of two English letters discovered in the Guildhall in the 1920s (see Appendix 2). There are also two letters in Latin, doubtless written by a secretary at San Quirico in the Val d'Orcia in 1377 but signed and sealed by Sir John, using a signet bearing a hawk and the inscription 'God Avail'.[2] This is the only evidence that Hawkwood used a motto, and it is significant that it was an English one, unlike Edward III's 'Honi Soit Qui Mal y Pense'.

Hawkwood was not a 'Renaissance man', but he certainly became fluent in spoken Italian. His Italian nickname L'Acuto was probably more than just a mispronunciation of 'Hawkwood': he deserved the name for his keen intelligence. According to the modern historian Guerri, the quality Italians value most is *furbizia* (cunning or slyness), and his contemporaries thought he had this in abundance.[3] Filippo Villani wrote that he was 'foxy, like all Englishmen' – an interesting comment when the English author of *The Life of Edward II* thought that all his fellow countrymen were 'crafty'.[4]

Leadership

The forces commanded by Hawkwood varied a great deal in size. It is clear that a Free Company was often comparatively small and the army put together by a league of Italian states much larger, but it is difficult to be exact when it comes to numbers. The figures given by the chroniclers are often approximations or exaggerations, but the men who hired Hawkwood and his kind were hard-headed businessmen who counted the cost of everything. Notaries were instructed to record the precise terms of the bargain, including numbers and rates of pay. Envoys were used to supervise the muster when the men enlisted and the figures they used had to be more than an estimate, or the books would not balance. Heralds were employed, whose job was to assess the numbers present on the battlefield, as well as count the dead. The chronicler Azario was an accountant (*contabile*) with the Visconti army, and the figures given by the two Gatari chroniclers of Padua seem particularly precise.

Hawkwood had his own brigade (*brigata*), though it might sometimes be called a band (*manu*) or retinue (*casa*), just as the larger Company might be called either a *societas* or a *commitiva*. During the late 1360s and early 1370s, when he was fighting for Bernabò Visconti, the brigade was probably small in comparison with the numbers of Germans whom the Milanese employed, but when he first served the Pope in 1371 he may have had as many as 500 lances (1,500 men). In June 1379 a brigade of 1,000 lances (600 German and 400 English) is mentioned, but not long afterwards only 300 seem to have remained. When the Carrara of Padua sent Giovanni degli Ubaldini to Faenza in 1387, with orders to enlist the Englishman for a war with Verona, he came with 500 men-at-arms and 600 archers, numbers not dissimilar to the retinue John of Gaunt took with him on the 'Great March' from Calais to Bordeaux in 1373. Yet, ten years later, an agreement with the Florentines provided for a mere sixty lances. Perhaps the last figure gives the best indication of the number of truly English troops Hawkwood still had round him at the end of his career. We know that some of them did stay to the end, because there was an English guard of honour at his funeral.

In 1363, when Pisan ambassadors arrived at Novara to hire the English Company, it numbered 3,500 horse and 2,000 foot, but in 1390, when Hawkwood arrived in Bologna to take charge of the Florentine army, he arrived with an escort of only fifteen lances, though he quickly assumed the joint command of a total force of 1,200 lances and 3,000 men. In the first case, the army was about 5,500 strong, in the second 6,600, though the English brigade was far smaller. A Roman legion comprised 6,000 men. It is a small number compared to many football crowds today, and it was small then in comparison with the 15,000 men Edward III took to France in 1346, or the 32,000 he mustered for the siege of Calais the following year, but those were exceptionally large armies. Very often, English forces in France were far less numerous, not least because the royal strategy was to attack on several fronts. Six thousand is also the size of the Black Prince's army at Poitiers in 1356, and only a little smaller than the one he led across the Langue d'Oc in 1355. It is also the size of the army commanded by Gaunt in 1373.

An army including citizen or peasant militias, or Italian allied forces, could be much larger again. When the Veronese decided to pursue Hawkwood and the Paduans in 1387 they are said to have amassed a force of about 16,000 men – four times as many as the Paduans had been able to concentrate, and we also find large forces involved in the confrontations between Florence and Milan in 1390–1. By January 1391 the allied army in Padua consisted of Florentines, Bolognese, Paduans and other mercenaries commanded by the *condottieri* Giovanni da Barbiano, Konrad von Landau junior and Astorre Manfredi. Admittedly, estimates of its size varied according to the allegiance of the chronicler. A Florentine wrote that there were 1,400 lances in the service of Florence, with only 600 from Bologna and 200 from Padua; but a Bolognese counted only 200 from Florence and under 3,000 cavalry in all. On the other hand, Galeotto Malatesta estimated there was a total of 9,000 cavalry and 5,000 infantry. For the defence of Tuscany in 1391 Hawkwood was put in charge of 3,300 lances and 3,300 infantry (over 13,000 men), but, when Florence itself came under attack, the Florentines fielded an extra 10,000 militia (said to be one from each house of the districts which owed her allegiance). With his back to the wall, Hawkwood was given more men than ever before to command, and more than he was ever to command again.

Does the commander lead from the front always, sometimes or never? In Hawkwood's case, the answer to the question posed by John Keegan is that – like Edward III and Henry V – and unlike Charles V of France and Gian Galeazzo Visconti in Milan[5] – he always led from the front. Hawkwood's style is epitomized in the story that, at the critical moment during the Battle of Castagnaro, he threw his commander's baton into the fray and charged after it. There were other occasions too when he led by example. Perhaps the most important moment in his Italian career came in 1364, when he was in command of the White Company and under contract to Pisa. The Florentines bribed most of his men to break their contracts. They paid 9,000 florins to Hanneckin von Baumgarten, 35,000 to his German followers, and no less than 70,000 to the English – of which 5,000 was for Hawkwood's colleague Andrew Belmont. Hawkwood stood aside from this double-dealing and even tried to persuade Baumgarten to keep his word. He remained at his post in Pisa and served to the end of the contract, though relatively few others did. This seems to have been the origin of his enduring reputation for reliability, and it was also a good example to set the men.

Hawkwood had to be a good manager, of men, horses, food supplies, tents, and equipment, because membership of the mercenary companies was fluid. They consisted of many contingents, which came together for an agreed period or purpose and separated at the end of it. In this world, success went to the commander who could attract the best men and keep them together. He had an eye for a good man and a good unit, and knew how to look after them once they had enlisted. Records show how he recruited a group of six English knights led by Hugh Despenser in 1373. These men had previously taken service in Padua, but were made redundant by a peace treaty agreed between the Paduans and the Venetians. Sir John's agent in Pisa arranged to forward 900 ducats to Padua, which enabled the Englishmen to settle their debts and keep out of the debtors' prison. Hawkwood forwarded a further 1,700 ducats to Despenser the following year through his proctor in Bologna, Andrea da Arezzo.

There is also evidence of how Sir John cared for the men he commanded. In 1378 he wrote from Parma to Gonzaga of Mantua, asking for a skilled doctor to cure a comrade who had been wounded. His correspondence shows that he tried hard to free a man who had been imprisoned in Siena in 1382. We also know that he sometimes lent money to his fellow *condottieri*, because on one occasion he forgot to pay the tax demanded by the Florentine exchequer in respect of loans. He must have been popular, for in 1388 some elements of the White Company who had engaged to fight in Naples reported for duty in Florence instead, saying they had *chosen* Hawkwood for their captain.[6]

English records show that Hawkwood had influence in London from the late 1370s and that he used it to benefit his men. The Patent Rolls contain details of a pardon granted on 12 April 1379 'at the request of Hawkwood to William son of John, son of Simon of Gaytescale, of all felonies and trespasses whereof he is indicted, charged or appealed, except treason, homicide, rape and common larceny'. (This is almost certainly our Hawkwood, since his brother of the same name was usually referred to in official documents as 'John the Elder'.) The Close Rolls record that on 30 July the same year, the King also granted his request that Sir William Coggeshall be allowed to postpone doing the homage due on his coming of age, on the ground that the young knight was overseas with Sir John.[7]

Discipline and Punishment

The French historian of medieval warfare Philippe Contamine wrote that Hawkwood never suffered a mutiny. Sir John deserved the compliment, because indiscipline was a problem, even in the royal armies commanded by Edward III. Armies always have aggressive young men in them, and Edward's had both English and Welsh contingents, who tended to quarrel with each other. In addition, the King regularly pardoned criminals as a method of recruitment – it has been estimated that between 2 and 12 per cent of recruits may have been former outlaws. Similar methods were used in Italy. In September 1391 when Jacopo dal Verme's Milanese army threatened Florence, the city revoked the sentences passed on persons convicted of criminal offences, if they would only join Hawkwood's army for the defence of the homeland.

In 1363 Hawkwood received a letter from a constable called Swiler, who wrote to him from Perugia. Swiler offered him the services of fifty lances and suggested a price of 1,000 gold florins (plus 500 for his own services), but he wanted an assurance that his men would not suffer from 'brawls or enmities' at the hands of the English, Germans and Italians already under Sir John's command. It was difficult to control the English when they were abroad: when Henry Bolingbroke was in Prussia, the English crusaders there repeatedly quarrelled with their French and Scottish counterparts. We also know that, when the Italian cities negotiated rates of pay with the English, they sometimes retained two months' pay, as a security against damage done. Villani contrasted the behaviour of the English in the field and in camp. He wrote that they were:

Very obedient to their commanders ... in matters of discipline ... [but] in their camps or cantonments, through a disorderly and over-daring boldness, [they] lay scattered about in great irregularity, and with so little caution that a bold resolute body of men might in that state easily give them a shameful defeat.

The presence of women often gave rise to trouble. During the winter of 1363–4, the English were allowed to stay in Pisa, rather than having to take up winter quarters outside the walls. Bruni tells us that this concession was not conducive to harmony:

For soldiers dwelling inside a single wall in such a multitude left nothing free for the citizens: neither city, nor building, nor families, but they would never obey, alleging now lack of money, now the bitterness of the winter.

Sozomeno, the historian of Pistoia, was more explicit. He wrote that the main cause of complaint was that the English 'insulted the wives of the Pisans with intercourse and adultery, with or without consent.'[8] The situation is said to have become so bad that some of the Pisans sent their wives and daughters to places of safety in Genoa and elsewhere.

There were other causes of indiscipline. It goes without saying that the men fell out with one another when drunk, and gambling too frequently occasioned trouble. The English royal family was very fond of dice but there were Italian writers who thought it a particularly vicious game – 'an insult to God, a source of pride, avarice and anger, leading to insults, duels, robberies and homicides'.[9] Questions of honour frequently arose. In *As You Like It* Shakespeare refers to the soldier:

> Full of strange oaths, and bearded like the pard,[10]
> Jealous in his honour, sudden and quick in quarrel,
> Seeking the bubble reputation
> Even in the cannon's mouth.

Apart from the reference to cannon, this could just as easily have referred to fourteenth-century Italy. Sacchetti has a story of a quarrel between a German and an Italian knight over the right to bear a coat of arms, which included a bear and the motto 'Don't mock the bear, if you don't want to be bitten'.

During the first part of his career, Hawkwood would have become used to the English system of military discipline. One feature of this was that the commander-in-chief issued Ordinances, seeking to impose common rules on an army drawn from many parts of the country. The problem must have been worse in Italy, where there were many states and many allegiances. A Florentine Code of 1368 attempted to regulate the behaviour of Germans (Teutonici), Burgundians (Borgognoni), Hungarians (Ungaresi), English (Anglici) and Italians (Taliani).

In theory the captain was expected to keep order and resolve disputes between his men. The Florentine agreement with Albert Sterz and the majority of the White Company in July 1364 expressly provided that: 'The trial and judgment of each and every complaint and controversy, and in what fair way it may be settled among those concerned, provided they are of the said company, is the responsibility and duty of the captains or marshals.'[11] Other *condotte* provided that 'the leaders of the companies are responsible for the crimes committed by the soldiers in camp, while the Commune shall judge those committed in the city or to the damage of the republic.' The title 'captain-general' implied both military command and legal jurisdiction, and this probably continued to be the case even when the captain commanded a company of freelances. Hawkwood certainly needed to remind his men of the 'rules of engagement'. During the advance on Milan in the spring of 1391, he ordered his troops to abstain from setting fire to buildings, and not to take prisoners, because the allies needed the friendship of the local population – an example of a 'hearts and minds' approach at work. His order was similar to clause 3 of the English Ordinances for the Scots campaign of 1385, which purported to exempt clerks, women and unarmed labourers from pillage and other acts of war.

There are some situations which require tact rather than tactics. During the campaign which Hawkwood conducted for Bernabò Visconti against Verona in the spring and summer of 1378, the English camped at various places to the south of Lake Garda, including Piadena, Monzambano on the River Mincio, and Villafranca di Verona. Some of the places they passed through belonged to the lords of Mantua, an independent state ruled by the Gonzaga since 1328, but allied with Milan. Hawkwood had ordered his troops to treat Mantuan territory 'like that of our Lord the Lord of Milan', but there were bound to be problems, since there were few natural boundaries in the Plain of Lombardy, and it was difficult for the English to distinguish a Mantuan from a Veronese. Property was damaged on both sides, and offence was taken. We still have some of the correspondence between Hawkwood (and his deputy William Gold) and Lodovico Gonzaga (1334–82), the lord of Mantua. In it Gonzaga complains, for example, that some English have attacked his Castle of Caneto near Piadena. Hawkwood complains to Gonzaga that an English horse with 'a long star on his forehead' has been stolen; on another occasion that, although the English may have killed a Mantuan subject, the victim had wounded some horses. He further complains that the Mantuans have seized his cattle. The Constable Gold writes that a German servant has deserted the English camp, taking with him 'a bay horse, a breastplate, and a flask set in silver belonging to his master', and later that a senior officer has been robbed of his horses and travelling bags, while on Mantuan soil. Throughout these exchanges, Hawkwood is anxious to maintain Gonzaga's goodwill – he even offers to make amends when there is fault on both sides.[12] This was tactful, but it was also a matter of self-interest. If he needed to retreat towards Milan, his troops could easily have been cut off by forces sent out from a hostile Mantua.

The power of the purse gave the hirer some degree of control over his mercenaries. There is a Table of Fines from 1368 showing how Florence punished her 'stipendiaries' if they failed to bring the right equipment to the muster. There was also the possibility of summary dismissal. A Florentine contract with Hawkwood in June 1389 stipulated that 'at the request of the commander the notary of the troop shall dismiss those stipendiaries who are not obedient, or do not give true service.' Yet fines and expulsion are unlikely to have been enough to maintain discipline in a medieval army. Richard II's Ordinances of 1385 provided that serious breaches of discipline were punishable with death, and John of Legnano advised that the normal penalty for many military offences was death, though (as lawyers do) he drew some nice distinctions:

Death is the punishment for those who lay hands on an officer, who are disobedient, who are the first to take flight in the sight of the others; for spies

Adige

The Adige rises in the Alps, near the Brenner Pass, and is the second longest river in Italy after the Po. The two rivers make their way side by side to the Adriatic, through high embankments of outstanding importance to medieval engineers and modern ecologists. Between the Adige and the small town of Castagnaro lies an area which is particularly flat, green and fertile. Nowadays this is an agriculturist's paradise, planted with cereals, vines, fruit trees and cabbages, though the surrounding area is also home to many small industries, and a local *graffito* urges the voter to support the Northern League. This is not the rural idyll that the English yearn for.

In 1387 Castagnaro was the site of Hawkwood's most famous battle. The battleground is visibly large enough to accommodate several thousand men, though not the tens of thousands who were present according to some accounts. Looking from the banks of the Adige across to the bell-tower in Castagnaro, we can imagine Hawkwood deploying his English brigade here, as part of the army of the Carrara, as the Paduan chroniclers describe.

The bell-tower has a nineteenth-century inscription, boasting of the victory which the Paduans won that day:

On the 11th day of March 1387, in this plain between the Adige and the Castagnaro canal, the Veronese troops of Antonio della Scala suffered a memorable defeat at the hands of the army of the Carrara commanded by John Hawkwood, which heralded the end of the Scaliger lordship.

The last part of this inscription is very misleading. The Scaliger lordship in Verona did come to an end in 1388, the year after the battle, but this was not because the Veronese had been defeated by the Paduans at Castagnaro. It was because Verona fell into the hands of Gian Galeazzo Visconti, lord – and soon to become Duke – of Milan. The inscription tells us more about the nineteenth century than it does about the fourteenth. Those who wrote it assumed that their medieval ancestors must have looked forward to the end of the rule of the local *signori* with as much enthusiasm as they welcomed the Risorgimento and the re-unification of the Italian homeland in their own time.

who betray secrets to the enemy; for malingerers who feign illness from fear of the enemy; for those who wound a comrade with a sword, who wound themselves without cause, or attempt to commit suicide ... One who does not defend his officer when he could do so is punished with death ... Also one who refuses to go scouting when the enemy are pressing on, or who retires from a trench is punished with death even if he acted with good intention. A deserter in time of war is punished with death; in time of peace a horseman is degraded, a foot-soldier is discharged.

In Hawkwood's day, execution meant either hanging or beheading: there was legislation in Italy which prescribed that males became eligible for decapitation at the age of fifteen.[13] The Great Company of Werner von Urslingen carried a gallows with it as it rampaged through Italy in the 1340s. When the artist Lorenzetti depicted the effects of good government in Siena's Palazzo Pubblico, he depicted the figure of Security with a gibbet. The poet Sacchetti tells a story of how, as *podestà* of San Miniato in 1392, he came across some lost poems, screwed up in a gauntlet he was putting on to attend a 'corporal execution' (*essecuzione corporale*).[14] When Hawkwood's army approached Verona in 1391, the men were ordered to refrain from taking anything other than hay and straw 'under pain of the gallows'.

Chivalry and Morale

Writers like Philippe de Mézières, Honoré Bonet and Christine de Pisan all regarded the Free Companies as a perversion of chivalry, but for the field-commander chivalry was still an ethic which could be appealed to, a way of encouraging solidarity and loyalty.

The most widely respected kind of brotherhood among laymen was the order of knighthood. Unlike many *condottieri*, including von Baumgarten, the Landaus, Alberigo da Barbiano and Astorre Manfredi, Hawkwood was a commoner. However, the Italian chroniclers knew him from the start as 'Messer' Giovanni Acuto and the letters he wrote home at the end of his life were signed 'Chivaler' (see Appendix 2). In English terms, he remained a 'bachelor' knight and he never became a banneret, let alone a member of any exclusive order of chivalry like the English Garter. In the Willement Roll compiled in 1392–7 his name appears in 152nd place (the total being about 600) and the heralds refer to him as plain 'Monseigneur', not 'Sire'. He was never Sir John Hawkwood *of* anywhere, though later ages sometimes called him Sir John *de* Hawkwood.

As a knight, Hawkwood was in a position to confer the dignity on others, and knighting several men at once was a recognized way of strengthening the bond between a leader and his followers.[15] In 1370, when he had failed to relieve San Miniato, he rode under the walls of Florence and dubbed knights there – perhaps to keep up the men's spirits after the setback. The Gatari chroniclers record that he and Francesco Novello dubbed several officers before the Battle of Castagnaro. According to Ghirardacci, he made twenty of his bravest men 'golden knights' (*cavalieri aurati*) after the fighting retreat across the Adige. In Italy the 'golden knights' were the ones who were dubbed with full ceremonial.

Hawkwood's coat of arms are depicted in Uccello's portrait in Florence. It has to be said that they are relatively plain, compared with the spectacular coat of arms of the Visconti family Hawkwood married into, which were 'Argent a serpent vert (crowned) swallowing a child gules' (a green viper with a crown, swallowing a blood-stained child). Sir John's arms are simply 'Argent on a chevron sable three escallops of the field' (a silver shield, with a black chevron and three silver scallops or shells, of the same colour as the background). The colours used were regarded by Christine de Pisan as the most 'humble' in the chivalric palette,[16] and the arms bear no personal motto. We do not know why he chose the shell, though this was widely used as a badge by pilgrims travelling to Santiago. The arms are first recorded in an Anglo-Scottish tournament roll of 1357–61, and appear on the Willement Roll compiled in the 1390s, and it seems likely that Sir John first adopted them when he became a knight. There is no sign that he ever displayed them – or those of his Visconti wife – on the walls of the castle at Montecchio Vesponi.

Ceremony and spectacle played an important part in maintaining morale, and the Italian chronicles contain many references to the holding of a *palio*. This is now familiar as a world-famous horse race which takes place twice a year in Siena, but *palio* originally meant no more than the flag or standard presented to the winner of a competition, and 'palios' were held throughout the Italian states. They took many forms, not all of which involved horses, though horse racing is very exciting – especially when the jockeys ride bareback, as in Giovanni Sercambi's illustration. Machiavelli tells us of an occasion in 1325 when Castruccio Castracani staged no fewer than three 'events', one for the horses, one for the men, and one for the whores – *femmine meretrici*. The last of these was a specialized sort of race which Hawkwood also thought of organizing in front of the papal fortress of Viterbo in August 1368.[17]

Sometimes the *palio* was more than a competition: it was a way of showing one's contempt for the enemy. During the attack on Florence in 1363, the Pisans and their English allies delivered various snubs to the Florentines. They re-minted Florentine coins (and stamped Pisan designs on top), hanged three asses with placards displaying the names of prominent Florentines, and ran a *palio* in the streets. The Florentines responded in kind when the tide turned and they swept down the Arno to the gates of Pisa. They held a *palio* of their own, re-minted coins and hanged donkeys, rams and dogs in a macabre tit-for-tat. Hanging the dogs was thought to be a suitable kind of revenge (or *vendetta*) because the Pisans had treated the Florentines like dogs the previous year.[18] The *palio* could have a strictly military purpose, for – if one was lucky – it might provoke the enemy into mounting a *sortie*; but there was probably a good deal of pleasure to be had from simply delivering a well-judged insult. In Italy the authorities were prepared to spend good money on having defamatory portraits painted. When the War of Eight Saints was drawing to a close in 1377, the Florentines were so enraged by the desertion of Ridolfo of Camerino that they had him painted upside down on the walls of their city.[19]

The monarchs of western Christendom had founded several Orders of chivalry by the time Hawkwood arrived in Italy. Alfonso XI of Castile had founded the Order of the Band; Edward III, the Order of the Garter; John II of France, the Order of the Star (for which Geoffrey de Charny wrote his *Book of Chivalry*); and the Emperor Charles IV, the Order of the Golden Buckle. Charles of Durazzo founded an Order of the Ship. This helps to explain why the *condottieri* – in conscious or unconscious imitation – sometimes gave grand names to the Free Companies. These were in no sense full military orders, with formal constitutions, elaborate rituals and distinctive dress, but they were fellowships of a kind, similar to the confraternities which men and women of lesser rank established in great numbers in the late Middle Ages. We find Hawkwood in command of a Company of St George in the late 1360s, the Holy Company in the 1370s, and a Company of the Rose in the 1380s. He was not alone – Astorre Manfredi, his rival in Romagna, organized a Company of the Star in 1379.

Naming a Company was a way of giving a sense of belonging to men of different nationalities who came from many different places. Another way of doing the same thing was to display a banner or standard, and standard-bearers played a crucial role in late medieval warfare. Before the Battle of Crécy the French unfurled the Oriflamme, which indicated – in an English chronicler's phrase – 'that the mercy of the French was entirely consumed' and hence that no prisoners would be taken. Not to be outdone, King Edward 'ordered his standard unfurled, on which a dragon was depicted clothed in his arms; hence it was called the dragon standard.'[20] The critical moment during the Battle of Poitiers came when the Black Prince shouted the order for the counter-attack: 'Banners, advance!'

Banners were just as important in Italy. Perhaps the most important use of a *carroccio* was to carry them to the scene of the fighting. One of Charles of Durazzo's regulations for the Order of the Ship provided that for every major battle in which he displayed his banner, a knight could add a rope of rigging to his coat of arms. Sacchetti tells of an incident in 1358, when soldiers quarrelled over the right to carry a banner displaying the Crucifix.[21] During the invasion of Lombardy in 1391 the allies assembled under the red lily of Florence, the *carroccio* of Padua and the cross and lily of Bologna. Hawkwood had his own banners in Italy: Giovanni Sercambi shows him outside the walls of Florence in 1375 displaying the cross-keys and triple crown of the Pope and his own triple cockleshell arms (and the troops are shown with both the triangular pennons and the square banners which were the exclusive prerogative of the bannerets in England).

The loss of a banner was shameful. Bruni noted that when the Pisans were defeated at Barga in 1363: 'Their loss was not a slight one, as they were slaughtered in great numbers and lost several military standards.' Conversely, when Hawkwood defeated the Florentines at Second Cascina, he sent the standards captured there back to Bernabò Visconti as trophies, and the event was celebrated as a triumph in Milan. After the leader of the Peasant's Revolt was killed in 1381, Richard II insisted that he 'wanted his banners back', to show that he was once again master of his own kingdom.

Music was important in boosting morale. At Ripoli in 1363 the English raised their standard on the parish church and saluted it with a grand fanfare of trumpets. In the following year in Fiesole, they celebrated the making of knights with music in the piazza, and they sent drummers and trumpeters down to one of the city's gates to annoy and alarm the Florentines. The Florentine Military Code of 1368 confirms that every group which mustered under a banner was expected to have a trumpet and a set of pipes, or a man who could play the castanets or bagpipes. In 1377 Hawkwood made several complaints about the behaviour of the Perugians, who were then his allies. One related to their refusal to allow him to recruit more archers, but another was that they had refused to send drummers and cymbalists to him.[22] On the other hand, a *condotta* signed in May 1390 specified that he had to pay the pipers. At around the same time, he employed a trumpeter called Zuzzo.

Even the lawyer, John of Legnano, recommended 'the daily practice of arms'. This was scarcely realistic in the medieval world, where there were very few standing armies, but jousting and tournaments provided training for men at arms, both individually and in groups. Indeed, jousting was an international sport. Edward III had been a keen jouster in his youth, and his grandson Henry Bolingbroke was a champion who participated in the greatest of international tournaments. Boccaccio thought that the French introduced the tournament into Italy in the late thirteenth century, but if that was so, the Italians took to it quickly. The Green and Red Counts of Savoy staged tournaments regularly, and participated in them with enthusiasm. No fewer than three of Sacchetti's poems are dedicated to a great Italian champion who, like a modern wrestler, went by the name of Tacone ('Big Heel'?). Between 1387 and 1434 there were at least a dozen jousts in Florence, and many Italian cities have revived the sport on feast days.

There is no direct evidence of Sir John jousting in Italy, though an English roll of arms of 1357–61 may suggest that he had taken part in a tournament between English and Scots at Smithfield in London in 1358. When he married Donnina Visconti in 1377, the wedding was certainly celebrated with a tournament in Milan, but Hawkwood was probably a mere spectator. Jousting was a young man's sport, and he was now in his late fifties. One of Sacchetti's stories suggests that it was regarded as something of a joke if an older man attempted to take part.[23]

In February 1392, Konrad von Pressburg jousted in the main square in Bologna, to celebrate the treaty which had ended the first great war between Florence and Milan. Given Hawkwood's position as Florentine commander-in-chief and the knight who had dubbed Pressburg the year before, it is likely that he attended this event. We are told that:

> After dinner in the presence of all the people the famous captain Konrad von Pressburg appeared with a band of thirty-four Italian soldiers, equipped in white armour with his grand white ensigns. The opposite band was of thirty-three German horsemen with red doublets, who were commanded by Prendiparte della Mirandola. They tourneyed worthily with lance and sword. The senate distributed money to the soldiers and a cap entirely covered with the finest pearls to each of the captains.

Three months later, in May 1392, Pressburg took part in another joust to celebrate the signing of the peace treaty, this time in Piazza Santa Croce in Florence. This time, eighty knights were divided into two groups, with a prize for the winner in each, and Konrad won the prize for the red team, which was 'a little lion covered with pearls'. The hero of the joust seems to have been popular with the ladies, and Pressburg was betrothed to Hawkwood's younger daughter in November 1393. The couple were married in Florence the following January.

The Bloody Gauntlet

Men often quarrelled and fought over questions of honour. A judicial combat described by a modern historian as 'the last duel' took place in Paris in 1386, as a result of an allegation that one man had raped the other's wife, but many duels took place without these formalities. However they came about, duels were usually preceded by a challenge, which could involve one man throwing down a gauntlet and the other picking it up, or both men throwing down their gages and an official picking them up. In 1384, John of Gaunt sued Sir Edward Dalyngrigge of Bodiam, alleging trespass to property he held in Sussex, but Dalyngrigge interrupted the trial by repeatedly throwing down his gauntlet. In the same way, Bolingbroke challenges Mowbray at the beginning of Shakespeare's *Richard II*:

Pale trembling coward, there I throw my gage.

In Italy the delivery of a gauntlet, and specifically a *blood-stained* gauntlet had a wider military significance. In 1382 Hawkwood and his men came face to face with Alberigo da Barbiano and the Italian Company in the Val di Pesa. The Italians sent Hawkwood a glove of defiance (*guanto di sfida*), otherwise known as the glove of battle. The meaning was obvious. It was an invitation to come out and fight. In April 1383, when Hawkwood was captain-general for Charles of Durazzo in Naples, Charles sent a glove to the Duke of Anjou and the challenge was accepted, though the battle never took place.

When Hawkwood sent the bloody gauntlet, it was more than a matter of vindicating his personal honour. It was a challenge to battle but it was also a form of psychological warfare. During the invasion of Lombardy in 1390 he repeatedly defied the Milanese in this way, even when they were numerically superior. At an early stage in the campaign he sent his herald and trumpeter Zuzzo to Jacopo dal Verme's camp at Casalecchio di Reno near Bologna on several occasions, and each time Zuzzo took a glove smeared with animal blood. Dal Verme repeatedly refused the challenge. On the last occasion he detained Zuzzo while he made preparations to decamp. Once the Milanese had gone, the trumpeter was left to report the disappointing news.[24]

The Italians were familiar with the power of psychology. Gian Galeazzo Visconti is said to have remarked that Coluccio Salutati's pen did him more harm than thirty troops of Florentine cavalry.[25] One of Sacchetti's Novelle tells how Marabotto da Macerata intimidated a German by telling him that, if the latter wanted a fight with picked champions, Marabotto would pick 10 per cent fewer men than his opponent. In other words, he was ready to fight with one hand tied behind his back: Sacchetti thought that this letter was worth 300 horsemen.[26] The gauntlet which Hawkwood repeatedly sent to dal Verme was a challenge of the same kind. It certainly rattled the Milanese, who was provoked on one occasion into sending Hawkwood a fox in a cage. This was a coded way of saying 'you may be cunning, but you are caught in a trap'. Hawkwood responded by breaking the bars of the cage and letting the animal go free. Dal Verme would have got that message too.

It was sometimes proposed that the most serious of quarrels be resolved by single combat between the individuals concerned, or between picked champions. In 1340 Edward III challenged his arch-enemy Philip of Valois to trial by battle as a way of deciding who was the rightful King of France. Alternatively, he suggested that they should face ravenous lions, or attempt to perform the miracle of touching for the King's Evil.[27] Galeotto Malatesta challenged Cardinal Albornoz as a way of ending the war in the Papal States, and in 1372 Hawkwood

– who was then in Milanese service – suggested to his opposite number that they arrange a combat between six champions on either side. In 1391 he made a similar proposal, involving four captains and sixty men on each side, as a way of ending the war between Florence and Milan. Temple-Leader and Marcotti say that this was a 'remnant of chivalric military customs', but it was not a mere remnant. Chivalry still meant something to the so-called 'mercenaries', just as it had to the knights, for the two were often one and the same. When Hawkwood sent his opponent the bloody gauntlet in 1390–1, as when he suggested combat between champions, it was a demonstration of his confidence that he could beat the Milanese, whatever the terms might be, and it also made the quarrel personal. His invitation was nearly always rejected, but that is beside the point. The act of defiance was a bold one, designed to impress his own men and humiliate the enemy, who lost face by their refusal to fight.

Fighting and Friendship
Dante knew of men who loved fighting:

> I tell you that I find less pleasure
> in eating, drinking and sleeping,
> than in hearing the cry of 'Charge!' ...
> and seeing the dead with bits of lances
> and banners protruding from their sides.[28]

Froissart's chronicles are full of stories about men-at-arms who clearly enjoyed war. His Duke of Gloucester denounces Richard II on the ground that 'England hasn't a king who wants war or enjoys fighting.' Some went to great lengths to pick a fight. In 1352, during a lull in the war with the Valois, Henry of Grosmont went on crusade to Prussia. He was disappointed, because the expedition was called off, but on his way back he was able to challenge Otto of Brunswick to a duel in Cologne. A few years later, at the siege of Rennes, Nicholas Dagworth fought Bertrand du Guesclin in single combat. They fought three 'courses' (rounds) with lances, three with battle-axes and three with daggers.[29]

Medieval fiction has little to say about tactics or strategy because it delights in individual feats of prowess, but for the same reason it does sometimes contain glimpses of the techniques employed by individual warriors. Sacchetti has a story in which a short-sighted knight charges down his own manservant during Louis of Anjou's invasion of Naples in 1384. When the knight first rides out of his city, he carries his lance in the 'soft' position (*lancia molla*), which means vertically, supported by the left hand, resting on the right thigh. When the enemy is sighted and the knight wants to charge, the base of his lance is engaged in the lance-rest (*gancio*) – a hook mounted on the right side of the breastplate – and he plunges forward, gathering speed.[30] This is the standard technique used by the Knights of the Round Table in Malory's *Morte d'Arthur*, where there is even a technical term for fixing the lance in its rest, which is 'feutre'. It is generally thought that a knight in full armour, charging in this way, must have arrived at the enemy's positions with the force of a small tank.

We can believe Malory when he describes the brutality of fighting. In one of his tales, Sir Lancelot kills Sir Turquine when the latter lowers his shield from weariness:

> [Lancelot] leapt upon him fiercely and gat him by the beaver [visor] of his helmet, and plucked him down on his knees, and anon he rased [cut] off his helm, and smote his neck in sunder.

In much the same way Jean de Carrouges butchered Jacques le Gris in a judicial duel held in Paris in 1386. Pinning him to the ground at the end of a long and exhausting combat, he hammered open his enemy's visor with the hilt of his sword and sank his dagger into his throat.[31] Literary accounts of fighting have been illuminated by the excavation, in the late 1990s, of the burial pit at Towton in Yorkshire. The skeletons there displayed horrific wounds, above all to the facial and cranial areas of the skull, and they include gaping holes as well as irreparable fractures. There is no reason to think that warfare was any less brutal in Italy.

There was compensation for the risks involved in fighting in the friendships which soldiers made. This is very evident in the way in which the Bascot of Mauléon spoke about the war. He looked back with great fondness on the time he had spent with 'the boys', and one of his stories specifically puts male friendship above the love of women. He tells the story of two members of the Free Companies, Louis Roubout and Le Limousin – both of them wanted men, whom the French authorities would have liked to arrest if they could. They were brothers-in-arms, but fell out because Le Limousin made love to Louis Roubout's mistress when he was away. When he found out, Louis had his friend flogged in public and banished, but eventually the tables were turned and Le Limousin captured Louis and handed him over to the authorities for execution. Before doing so, he told his old friend how surprised he was by Louis's previous behaviour:

> Louis, Louis, this is where friendship ends. Remember the shame and disgrace that you brought on me at Brioude, because of your mistress. I would not have thought that for a woman, if she was willing and I was willing, you would have made me take what I did take. If you had done the same thing to me, I should

never have minded, for two companions-in-arms, such as we were then, could surely, at a pinch, have overlooked a woman.

Fraternal sentiments can be felt by any band of men, whether or not they operate within the law. The story of Louis Roubout and Le Limousin shows that the special relationship of brotherhood in arms was to be found in the Free Companies, as well as elsewhere. We cannot be sure that Hawkwood ever entered into a formal relationship of this kind, but in his last testament he expressed the wish that money be found for two chantries, for the benefit of the souls of those who had been 'slain for his love', which indicates a close tie to those concerned, and, as we saw, there are six shields on Sir John's sarcophagus in Sible Hedingham. Though the coats of arms have long since faded and we no longer know the names of those commemorated, these men were once the knight's friends and companions, and the chantries Hawkwood wanted to establish were indeed founded in 1409, with the proceeds of sale of his property in the City.[32]

Chapter 8

Chevauchée and Battle

But if you frown upon this proferr'd peace,
You tempt the fury of my three attendants,
Lean famine, quartering steel, and climbing fire.

Shakespeare, *Henry VI*

Shakespeare's history plays take many liberties with the facts, but his poetry describes, as nothing else can, the reality of medieval warfare. This quotation is taken from Sir John Talbot's speech to the citizens of Bordeaux in 1452, when he calls on them to surrender their city. The devastation he threatens to unleash was part of the centuries-old strategy of attrition. Recommended by Vegetius, it was typical of Anglo-Norman warfare and normally employed throughout the so-called 'Age of Chivalry'.

Foraging and Ravaging

The term *chevauchée* simply referred to a mounted raid or expedition. The word was in use by the 1220s when the *Life of William Marshal* was written, but it came to refer to the type of large-scale and long-distance ravaging adopted in France a century later, though the term *voyage* was used by the witnesses in *Scrope v Grosvenor*, whose testimony was recorded in French. The strategy brought Edward III considerable success between 1340 and 1360. In 1358–9 Sir Robert Knollys famously devastated the district of Orléans and the Upper Loire, burning so many villages on the line of march that they became known as 'Knollys's mitres'. The *chevauchée* proved much less effective when the French devised ways of limiting its impact in the 1370s and 1380s, and it was largely abandoned after Agincourt (1415), when the English decided to conquer and occupy Normandy. For speed, the *chevauchée* has been compared to the *Blitzkrieg*, but a better modern parallel is Sherman's March to the Sea during the American Civil War, when a deliberate policy of attrition made the towns of Georgia into so many 'Chimneyvilles', like 'Knollys's mitres' before them.

Parts of Italy, especially the North, were very intensively cultivated and Hawkwood and his companies could employ the same strategy there as had worked so effectively in France before 1360. They 'foraged' and ravaged – at least when in hostile territory – not only as a means of supplying themselves and the horses, but also as a means of putting pressure on the enemy. An expedition like this was described in Latin and in Italian as a *cavalcata* – which can be translated in a somewhat mealy-mouthed way as 'ride' or by the more stirring *chevauchée*. It does seem to bear this more technical meaning in Cardinal Albornoz's *Egidian Constitutions* of 1357 and in the Sercambi illustration, which shows Hawkwood outside Florence in 1375: 'Johanni aguto chavalcò insulterreno e contado di firenza.' This sentence could be translated as 'Hawkwood rode into the territory and country of Florence' or as 'Hawkwood launched a *chevauchée* into the territory and country of Florence.'

Sacchetti tells us of a clash between his favourite *condottiere* Ridolfo of Camerino and Francesco of Matelica, when one of Francesco's captains (called Foscherello) launched a *cavalcata* against Ridolfo's territories and rode home with 800 pigs. He tells us that the raid was a routine part of making war: 'come s'usa per le guerre'.[1] When Pope Urban V issued a bull in 1364, promising an indulgence to anyone willing to take up arms against the Free Companies, he condemned them for 'methodically devastating the country and the open towns, burning houses and barns, destroying trees and vines, obliging poor peasants to fly; assaulting, besieging, invading, spoiling, and ruining even fortresses and walled cities.' Note the word 'methodically'.

The principal weapon was fire. In the poem *Vows of the Heron*, several of the guests present at a feast supposedly held in 1338 boast of their prowess by telling how they will 'set the land ablaze' when they reach France, as does King Edward. In 1362, when Hawkwood was serving the Marquis of Montferrat in Piedmont, the chronicler describes a grim competition between the English and Konrad von Landau's Germans in setting fire to castles and villages. The English were accounted the winners because the Germans only managed to burn twelve places, while they ignited fifty-two. In 1363 the Pisan army sent to invade Florentine territory included about a hundred men specially provided with tinder, flint and a steel (*acciaiuolo*), to start fires along the Arno. The illustrator of Giovanni Sercambi's chronicle drew vivid images of castles in flames. It is perhaps no accident that the Italian for 'putting a country to the sword' is 'mettere un paese a ferro e fuoco' – which adds 'fire' to 'sword' as a matter of language. Henry V is said to have remarked that 'war without fire is as worthless as sausages without mustard'.[2]

In 1389 the Florentines hired both Hawkwood and one of the Landaus. It was a term of their *condotta* that the army do no damage to territory belonging to

Florence, Perugia or other allied communes. The result was that Hawkwood invaded the Sienese domains instead, as a means of supplying and rewarding his troops. Indeed the Florentines secretly ordered him to remain there for a month 'doing as much damage as possible', because Siena was an ally of Milan. They even offered him inducements to do so: a payment of 1,000 florins, reinforcements, supplies, and intelligence about the disposition of Sienese forces.

The victims sometimes resorted to a scorched-earth policy. This happened in March 1366, when the Sienese burnt their hayfields, to deny supplies to Hawkwood and Johann Hapsburg. The burning of hay deprived the invaders of vital fodder for the horses. The burning of other crops denied food to everyone in the area for a season. If vines were destroyed, it meant the loss of the wine harvest for years to come, and if watermills were wrecked the local economy as a whole was affected.

Those on the sharp end of Hawkwood's activities could hardly be expected to think well of him. In 1369 the Tuscan chronicler Sardi wrote with great bitterness:

> At my place they pulled the portico at Oratoio down to the ground, set fire to the woodwork and cut the poles. They burned a great deal of my stores, with beams, benches and cupboards, bedsteads, stools and wardrobes, which were worth altogether more than 200 lire. The Lord destroy them all!

Three years after Hawkwood's death, Francesco Sacchetti suffered the same treatment at the hands of Alberigo da Barbiano, later to become a favourite *condottiere* with Italian nationalists. He complained that at his property at Marignolla:

> all my possessions and the furniture of five rooms was completely burnt, except for the bed linen and something else; the jars were broken with about 120 florins worth of oil in them; 100 florins' worth of wine was spilt; twenty big sweet orange trees were cut, and the workers' dwellings were burnt with all their goods and fittings.[3]

Skirmishing, Ambush and Battle

In England, Hawkwood is not remembered for winning battles in the same way as Cromwell, Marlborough and Wellington. The opposite is the case in Italy, yet much depends on what one calls a battle. In the Middle Ages groups of armed men encountered one another on innumerable occasions, but not all encounters were regarded as battles, and of those that were, not all were pitched battles. Geoffrey de Charny distinguished between a *bataille*, a *rencontre* and a *besogne*,[4] but that is perhaps too logical. The Battle of San Romano of 1432, which features large in the history of art because it was immortalized by Uccello, was not regarded as a battle at the time.

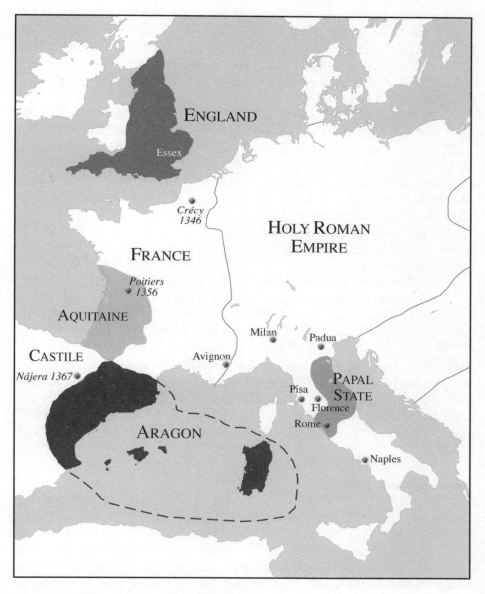

The Hundred Years' War and the Italian States.

During the late 1370s Hawkwood and Landau were engaged in a campaign for the Visconti near Verona. They encountered Hungarian mercenaries employed by the Scaligers, led by the Voivode of Transylvania and the Ban of Bosnia, and deployed at the river crossings in the Plain of Lombardy. On one occasion, Hawkwood and Landau received warnings about the enemy's movements. They crossed the Adige by night and waited in ambush by the river, falling on the Hungarians and Scaligers when the latter attempted to ford the water. They got the better of their enemies and recovered many comrades who had previously been captured. None of this skirmishing was dignified with the name of a 'battle', though the tactics employed were very successful.

As Vegetius and Christine de Pisan both warned, an army was very vulnerable when fording a river. When the Florentines forded the Arno near San Miniato in 1328, 'the infantry had to wade through water that came up to their shoulders, while the cavalry had water up to their saddles', and as soon as they came ashore, they were set upon by Castruccio Castracani and his men.[5] Hawkwood's adversaries tried to take advantage of the fact that he had to cross several rivers when in retreat from Milan in 1391. As he approached the Oglio, he found Taddeo dal Verme waiting for him, with 700 horsemen out of Brescia. He countered this threat aggressively by placing Landau junior in hiding with 300 lances and ambushing the enemy. He took 100 prisoners, and 300 of dal Verme's men were drowned or killed, but none of this fighting has been dubbed a battle.

The chronicler in Treviso calculated that Hawkwood was beaten in only one of *twenty-three* battles[6] and Filippo Villani called him 'grand master of war'. Favourable verdicts were returned by many later Italian writers, notably Vergerio (1370–1444), Giovio (1483–1552) and Ammirato (1531–1601). There is a tendency to exaggerate here, since Hawkwood lost more battles than many allow: he took a bad beating at First Cascina in 1364, and was defeated at Perugia in 1365 and Arezzo in 1368, but it remains true that his record in pitched battles was impressive. The chronicles allow us to give a reasonably detailed account of four of these. All four took place in the North of Italy, in the valleys of the Arno, Adige or Chiese.

Second Cascina, 1369

The Second Battle of Cascina was fought between the Milanese and the Florentines when Hawkwood was in the Visconti service. It was fought in December 1369, when the enemy might well have expected Sir John's forces to be in winter quarters. Sacchetti remarked on the timing of the campaign, taking the opportunity to castigate Hawkwood's master, Bernabò. Likening him to the viper, central emblem in the Visconti coat of arms, he condemned him for fighting at the wrong time of year:

Apennines

As British prisoners of war who escaped into them found to their cost – though also to their advantage – the Apennines are very different from the Pennines of northern England. They are far more extensive, higher and more rugged. There are many places to hide, but it is altogether a wilder place, with a more extreme climate. The chain of mountains is between fifty and seventy miles wide and runs down the spine of Italy for over 600 miles, separating the Plain of Lombardy from Tuscany and Umbria. The peaks can reach 7,000 feet and the Futa and Giogo passes, which lie between Bologna and Florence, are at 3,000 feet as high as any mountain-top in England. The slopes are heavily wooded, though nowadays they are home to both wild boar and skiers. In the Middle Ages they were a source of manpower for local families – including the Guidi and Ubaldini in Tuscany and the Manfredi in Romagna.

In the early fourteenth century, the Florentines built a new road across the Giogo and protected it with fortresses at Scarperia on the south slope of the Apennines (1306), and Firenzuola ('little Florence') in the middle of the range (1324). The Giogo route was more secure than the old one over the Futa, though the Ubaldini still managed to capture Firenzuola twice and close the pass altogether on several occasions, until they were finally put down in 1373.

Despite the attentions of the Ubaldini, Scarperia and Firenzuola were bastions of Florentine power – places where travellers could rest and soldiers could pick up supplies, before tackling the next section of the road and the wilderness. The bottom half of the front of the Palazzo Pretorio at Scarperia is almost entirely covered with the coats of arms of the 'vicars' the Florentines appointed to govern the town. They held office for a mere six months, so the number of coats of arms multiplied rapidly. They must have needed to apply a firm hand to keep law and order in the mountains.

In 1390, when Hawkwood crossed the range from Florence to Bologna, he and his men left on 9 May and arrived on the 14th. He may have travelled via the Futa pass, which is the more direct route, or taken the Giogo route for greater security. Either way the total distance is about 65 miles, or thirteen miles a day. This is not especially fast but the difficulty and height of the passes needs to be remembered. Thirteen miles on a high mountain road was not like thirteen in Lombardy or in what later became known as the Veneto, unless there had been flooding.

Mountainous terrain enabled local people to fight back against professional men-at-arms. The Battle of Le Scalelle, in the upper Val di Lamone, was won when local men and women took revenge on the mercenaries by rolling boulders down from the peaks. The event is remembered to this day in

Marradi, where there is a Piazza Scalelle, and the site of the battle is marked by a classical column and a plaque erected in 1931. The inscription, written in the ninth year of Mussolini's new Fascist 'era' (but two years before Hitler came to power) celebrates the victory of local Italians over soldiers led by a German *condottiere* whom Hawkwood was later to defeat at the bridge of Canturino:

On 24th day of July 1358, these mountain slopes saw the bullying arrogance [*prepotente baldanza*] of the free company led by Count Konrad von Landau annihilated by the ardour of the valley dwellers.

The Commune of Marradi, in perpetual memory. July 1931 – Year Nine.

In 1943 the Italian government signed an armistice with the Allies but the Germans took control of northern Italy and Field-Marshal Kesselring succeeded in holding up the Allied advance for two winters. His forces built successive lines of fortification across the peninsula. The most formidable of these was the Gothic Line, a belt of forts, gun emplacements and traps stretching right across the Apennines, which was made ready for the winter of 1944–5. The Gothic Line centred on the Futa pass, but the Allies launched a two-pronged attack, in the east and in the centre up the Giogo route, to take Firenzuola. Before doing do, they did their best to flatten the town; and only the Porta Firenze and the Porta Bolognese were left standing. The work the Florentines had first completed in 1324 had to be redone after the war.

You snake, enemy of human reason,
who in winter, while others are underground,
goes on biting and making war ...

The battle took place in the cockpit of the Arno, where the Florentines had defeated the English five years before: Cascina, in the broad valley bottom, midway between Pisa and San Miniato, was now the site for a 'return match'. On this occasion Hawkwood had the advantage of being allied with the Germans Johann von Rieten and Flachsen von Riesach (who had beaten him at Arezzo the previous year), but the Italian writers seem agreed that he defeated the Florentines by means of a trick, rather than because of superior numbers. Sozomeno of Pistoia, who had no reason to like Hawkwood, had no doubt that the victory was due to the Englishman's 'prescience and sagacity'. He wrote that Hawkwood ordered some of his men to pretend to flee, once the battle had begun, while holding his main force in reserve.[7]

There is a more detailed account of this battle, which emphasizes the importance of the youths who were a normal part of the three-man English 'lance'. Normally, these 'boys' or 'pages' had the job of looking after the horses – a necessary task since it was normal in English armies for each knight to have four horses, a squire three and a mounted archer two.[8] Second Cascina shows how these young soldiers, generally non-combatant, could be deployed tactically. The river is broad at Cascina and, in this account, Hawkwood ordered the pages to take their mounts down to the river and pretend to be looking for a ford. He also ordered them to put on the armour which they normally carried and polished for others, so as to give them the appearance of men-at-arms. This fooled the enemy into thinking that the whole Milanese army was on the move, indeed in retreat, when the more experienced men were in fact held in reserve. The Florentines, led by Giovanni Malatacca, fell into the trap. They pursued the boys and were attacked by the men, who ambushed them with devastating effect. Eight hundred Florentine horsemen sank in the soft earth of the riverbank and a larger number were captured.

The 'false retreat' was not an original tactic: William the Conqueror had used it at Hastings in 1066, with incalculable consequences for English history. To pull it off required organization, training and discipline, and a leader who commanded obedience and exercised control over both infantry and cavalry. It may also have helped that by the end of 1369 Hawkwood had extensive experience of fighting in the lower Arno (especially in and around Cascina) and knew the ground well.

Montichiari, 1373
Our second battle was fought at the start of the campaigning season, in May 1373, at Montichiari on the River Chiese, to the south of Lake Garda. On this occasion Hawkwood commanded an allied army, consisting of soldiers loyal to the Pope, followers of the Green Count of Savoy, and some French troops. The latter were led by Enguerrand de Coucy, a French nobleman who had travelled to England as a hostage after Brétigny, stayed to marry Edward III's daughter, and become known to the English as Sir Ingelram. Hero of Barbara Tuchman's doleful history of the fourteenth century, *A Distant Mirror*, Coucy was known in Italy as Inghiramo, or as the Siri di Così.

The allies marched to relieve the Count of Savoy, who had become trapped at Brivio on the Adda. Ranged against them were forces deployed by both Visconti brothers, Bernabò and Galeazzo, and commanded by the latter's young son Gian Galeazzo and Hanneckin von Baumgarten. Hawkwood was outnumbered, for he and Coucy had only 600 lances and 700 archers, though there were also some *provvisionati* and town militia under one of the Malatesta. The Visconti forces are said to have numbered 1,500 lances, mainly Germans and Hungarians, with 4,000 foot in all.

French cavalry was already infamous for the *charge en masse*, a phenomenon noted by the Byzantines at the time of the First Crusade, though the expression *furia francese* seems to have been coined much later, during the Italian wars of the sixteenth century. The enduring reputation of French cavalry for recklessness survived its setbacks at the hands of the English during the Hundred Years' War, and reached its zenith during the Napoleonic Wars. The nadir only came when Napoleon III's armies were out-generalled and out-railwayed by the Prussians in 1870–1. The problem it posed for the medieval commander was that, once the horsemen had charged, it was extremely difficult to recall them, or to rearrange one's forces so as to withstand a counter-attack. This endangered the whole army, for as Philippe de Mézières complained, 'battles are decided in an hour or two, even less, and we often see that the side apparently beaten takes heart and wins the day.'

In Froissart's version, the Battle of Montichiari started in predictable fashion, and badly for Hawkwood, when de Coucy's French launched a cavalry charge, hoping as ever to prevail by 'shock and awe'. This triggered a general encounter and obliged Hawkwood to follow, though he is unlikely to have approved, or approved of, the French tactics. As often happened, the charge did not prove decisive and the allies were beaten back. The Visconti even assumed that they had won the day, and their *saccomani* started to gather the spoils of war from the battlefield.

Troops who see their friends and colleagues swept from the field tend to break and run, and Hawkwood did well to stage a recovery. He had taken refuge on high ground and, although he now had few professionals left, he was able to rally those he had and lead a counter-attack, with the help of the *provvisionati* and militia. This caught the Visconti by surprise. Von Baumgarten's Germans fled and the resistance of the remaining Italian troops on the Visconti side was feeble. Hawkwood succeeded in capturing the enemy camp and took some 200 prisoners. Young Gian Galeazzo Visconti was thrown from his horse and lost his helmet and his lance. He was nearly captured, but managed to defend himself long enough to find another horse.[9] He fled from the battlefield.

In Froissart's account, Hawkwood not only snatched victory from the jaws of defeat, but saved Enguerrand de Coucy's life, though the latter had put everyone in danger by his ill-timed bravado. We are told that Sir John's only reason for going to de Coucy's assistance was that the Frenchman was King Edward's son-in-law. The chronicler also tells us that, in his opinion, Montichiari was 'a really fine day's work': 'une très belle journée'.

There is a much less inspiring version of this battle: William Caferro points out that, according to Italian chroniclers and contemporary letters, it was Gian Galeazzo who attacked first. If this is right, the early difficulties cannot be blamed on the 'confident and over-lusty French' – as Shakespeare calls them in *Henry V.* But by all accounts, the day was won in the end by the prudence of an English commander, who had the difficult and unusual task of deploying French cavalry, and still won the day.

Castagnaro, 1387[10]

Castagnaro is the best known of all Hawkwood's victories, perhaps because it was a major encounter between two armies drawn up for battle, of a kind which Tizzana was not, and won by sound strategy and tactics, rather than by a trick, like Second Cascina. It was also recorded very fully by the two Gatari, though we should remember that they worked for the Carrara of Padua, whose army won the day. At least two modern accounts (Strickland and Hardy's and Caferro's) come accompanied by detailed maps, showing – perhaps too precisely – how the armies are supposed to have manoeuvred. The battle was fought on 11 March 1387.

Sir John had been hired by the Carrara, who were at war with the Scaligers of Verona. He even laid siege to Verona, but was forced to fall back along the south bank of the Adige, thereby getting more and more cut off from his base in Padua. The men began to suffer from a shortage of supplies and they were reduced to eating horsemeat and turnips. After discussing the situation in a council of war, Hawkwood decided to stand and fight, rather than try to cross the Adige at Castelbaldo, though the bridge there had been recently rebuilt, and there was a depot containing supplies, which attracted some deserters. The halt allowed time for the army to rest, but it also allowed the commander to choose his ground and draw up his battle-lines to best advantage. Vegetius had advised that 'a large part of the victory depends on the actual place in which the battle is fought', and on this occasion Hawkwood chose a location on flat land near the village of Castagnaro, taking up a position on the south bank of the Adige behind a dyke, at a point where there was also a canal to the rear. His position was therefore protected by moats, natural or artificial, except on the left flank, where there was a marsh.

Sir John arranged his army in eight battalions (*schiere*), some consisting of as many as 1,500 horsemen, some not exceeding 500. His own consisted of 500 cavalry and 600 archers, all Englishmen. He dismounted six of these battalions, forming two lines of 3,000 men each along the line of the dyke in front. The Paduan *carroccio* was put in a place of safety at the rear. The right flank was protected by Italian crossbowmen, with their shields. Sir John had about 1,000 Paduan *provvisionati*, usually of doubtful quality, but on this occasion trained men, since the Paduans had a small standing army. On the other side, the Veronese – who almost certainly outnumbered the Paduans – were also dismounted and drawn up in two lines, with reserves of cavalry and foot in the rear. This was also where the Veronese had their precious *carroccio*. The Veronese in the front line prepared bundles of reeds, to fill the watercourse separating them from their enemies.

To boost morale, Francesco Novello knighted five Paduans and Hawkwood knighted some English, and it is possible that he made a speech. Some say he mounted a Thessalian charger and invoked the assistance of the patron saints of Padua – Prosdocimus, Justina, Daniel and the more famous Anthony, still widely revered as the patron saint of lost objects. More practically, he precipitated the battle by using skirmishers to harass the enemy, who responded by launching the first attack. Though held up by the dyke, the Veronese had superior numbers and they started to gain ground, but, as the Paduans fell back, the Scaliger troops were exposed to missile fire from English archers and Italian crossbowmen. Their general Giovanni dei Ordelaffi, who was from an old family in Forlì and had two members of the dal Verme family with him, then made the mistake of feeding his second line into the fray, so that almost his entire main force became engaged. Hawkwood saw what was happening and now delivered the *coup de grâce*. He took his 600 mounted archers, crossed the dyke to his right, rode along the raised bank of the Adige, and charged down it, wheeling round and outflanking the enemy left wing. He and his English were now in a position to attack the hapless Veronese from the rear, while the Paduans continued to resist their front line.

At one point, Hawkwood is said to have thrown his baton into the enemy ranks, drawn his sword and charged in where the action was. It has even been suggested that the baton was thrown as an inducement to his troops to retrieve it – as one might throw a stick for a dog, but it seems much more likely that this was the signal to charge. Sir Thomas Erpingham commanded the archers to fire at Agincourt in much the same way, by throwing his baton high into the air. Whatever the precise significance of Hawkwood's gesture, the Veronese army collapsed under the battering it received from two directions at once. The Paduan heralds made a tally of the damage inflicted on the enemy. They had taken over 5,000 prisoners, including the enemy commander and eighty of his captains, 4,620 hired cavalrymen (*soldati da cavallo*) and 840 locally raised and hired infantrymen (*provvisionati e soldati da piè*). They captured 424 wagons and carts laden with supplies and armoury of various kinds – bread, wine and maces filled with lead; twenty carts laden with axles, pack-saddles and assorted ironmongery; twenty-four 'bombards', large and small; and three battle-wagons containing those frightening 'Stalin-organs' with which the Veronese had hoped to intimidate and destroy their enemies (see Chapter 5). The heralds found over 700 Veronese dead, either on the battlefield or in the adjacent dykes. The Battle of Castagnaro had lasted only two hours: Francesco Novello wrote to Treviso that it had begun an hour before sunset and finished an hour afterwards, but it had taken a terrible toll.

Castagnaro has been much misunderstood. In their recent work on the longbow, Matthew Strickland and Robert Hardy credit archery with playing a significant part in the victory, but what seems to have been critical was the final charge by Hawkwood's mounted reserve. English archers often rode to the battlefield but they were not horse-archers, trained from boyhood to shoot from horseback, like the Huns and Mongols of previous centuries, or the Ottoman Turks who defeated the crusaders at Nicopolis in 1396. In any case the English missile weapon was the longbow, which could not be used in this way. Hawkwood's charge at Castagnaro must have succeeded because of the shock it delivered, not because of the skill of the English bowmen. Benjamin Kohl, the historian of Padua, tells us that the archers 'rained arrows from the bank',[11] but this seems to be based on a single phrase in the chronicle of the senior Gataro, and it seems unlikely that the archers would have had time to break off and engage in a spot of archery during a cavalry charge. However, it would seem that Andrew Ayton and Michael Mallett are each wrong to attribute the victory at Castagnaro to the use of cannon. Hawkwood may have had a few cannon with him, but it was the Veronese who brought along the big guns (though even they did not use them). They are also wrong to describe Castagnaro as in any sense an 'ambush'. It was a classic pitched battle, if ever there was one.

One cannot really explain Hawkwood's success better than Temple-Leader and Marcotti did, over 100 years ago:

> Hawkwood had shown the finest qualities of a first rate captain: constancy in peril, rapidity in conceiving a good solution to a problem and in modifying the plan chosen according to circumstances, resolution in action, a judicious use of the different arms, an exact valuation of the opposing forces, above all things a conscientious study of the ground and knowing how to make use of it to attain his object, together with the personal courage to lead his men-at-arms at the decisive moment.

Castagnaro is reminiscent of the Black Prince's victory at Poitiers in 1356. Although that battle – along with Crécy and Agincourt – has become famous as one where a combination of English infantry and archery decimated a French cavalry charge, it had a 'second half', according to Froissart, when the English and their Gascon allies *got back on their horses*. It seems quite clear from his account that it was only when the Captal de Buch rode round the rear of the French army, and the Black Prince mounted a cavalry charge from the front, that the real damage was done.[12] In the same way, Hawkwood's final wheeling manoeuvre at Castagnaro required the speed which only horses could provide. In this sense Castagnaro was won in the old-fashioned 'chivalric' manner, not by the new English methods which had so impressed Filippo Villani in the 1360s.

Tizzana, 1391[13]

The last of our four battles is not so well known as Castagnaro; indeed it is not even mentioned by Frances Stonor Saunders (2004) and it appears only briefly in William Caferro's biography (2006), perhaps because it was not a pitched battle, but more of an attack on an army on the march, such as the Seljuks had often launched against the Crusaders in twelfth-century Palestine.[14]

It was fought in September 1391 near Tizzana, now a 'fraction' of Quarrato, when Hawkwood was commander-in-chief of the Florentine army. The allied armies had now been defeated, or driven out of Lombardy. Jacopo dal Verme had crushed the Count of Armagnac at Alessandria and then invaded Tuscany. He took the coastal route via Sarzana and arrived in Pisa via Lucca. This invasion was extremely dangerous for the Florentines, because Gian Galeazzo had popular support in some areas, at least with some classes of men. Hawkwood travelled south from Bologna to Pistoia, taking a route through the Apennines via Sambuca Pistoiese, and took up a position at San Miniato al Tedesco.

A series of manoeuvres now took place in the lower Arno, a war of movement and counter-movement where the honours seem to have been largely equal. Dal Verme moved from Pisa to Cascina, while Hawkwood moved from San Miniato to Montopoli and San Romano, where he had built the dyke and the tower a year before, but the Milanese simply walked and rode around these static defences. Dal Verme temporarily billeted his men at Poggibonsi and other places in the valley of the Elsa, some way to the south, but then moved swiftly back to the north bank of the Arno and laid siege to Santa Maria a Monte near Pontedera.[15] Finally he moved across Monte Albano and took up a position at Poggio a Caiano – only ten miles or so from Florence. Hawkwood marched along the south bank of the river and, between 20 and 21 September, crossed it at Signa, at that time the limit of navigation for barges and now a railway station in greater Florence. Sir John made camp at Tizzana, on the slopes of Monte Albano.

The two armies now faced each other, and the danger to Florence was thought to be so intense that the authorities reinforced Hawkwood with 10,000 *distrettuali* – citizens and peasants from districts owing allegiance to the city. Ten thousand sounds an impressive number, but large numbers were not necessarily an advantage, especially when the nucleus of the army on both sides consisted of professionals. It does show how worried the Florentines were.

Perhaps the risks were not so great as Florence feared. By taking up a position at Tizzana, when dal Verme was at Poggio a Caiano, Hawkwood had at last succeeded in outmanoeuvring dal Verme, for his army now blocked the way home to Milan. This may explain why dal Verme drew back, without laying siege to Florence or seeking battle. Instead he began to move his men away in the direction of Pistoia. Since the Florentine army was literally in the way, he went west and north, but this involved recrossing Monte Albano and heading for the Val di Nievole. It was now that Hawkwood decided to act. As the enemy marched and rode across the mountain, he detached an elite force of 1,000 lances (some 3,000 men, or 2,000 combatants) to attack it, while he followed with the main force. This was a situation where local knowledge was of vital importance, since the Florentines must have known the mountain tracks better than the Milanese, and a vanguard could follow the scouts more quickly on its own.

The plan worked and Hawkwood's men caught up with the enemy rearguard led by dal Verme's cousin Taddeo, and gave it a mauling in the hills. Taddeo was captured, together with his senior officers. The casualties included 2,400 dead and some 200 prisoners. Hawkwood and the Florentine infantry continued the pursuit of Jacopo and the main body of the Milanese army, picking up equipment and stores abandoned by the enemy near Pescia (now famous for cut flowers and Pinocchio), but Jacopo got away. Eventually, both sides took up positions very close to where they had started off a short time before – Jacopo in the plain at Cascina, Hawkwood near the fortress of San Miniato, but within weeks the Milanese withdrew to Lucca and eventually back up the coast into Liguria, while Hawkwood took up winter quarters in the Val di Nievole. His generalship had enabled the Florentine republic to survive.

Chapter 9

Strategy, Spies and Luck

And whosever would know in general and in particular about the office of captains of war … should read the fine book by Vegetius entitled On Military Matters, and there he will find the best rules relating to strategy and to all chivalrous endeavour, and how to obtain the victories he desires in a worthy manner.

Philippe de Mézières, *The Dream of the Old Pilgrim*

Italians constantly looked back to the classical world for inspiration. Vegetius and other Roman authors were widely read, and Pier Paolo Vergerio compared Hawkwood to the commanders of ancient Rome. The epitaph for Uccello's portrait, commissioned by the Florentines in 1436, was written by Filippo Fortini in Latin, and employed classical vocabulary and allusions:

Johannes Acutus eques Britannicus dux aetatis suae cautissimus et rei militaris peritissimus habitus est.

Hawkwood, a British Knight, regarded as the most prudent commander of his age, and the most experienced in military affairs.

This is a handsome tribute, though not a summary of the knight's career, such as we might have found on an English brass. How far did he deserve the compliments which the Florentines paid him?

'Most Experienced Commander' *(Dux peritissimus)*
Leonardo Bruni, who was in his teens when Hawkwood lived in Florence, thought that knowledge of military affairs (*scientia rei militaris*) was unusual even in professional soldiers, 'let alone in commoners who are used to leisure and mercantile activities'. Yet he thought that Hawkwood was already 'an extremely experienced and crafty war leader' (*peritissimus et callidissimus bello dux*) in the 1360s.[1] In 1387 Giovanni degli Ubaldini, who was an experienced soldier

himself, renounced the command of the Paduan army in Hawkwood's favour because he recognized that the Englishman had a better claim.

This was partly the result of longevity. Hawkwood was already forty when he arrived in Italy but his career there was as long as the whole of the Black Prince's, and he spent more time fighting. Shakespeare's 'time-honoured Lancaster', John of Gaunt, died at the age of fifty-nine – the average age of the thirty-four Italian *condottieri* whose biographies were related by Claudio Rendina in the 1980s. Henry of Grosmont was probably Edward III's most experienced commander, but he died in his early fifties. The length of Hawkwood's career was not unique – Richard Le Scrope of Bolton Castle in Yorkshire was present in every major English campaign between 1346 and 1384 – but it was nonetheless remarkable. To find a parallel in modern British history, one would have to find someone who fought in the ranks in the Second World War and was an officer in the Falklands War of 1982.

Hawkwood's experience must have been a great advantage to the forces he commanded. He was fifty-three at the Battle of Montichiari in 1373, when Gian Galeazzo was a mere twenty-two. By the time of Castagnaro he was sixty-seven when his opponent Ordelaffi was only thirty-two. At Tizzana he was seventy-one, when both his Milanese opponents, Jacopo and Taddeo dal Verme, were in their early forties. In short, he was sometimes twice as old as the commanders he defeated. Such an age difference would be thought a great disadvantage today, but it was clearly no handicap then. Age brought experience, in particular in the handling of men. Military historians are very interested in whether infantry or cavalry was the predominant 'arm' in any particular period, but in Hawkwood's case the question is largely irrelevant – he knew how to deploy both, and how to combine them. Versatility was the key.

Machiavelli recommended that the commander should familiarize himself with local geography, but Italy is a very different country from England or France. Yet, Sicily and Venice apart, there were few parts of the Italian peninsula which Hawkwood did not campaign in. The tributaries of the Po – Lanzo, Ticino, Panaro, Adda, Chiese, Oglio and Mincio – are mentioned repeatedly by the chroniclers, as are those of the Arno. He fought many times in the plain of Lombardy, in Tuscany, in the Papal States and in the Kingdom of Naples, and he crossed the mountains and rivers repeatedly. Use of ground is a basic tactical skill which he would have acquired in France, long before he crossed the Alps, but he also had long years in which to accumulate detailed knowledge of Italian topography.

He could also buy in local knowledge. Vegetius had urged the commander to

find out everything from intelligent men, from men of rank, and those who knew the localities, individually, and put together the truth from a number of witnesses. Furthermore, ... collect ... able guides, knowledgeable of the roads, and keep them under guard, having given them a demonstration of punishment and reward.

We know that Hawkwood acted in accordance with this advice, whether or not he ever read Vegetius. When he commanded the Pisans at First Cascina in 1364, he attacked at an hour known to be suitable for an assault, because of the prevailing wind direction. In 1377 he complained when his allies in Perugia 'would not furnish him with mounted guides who knew the country, [making it] necessary to take fresh ones from one place to another.' The circumstances of his victory at Tizzana strongly suggest that he had guides who knew the area and the terrain better than the enemy.

Knowledge of men was equally important. Vegetius had advised: 'It is ... relevant to find out the character of the adversary himself, his senior staff-officers and chieftains', but Hawkwood had a rare advantage in that he sometimes knew the enemy commanders personally. His career was made up of a series of short-term contracts (interspersed with a good deal of freelancing) and in the course of this he often found himself alongside men whom he had occasion to fight later. This allowed him to see into the mind of his enemies. When he was employed by the Pisans in 1363, his fellow captains were the Germans Sterz and Baumgarten. Sterz was initially Hawkwood's commanding officer, though their roles were later reversed, but in the following year, when Hawkwood remained loyal to Pisa, both Germans defected to Florence. In 1365 they commanded a papal force which defeated the English at Perugia and in 1373 Baumgarten was on Gian Galeazzo's side when Sir John defeated the Milanese at Montichiari. In the same way, Hawkwood was a companion of Bernard de la Salle in France, and again when they served the Visconti, but when he attacked Naples in 1389, de la Salle and his Gascons formed the backbone of the French garrison there.[2]

Hawkwood also got to know many of the Italian captains. Sacchetti tells us, as if there was nothing remarkable about this, that Ridolfo of Camerino went to visit the Englishman some time in the 1370s at his camp outside Perugia, but we know that Ridolfo was captain-general for the anti-papal league during the War of Eight Saints, when Hawkwood was in command of the other side.[3] Like Sir John, Alberigo da Barbiano served the Visconti in the early 1370s and the Pope during the War of Eight Saints, and both men participated in the operations at Faenza and Cesena in 1376–7, but Alberigo was on the other side when the Englishman was employed to defend Florence against the Italian Company in 1382. Hawkwood fought alongside Giovanni degli Ubaldini at Castagnaro in 1387, but was on the opposite side soon afterwards, when Ubaldini signed a *condotta* with the Milanese, and again in 1390, when Siena allied itself with Gian Galeazzo and

Ubaldini led the Sienese against Florence. Hawkwood fought on the same side as Galeotto Malatesta at Montichiari in 1373, but the two were soon on opposite sides in Romagna, when Malatesta defended his lands round Rimini.

'Most Prudent Commander' *(Dux cautissimus)*

Hawkwood was not afraid of a fight, even when the odds were stacked against him, and on one occasion he was even prepared to risk the lives of his own children. For reasons which are now obscure, an illegitimate son of his was in Bologna in 1376, when that city joined the widespread urban revolt in the Papal states.[4] The Bolognese imprisoned the boy, along with several of Sir John's followers, in revenge for the Englishman's sack of Faenza, but Hawkwood took no notice. He attacked, laid waste to the countryside and took some 400 prisoners of his own. This paid off, and Bologna surrendered the child in return for a truce with the father and the return of her own prisoners. In view of this willingness to fight, it is at first sight a little curious that his Florentine epitaph describes him as *cautissimus* (most cautious, or most prudent). One might think that the Florentines would have valued him most as a fighting soldier, as Lincoln valued Grant during the American Civil War.

In reality there is no contradiction here. Prudence was one of the four cardinal virtues admired by Catholic theologians, and it was a necessary quality in time of war. Even in the twelfth century, when French cavalry was famous for its aggression, a Muslim writer remarked that 'Of all men the Franks are the most cautious.'[5] The most striking adverb in Matteo Villani's account of the battle of Marradi (1358) is *baldanzosamente* (arrogantly), which he uses to characterize the tactics of the German commander there. Hawkwood's prudent approach was the opposite of this.

A medieval general needed caution as well as dash. John of Legnano recommended that a commander should:

> keep his troops in camp, train them to the practice of arms ...; ... carry the keys of the gates, go round the watches, concern himself with the foraging of his troops, approve their food, punish fraudulent measurement, chastise offences, hear the complaints of the troops [and] inspect the sick.

Likewise, Geoffrey le Baker related how, on the *chevauchée* of 1356, the Black Prince pitched his camp in the right place, guarded it at night and moved on at appropriate intervals. He also told how this English hero was concerned to see that the 'fiery young men did not advance against orders', that the archers did not waste their arrows, and that a reserve was maintained when the battle-lines were drawn up.[6] Hawkwood saw with his own eyes, at Brignais in 1362 and at

Montichiari eleven years later, how the arrogance of the French nearly led to catastrophe.

Hawkwood's prudence was recognized during his lifetime. In the late 1370s Chancellor Salutati urged that he avoid battle:

> curb the generous impatience of your men so near the discouraged enemy, who being already reduced and enraged might fight desperately – wait till they are more demoralized, or till they rashly risk themselves in an insecure position – For the rest we trust in your prudence and well-known capacity.

The literary context is important. Sacchetti praised a personified 'Prudence' when the revolt of the Ciompi was suppressed in 1378, and the same Virtue is symbolized by a picture of a lynx in Fiore dei Liberi's enigmatic handbook of martial arts of 1410, *Flos Duellatorum*. The Florentines (who were a highly literate people) compared themselves with the Romans, and one of the generals they remembered was Fabius 'the Delayer'. Sir John mounted a great invasion of Lombardy for the Florentine republic and its allies in 1390, but it was his rescue of their army from the waters of the Adige, followed by his successful defence of their capital, which invited comparison with Fabius and which the Florentines remembered best.

In English terms Hawkwood's mentors were Edward III and the Black Prince, and the King in particular has recently been portrayed in quite a new way. The orthodox view, held for most of the twentieth century, was that he was 'a capable tactician but a poor strategist', but the historians Clifford Rogers and Andrew Ayton have more recently portrayed him once again as a highly successful, 'battle-seeking' general. Did Hawkwood emulate his sovereign in seeking out the enemy, or was he just good at winning battles when these could no longer be avoided? Any comparison with Edward III is bound to be a little unreal, since Edward was a sovereign as well as a general and fought almost entirely in France, at the head of Englishmen, Gascons and others who were his to command as of right. Hawkwood learned much from the war in France, but he had to practise what he learned in very different conditions. He served many masters and faced a greater variety of military problems, while commanding less homogeneous forces.

Temple-Leader and Marcotti were seldom critical of Hawkwood; but they did write:

> It has ... been noticed that Hawkwood always showed a great wish to fight when he knew his masters would not give him the means of doing so and likewise to drag out a slow war when they wanted decisive actions; such little hypocrisies were useful to the reputation of adventurers and served their interests.

Florence

Florence is one of the most beautiful and fascinating cities in Europe because she has preserved her medieval buildings as well as her works of art. Her skyline looks much as it would have done in Sir John Hawkwood's day, though the dominant feature – Brunelleschi's Dome – was completed forty years after his death, at the same time as his portrait was painted for the nave below. The city first became pre-eminent in cloth manufacturing, but she soon expanded into the service industries, notably banking. Her wealth fuelled a spectacular building boom and palaces went up in the city, villas in the surrounding countryside. The Palazzo della *Signoria* and the Duomo we see today were both begun around 1300. She was home to poets and storytellers like Petrarch (1304–74) and Boccaccio (1313–75) and many other writers and scholars. She had a highly educated elite and a largely literate populace.

For centuries after his death, Hawkwood's memory was principally preserved in paint rather than in print. Paolo Uccello's portrait is discussed in all the major histories of the Renaissance because of its technical virtuosity. It hangs side by side with a portrait by Castagno of Niccolò da Tolentino, who commanded the Florentines at the Battle of San Romano in 1432. Both portraits date from the early days of Medicean power in Florence, and both were commissioned to celebrate victories won by republican Florence over the Visconti 'tyrants' of Milan.

Uccello painted Hawkwood in fresco (though the painting was later transferred to canvas). The Florentines wanted to emphasize the Englishman's qualities of prudence and caution rather than belligerence, so he is dressed for the parade-ground. He carries the commander's baton in his right hand but wears a Florentine cap on his head, and his war-horse is unprotected by armour. On the other hand, he has the straight back of the soldier and the upright posture required for mounted shock combat and the tournament. The same is true of Gattamelata, whose equestrian statue bestrides the piazza in front of the Basilica of St Antony in Padua. Gattamelata shows us what Hawkwood would have looked like in three dimensions, if Uccello's vision of Sir John had ever been realized in stone. The inscription along the bottom of his painted sarcophagus makes a Caesar of Hawkwood, by using the language of ancient Rome. He is described as 'eques' (knight) rather than 'miles' (soldier), and 'Britannicus' rather than 'Anglicus' (though he was English, not British). The word 'dux' (leader or commander) is the one Vegetius used in his treatise on war a thousand years before.

It is recorded that Uccello had to paint Hawkwood twice and that his first effort was destroyed because it was not painted 'as it should be'. Some say this was because the stallion showed too much of its private parts, others that the rider's appearance was too martial. A hundred years later Vasari, in his *Lives of the Artists*, placed the work among the very best the Renaissance produced, though – as a fellow artist himself – he could not resist a final swipe at Uccello:

> In Santa Maria del Fiore, Paolo painted in commemoration of the Englishman Giovanni Acuto, the Florentine commander, who died in the year 1393 [sic], a horse in *terra verde*. Considered a very fine work, and being of extraordinary size, it showed the image of the commander on the horse in *chiaroscuro* with the colouring *terra verde*, and was placed within a frame ten arms-lengths high in the middle of one wall of the church. There Paolo drew in perspective a large sarcophagus, as if the body were inside, and above it he placed the image of the man in his commander's armour astride a horse. This work was and is still considered to be a most beautiful painting of this type, and if Paolo had not represented the horse as moving his legs on only one side – something horses cannot naturally do, since they would fall – this work would have been perfect, because the proportions of that horse, which is huge, are quite beautiful. Perhaps he made this error because he was unaccustomed to riding on horseback, nor was he as familiar with horses as with other animals.

This is unfair, since Hawkwood seldom shied away from a fight, though he often faced superior numbers. At Second Cascina in 1369 he probably only had 500 men-at-arms, reinforced by 2,000 horsemen and led by German mercenaries, while the Florentines had a force of 3,000 or so, plus 400 crossbowmen. At Montichiari he and Enguerrand de Coucy had only 600 men-at-arms and 700 archers, and were heavily outnumbered in terms of professional soldiers (though they had peasant levies and town militia as auxiliaries). At Castagnaro he may indeed have had comparatively large numbers at his disposal – possibly around 7,500 horse and 1,000 foot – but the enemy had larger forces again. During Hawkwood's last war with Milan, dal Verme was able to muster a force of 3,300 lances and 5,000 foot for his campaign along the Arno, whereas Hawkwood commanded a mere 1,200 lances and 1,000 crossbowmen, until Florence reinforced him with a large body of militia, when the enemy was at the gates.

To consistently take on superior numbers might seem like bravado, but to consistently succeed against such numbers required the application of prudent methods recommended by Vegetius centuries before, and again by Christine de Pisan only a few years after Hawkwood's death:

It is better to have a small number of men well instructed and skilled in arms through continuous training in all things that may happen in the dubious fortunes of battle than a very large number of rude and ignorant men.[7]

Speed and Subterfuge

When the White Company first arrived in Italy it impressed the Italian chroniclers with its speed of movement, but it is difficult to be precise about rates of march and journey times, because the evidence is hearsay, and we are usually only told that Hawkwood arrived in a certain place on a certain day, not the time of day. For the early sixteenth century, there are Venetian reports and journals showing how long it took travellers to cross the Apennines between Tuscany and Romagna, but this kind of evidence does not exist for the movements of English soldiers in the late fourteenth century.[8]

On English roads, soldiers travelling to the ports were expected to cover ten or thirteen miles a day. In France the army led by Edward III in 1346 averaged between ten and fifteen, while on the *chevauchée* of 1355 the Black Prince averaged ten, with a maximum of twenty-five. None of this sounds very fast, but we have to remember that there could be thousands of men on the march, many without horses. Wagons laden with equipment could be terribly slow, and even those who rode might be held up by the condition of the roads, the narrowness of bridges and the difficulty of fording the rivers.

On the other hand, when Hawkwood rode from Florence to Bologna in May 1390 the chronicler noted that he only had fifteen lances with him, and it is clear that men in relatively small groups could travel much more quickly than an army. (The *Commentaries* of Pope Pius II reveal that, when he made the same journey in 1459, he took four days, stopping at Caffagiuolo, Firenzuola and Pianoro on the way.[9]) Individual messengers could travel much more quickly again. The Florentine Military Code of 1337 required all mercenaries to swear on the Gospels that they would denounce 'machinations and conspiracies' on the same day they came to light, but the rule was relaxed if the soldiers were not in Tuscany at the relevant time. If they were still in Romagna (or for that matter in Bologna) the obligation was to report within three days. If they were in Lombardy or any other part of Italy, it was eight days. Eight days is not a long time to cover the distance between Milan (or Padua) and Florence when the Apennines lie in between.[10]

We tend to think that medieval roads were universally bad in comparison with those which the Romans had built, but they were probably better in Italy than they were in England or France, because of the great importance of trade and the wealth and political influence of the merchant class. Nevertheless, it does not seem that Hawkwood travelled much faster in Italy than the English King and his generals in France. In 1363 the Pisan army, stiffened by the arrival of the White Company, took almost a week to march from Pisa to the outskirts of Florence, taking the northern route via Pistoia. The two cities are about sixty miles apart and, assuming a march of five days, that is only twelve miles a day. During the winter march on Milan in January and February 1391, the allies made heavy weather of it, taking almost a month to cover the thirty miles from Padua to the Adige. When they tried again in the spring (leaving Padua on 10 May and crossing the Adige on the 15th), their rate of march was only six miles a day. One can imagine the excuses the commander may have given the Florentines for the lack of progress: it was a large army to drive forward; winter was a bad time to be moving large numbers of men; the rivers were swollen with meltwater; an army entering enemy territory had to take precautions; and so on.

However, there is no doubt that Sir John could make haste when he needed to. This was demonstrated in striking fashion, both at the beginning and towards the end of the war of 1389–91. On each occasion, the Florentines summoned Hawkwood back to the city. On the first they recalled him from Naples, and we can be quite precise about his rate of progress: he was seen passing through Grosseto on 27 April 1390 with 150 horses, 300 infantry and some fifty archers, and we know that he arrived in Florence three days later. The distance by road, using the most direct route, is about eighty-five miles, which would make his time just over twenty-eight miles a day, but we know that he in fact travelled back via the Maremma and Volterra, which is further. It does look as if, this time, he was travelling at twice the normal speed achieved by a medieval army.

On the second occasion, he was recalled from Padua when Jacopo dal Verme invaded Tuscany. He left on 12 September, with 1,200 lances and 1,000 bowmen, and must have arrived in San Miniato some time before the 17th (when Florence was enacting emergency legislation). By 20 or 21 September he was making camp at Tizzana, near Prato. Assuming a journey of five days from Padua to San Miniato, that is a marching rate of thirty miles a day – which, again, is double the average. These must have been forced marches, since the journey involves crossing the Apennines.

The lawyer John of Legnano advised that it was lawful to use trickery to win a war, and Christine de Pisan repeated this view in her *Book of Deeds of Arms and of Chivalry*, though she clearly had her doubts.[11] When the English wanted to return from Figline to take up winter quarters in Pisa at the end of 1364:

they sent messengers to the Florentines, indicating that they would come to the church of San Salvi on 12 November and they invited the Florentine priors to attend mass. This message, delivered with military *braggadocio*, was given so much credence that everyone anxiously waited for that day ... But the enemy had burned his encampment on that very day at Figline and got away unscathed over difficult passes and winding mountain roads with all his booty and all his captives.[12]

Hawkwood used a combination of disguise, false retreat and ambush to defeat the Florentines on the Arno in 1369 and he sometimes used spies to spread disinformation, but perhaps the best example of subterfuge comes from 1391. In June of that year, he arrived at the banks of the Adda, only ten miles from Milan, but in view of Armagnac's delay he felt obliged to withdraw. He wanted to cover that retreat if he could. He led dal Verme into thinking that he wanted battle by sending him a bloody gauntlet, but then his men gave the impression that they were there to stay, by tying banners on the trees around the camp, lighting fires and piling supplies in prominent places. He ordered trumpeters to sound confusing signals, and in the night his army stole away. In the morning the Milanese entered the camp and found it deserted.

Intelligence and Spies

Messengers travelled regularly between Italy and England, bringing information of all kinds. The Westminster chronicler recorded that in January 1386:

A squire who had for some time been in the company of Sir Hawkwood in Lombardy arrived at the king's court with a story about a man of religion living in those parts, who predicted that within the ensuing three years the English nation, because of its evil life, would be mercilessly punished, chiefly, so he said, by famine and pestilence, but that after this the country would be the happiest of all kingdoms.[13]

Not all information was for public consumption. In 1360 John of Legnano advised that the death penalty was appropriate for 'spies who betray secrets to the enemy', and in 1389 Philippe de Mézières recommended that one-third of all expenditure be laid out on espionage. It is interesting that, although his advice was chiefly directed to the French King, de Mézières still thought that

the best intelligence is to be gained from Lombard and other foreign merchants. It is their business either in person or through their agents or by correspondence to be in contact with all sorts of people.

Italy was as usual at the cutting edge.

The use of spies was almost universal. The English used extensive networks of them in northern France and the Netherlands before 1360, but also feared their activities in England, when invasion threatened. Naturally secret agents were not referred to as such in administrative records – they were called something else, for example *coureurs* (runners). Heralds and ambassadors were used to gather information more openly, while engaged in other public duties. When English ambassadors travelled to the court of Bernabò Visconti in 1379 (with orders to treat with Hawkwood) they were sent 'on the secret business of the King'. There were other ways of gathering information. One reason for holding tournaments was to discover more about the enemy and his dispositions.[14]

Espionage may have been relatively easy in Italy, since a common language underlay the multiplicity of dialects, and there were exiles and factions in many states, who could provide a potential 'fifth column'. Matteo Villani cited an old proverb: 'Those who are poor in spies are rich in shame', and the Florentines certainly knew the value of intelligence. Their Code of 1337 referred to spies used to keep watch over their own mercenary soldiers and auxiliaries. After the revolt of the Ciompi in 1378 a new agency, the Otto di Guardia, was established in Florence, perhaps the first secret police force in Europe.

John Hawkwood and Giovanni Acuto were one and the same man: he acquired a second identity. As Hawkwood he was an ambassador for the English King on several occasions during the 1380s and supplied the royal administration with information, but as Giovanni Acuto he also organized a military spy network for the Florentines. The historian Cavalcanti (1381–1451) tells us that

> he went most mornings to consult with the Ten of War and, more often than not, it fell out that the said captain gave advice to the Ten instead of the Ten giving orders to him.

It had not always been like this. Hawkwood had used spies to serve the interests of whoever employed him, and there had been times when he had used them against Florence. While operating near Incisa on the Middle Arno in October 1363, the English obtained information about a nearby Florentine force led by Ranuccio Farnese. In the guise of witnesses sent to observe a duel between one of their own knights and a Florentine, they reconnoitred the enemy's positions and used the information gathered to defeat Farnese the following day. By 1376 Hawkwood was under contract to the Pope and he schemed with some of the inhabitants of Arezzo to betray that city to the Church. The plotters managed to obtain a key to one of the gates, but the conspiracy was discovered and the mission had to be aborted.

Intelligence was a commodity. In 1379 Hawkwood fell out with his father-in-law Bernabò Visconti and, according to Stefani, he wrote to a citizen of Florence (whom the chronicler was unwilling to name), to warn the city of a great conspiracy. He said that he was prepared to release details of this, but only if he was paid. His starting price was 50,000 gold florins for full details of the plot – with the names of the conspirators – but he was willing to give the Florentines some information for only 20,000. The merchant Guccio Gucci came to see Sir John at his home in Bagnacavallo and was led into a room, lit only by a charcoal brazier, where negotiations were conducted. A price was agreed on, and Hawkwood revealed some part of what he knew: we are told that he became 12,000 florins richer and that many people were executed in Florence in the following days.[15]

We know that messages were sometimes sent in code. When Pope Gregory wrote to Hawkwood in January 1373, he wrote openly but referred to further instructions enclosed in secret letters which he enclosed, but which have not survived.[16] Other precautions were also used. In 1389 the Florentines were engaged in delicate negotiations with him while he was in Naples. They sent two messengers to him, carrying the same message but by different routes, because they feared that it might not get through.

Hawkwood learned to recognize a spy when he saw one. In 1387 Antonio della Scala of Verona sent an envoy when the Englishman was in command of the Paduan army. Ostensibly the messenger was sent to ask Francesco Novello to intercede with his father, with a view to opening negotiations, but Hawkwood suspected that there was no genuine desire for peace, and that the envoy was not what he seemed. Respecting diplomatic immunity, Sir John kept the messenger shut up in his tent all day but sent him away again when night fell.

It is in the nature of covert operations that they are intended to be kept secret, so that, if Hawkwood was successful in this department, one would not expect to find the evidence – the secret writing, codes, false names, and so on. The evidence is slender and circumstantial. Yet there is a macabre tale, which strongly suggests that he did indeed control spies from his castle of Montecchio Vesponi. The story goes that, while he was staying there in 1388, he learned of a plot to eliminate his brother-in-law Carlo Visconti, who was at that time living in exile in Cortona. Gian Galeazzo Visconti had paid the lord of Cortona's doctor, Goioso, 30,000 florins to kill Carlo by feeding him poisoned figs, but Sir John sent a letter warning of the danger and this was evidently received in time. The doctor was interrogated and admitted all he knew (before being horribly executed). It is difficult to see how Hawkwood could have discovered this medieval doctor's plot if not through agents deployed in Cortona and under orders to report back to him at Montecchio.[17]

Luck

Napoleon once remarked, 'I would rather have a general who was lucky than one who was good', and when the Marquis of Saluzzo wanted to pay Hawkwood a compliment, he assigned him one of only two seats in the Palace of Fortune.[18]

Sir John was indeed lucky. He took many captives, but was captured only once, and only held for a few months, whereas Bertrand du Guesclin was taken prisoner several times and Hugh de la Zouche spent four years as a prisoner in Italy. He suffered few defeats on the battlefield. He is not known to have had any serious illnesses, nor to have suffered any serious injury, unlike Federigo da Montefeltre who lost part of his nose in a tournament. He was lord of Montecchio Vesponi for some ten years, whereas Hugh Calvely's brief attempt to become a landowner in Spain ended in the courts. Above all – like the Abbé Siéyès during the French Revolution – he 'survived', in difficult and violent times.

Analysis of mid-fourteenth-century remains in London cemeteries suggests that almost 90 per cent of those buried there died before reaching the age of forty-five, which means that (statistically) Hawkwood should have died shortly after he left France for Italy. He was probably in his late twenties when the Black Death swept out of Italy, killing between a third and a half of the population, but Henry of Grosmont died of that very disease in 1361. Sir John also outlived many fellow soldiers who died of more mundane causes. Castruccio Castracani caught a cold at the siege of Pistoia in 1328 and died at the age of forty-seven. The Black Prince died at the age of forty-six, after more than five years when (according to Thomas Walsingham) he had suffered a monthly discharge of both blood and semen – the result of an illness contracted while fighting in Spain. Louis of Anjou succumbed to fever in Apulia when he was forty-five. The Count of Armagnac was thirty-two when he died after his ordeal at the Battle of Alessandria. Gian Galeazzo Visconti died of a fever at the age of fifty-one.

Many *condottieri* died violent deaths. Fra' Moriale was beheaded by the Roman dictator Cola di Rienzo in 1354. Count Konrad von Landau, captured at Marradi in 1358, was mortally wounded at the bridge of Canturino five years later. Albert Sterz was beheaded in Perugia in 1366. Ambrogio Visconti died in a peasant uprising near Bergamo in 1373. Giovanni degli Ubaldini died in June 1390 and – though the Florentine Vasari claimed that he 'became ill in the field' – the Sienese, Lucchese and Bolognese chroniclers all thought he was poisoned by the Florentines. Bernard de la Salle was ambushed and killed in the Alps in 1391. Enguerrand de Coucy was captured by the Turks at Nicopolis and died in captivity in 1397. Sir John's son-in-law Konrad von Pressburg was killed in battle in 1399. His old rival Astorre Manfredi was executed, on the orders of the Pope, in 1405, but Hawkwood died in his bed at the age of seventy-four.

Chapter 10

The Atrocities in Romagna, 1376–7

In law context means everything.
> Lord Steyn in *R v Home Office ex parte Daly* [2001] 2 All ER 447

Much of the opprobrium attaching to Hawkwood's name derives from the military operations he conducted for the Pope at Faenza and Cesena in 1376–7. These towns are now in the Italian province of Emilia-Romagna, but in Hawkwood's day they were in the Papal States. Even in normal times, Romagna was notoriously unstable and the papal writ did not run without the tacit consent of powerful local families – the Este of Ferrara, Ordelaffi of Forlì, Malatesta of Rimini, and the Manfredi, whose power base was in the Val di Lamone and who normally controlled Faenza. The province was also known as a nursery of mercenaries, some of whom – like the Barbiano Counts of Cunio – came from the upper echelons of society, while others, like the Sforza of Cotignola, had more humble origins. But the late 1370s were not normal times. In these years there was a widespread urban revolt, backed by Florence, in which Romagna played a key role. The irony is that, if Hawkwood had ever been arraigned in a court of law, he would have had a respectable defence to charges relating to what he did in Faenza and Cesena, whereas he would have found it impossible to maintain the same argument in relation to many operations he conducted as a freelance.

Hawkwood and the Laws of War

Brigandage (*il brigantaggio*) has been a persistent problem throughout Italian history. In the Scrovegni chapel in Padua, frescoed by Giotto in the early fourteenth century, the Vice of 'Injustice' is portrayed by a band of robbers who waylay a traveller and strip his corpse. In the late nineteenth century, when brigandage was a particular problem in the South of Italy, the German historian Gregorovius was affronted by the presence of Hawkwood's portrait in the Duomo: he protested that 'Florence, who denied Dante a resting place, erected a noble monument to a robber.' Terry Jones has castigated the Free Companies as 'bands of robbers on a nightmare scale'. But for much of his career Hawkwood's place was firmly within the pale of civilized society, even when he was engaged in bloody fighting. This is vividly demonstrated by an Italian chronicler's description of an incident in September 1391. It was recorded that, on that occasion, Sir John fought with 300 of Carlo Malatesta's infantry and that, 'contrary to *the custom of war*, they fought like barbarians, and each side made a miserable slaughter of the other' (my italics). Why should the chronicler make this remark, if certain standards of behaviour were not accepted as normal and customary, even in time of war?

Italy had known what real barbarians were like. When the Roman Empire fell, she had suffered at the hands of Huns and Vandals, and been invaded by Goths and Lombards. The depredations wrought by these peoples were more than just a folk memory. Buildings, histories and works of art survived, to remind later ages of what had been lost. The real barbarians had set fire to cities rather than merely plunder them, killed defeated soldiers rather than ransom them, routinely raped women and slaughtered children. The *condottieri*, on the other hand – even those who were foreigners – were all Christians who recognized the Pope as head of the Church, and they all came from the same civilization and culture. On some occasions they were ordered to respect the lives and property of the civilian population in the areas they invaded. On other occasions it was in their own interest to moderate the behaviour of their men. It made good economic sense to capture a man and ransom him rather than kill him out of hand, just as it was more profitable to sell a town back to the inhabitants, rather than destroy it. The *condottieri* were sometimes unpopular with their masters because of their habit of releasing rank-and-file prisoners *without* ransom.

Before the Battle of Halidon Hill in 1333 the Scots announced that they would take no prisoners and Edward III responded in kind: after he won the battle, he had 100 Scots prisoners beheaded. Geoffrey de Charny, who carried the Oriflamme at Poitiers to indicate that no quarter would be given, was one of the French who were killed in that battle. By contrast, Hawkwood was usually prepared to give quarter to his equals. In the fifteenth century Pope Pius II complained that Italian wars seldom involved a pitched battle because the *condottieri* usually terminated the hostilities by means of a negotiated settlement.[1] In the twentieth century the travel writer H V Morton remarked that they aimed to make war 'as safe as steeple-chasing or rugby football', but one can hardly blame professional soldiers for trying to avoid a situation where every fight was to the death.

Over forty years ago, Maurice Keen showed that knights and other men-at-arms in late medieval France operated according to a code of law, and it is strongly arguable that this 'did a great deal to ensure a humane standard of conduct'. The laws of war derived from the teaching and writings of jurists at Italian universities (of which the oldest was Bologna), and these ideas were current in Italy as well as in France and England. The *condotta*, after all, embodied the idea that both sides should behave according to law.

The starting point for the lawyers was that war was not unusual or wrong, and the established authorities in both Church and State considered it to be the normal state of affairs. In 1360, the year of the Treaty of Brétigny, John of Legnano, who was internationally respected and widely consulted, wrote that 'it would not be wrong, according to the teachings of natural philosophers and astrologers, to hold that the world could not continue without war and with peace alone'.[2] Legnano thought that God had positively *allowed* war between men. In France Honoré Bonet argued that 'War is not an evil thing, but a good and virtuous, for war by its very nature seeks nothing other than to set wrong right.' The soldier's profession was likewise regarded as honourable, and was approved by the Church. The fact that soldiers were now always *paid* made little difference to this. When Chaucer praised the hero of 'The Knight's Tale', he was not being ironic (as Terry Jones argued in *Chaucer's Knight*). He was reflecting the widespread view that the military calling was a noble one, and it did not cease to be so merely because the French wars brought unprecedented material rewards for the English.

In Italy the *condottieri* were part of the legal order. John of Legnano discusses many problems relating to the mercenaries and their terms of employment, and the answer he gives is by no means always that 'ex turpi causa non oritur actio' (from a base transaction, no legal action may arise). On the contrary, proceedings can be brought to recover the balance of a mercenary's pay, if the city which hires him is later seized by a tyrant, or if the mercenary himself is temporarily unable to fulfil his obligations, or even if he terminates his contract prematurely. Legnano also deals with the questions of whether a mercenary should be paid at the beginning or the end of the month, whether he can perform his services by a substitute, and whether he is still entitled to his pay when he is ill. Do a mercenary's heirs become entitled to sums due to him at his death? The answer (which perhaps surprises us) is yes. The jurist even illustrates his solution by reference to the case of Konrad von Landau senior – the German Count captured by peasants at Marradi in 1358 and defeated by the White Company at Canturino in 1363, though he is remembered by some Italians as the father of a whole tribe of brigands.[3]

Among professional soldiers, the sword was not the arbiter of every question. Hawkwood expected to be held accountable according to the terms of his contract, and also to have recourse to law himself if he was wronged. He followed the same rules as others engaged in businesses very different from his own. The contractual formalities were the same, and the assumption was that he would perform his side of a bargain, and even (on some occasions) pay damages if he was in breach of contract. He is known to have used the courts in Naples in 1382–3, when some prisoners he had ransomed and then released on parole refused to pay the balance that was due. However dreadful the events he became involved in, Hawkwood could therefore usually claim both that he was following orders and that he was acting in accordance with his contract. True outlaws do not behave in this way.

Hawkwood was never charged with any specific crimes, unlike Sigismondo Malatesta (accused in 1461 of rapine, arson, violent conduct, adultery, incest, parricide, uxoricide, sacrilege and heresy). From a legal point of view, however, there was a clear difference between operations conducted when he was under contract and what he did as a freelance. If he had ever been indicted and had the opportunity of a fair trial, he would doubtless have argued that what he did for his employers was done in pursuance of lawful war, but that defence would not have been available in relation to his activities with the Free Companies. There, he could only have pleaded a right to make private war and that what was done was necessary to enable him and his men to survive as a fighting unit. As he told the friars outside the gates of Montecchio in the 1380s, he 'lived by war' and by that stage in his life he clearly knew nothing else (see Appendix 1), but the jurists and the courts of the day would certainly have rejected these arguments. The argument of necessity has never appealed to the English common law, and Christine de Pisan summarized the commonly accepted view that only a sovereign prince – an Emperor, a King or a Duke – had the legal right to make war.[4] The jurist Bartolomeo of Saliceto had no doubts:

> What shall I say of those companies of men-at-arms who overrun the territory of our cities? I reply that there is no doubt about their position, for they are robbers … and therefore as robbers they should be punished for all the crimes that they have committed.

Most men did not analyze the situation in terms of legal principle. They did not distinguish between the activities of mercenaries when they were under contract and those undertaken outside the terms of a *condotta*. Accordingly, Hawkwood was often regarded as being little better than a thug. In Novella 181 Francesco Sacchetti damned all his activities, along with those of all mercenary captains, while as late as 1385 Coluccio Salutati described him as a robber,[5] though Hawkwood was one of Florence's best generals by that date. The insult does not do him justice, though it has to be recognized that he was a ruthless man, successful with employers precisely because he could be relied on to 'get the job done', and determined to keep his brigade together between contracts, regardless of risk or cost.

The Nun of Faenza, 1376

Faenza was the key to Romagna. It lay in the plain, but at the entrance to the Val di Lamone and at the centre of a network of important routes. In the late fourteenth century it was already acquiring a reputation for the manufacture of majolica, the glazed earthenware which had originated in Majorca but which was to become known as faience. The town had belonged to the Manfredi, but they had been forced to cede it to the Papacy in 1356, when Astorre Manfredi was a boy (though he made it his life's work to recover his ancestral lands).

In 1375 Faenza rebelled and joined the league led by the 'Eight Saints' of Florence, in an attempt to throw off what was portrayed as a papal yoke. Hawkwood, who was in Granarolo near Bologna, and Alberigo da Barbiano, whose family home was close to Faenza, were employed by Pope Gregory and his local representatives to suppress the rebellion. This was a routine military operation for them, and the Pope later justified it to the Florentines as the restoration of legitimate authority – in fact he even blamed Florence for fomenting the rebellion in Bologna, which had caused Hawkwood to move on to Faenza. Whoever was responsible, the recapture of Faenza proved disastrous for the civilian population.

A central allegation – accepted by Sozomeno of Pistoia, the chroniclers of Bologna and Reggio and by Stefani of Florence – was that in retaking the city, the English and their allies drove out the men, the children and the women who were too old or unattractive (*rustiche*), but kept the attractive younger women in the town, to use for their own pleasure.[6] At this point in their narrative Temple-Leader and Marcotti could not even bring themselves to translate their own disgusting quotation, which gave details of what the English soldiers did – 'trattando ignominiosamente le vergini e le matrone a guisa di meretrici e di schiave vilmente vendute'. It means 'treating virgins and married women ignominiously, as if they were prostitutes and slaves to be basely sold'.

There is an even more horrifying version of these events. The Sienese chronicler Donato di Neri relates that, while the soldiers were rounding up the young women, Hawkwood found two of his constables duelling over a nun. By way of a solution to their quarrel, he plunged a dagger into the woman's body, restoring order at the cost of a human life.[7] This story is almost certainly propaganda, since it is recorded under 1371 – the wrong year – and the Sienese hated Hawkwood for his repeated raids on their territory, but even this tall tale has grown in the telling. Ricotti and Temple-Leader each added the detail that, when he drove the knife home, Hawkwood shouted 'Half for each!' (a brutal command, but one which appealed to the contemporary liking for Old Testament parallels, by inviting comparison with the judgement of Solomon). When Barbara Tuchman and Richard West repeated the story in the late twentieth century, they embellished it even further with the unlikely detail that Sir John *ordered the woman to be cut in half.* Women, including nuns, were certainly abused by the mercenary companies, both in Italy and in France, but the latest version of the story of the nun of Faenza beggars belief. Bruni's account is chilling enough, and highly critical of Hawkwood, but it says nothing about nuns:

> The English, thanks to the incredible perversity of their leader, once inside the walls inflicted everything on its citizens that is usually inflicted on stormed and captured cities. For everything was laid open to pillage, the men were either beaten or killed, the women raped, and things both sacred and profane were wretchedly and impiously polluted by the cruelty of the barbarians. Finally, when it had at last been stripped bare of everything, leaving only the town walls and houses, the evil captain sold the place itself to the rulers of Ferrara.[8]

The horrors supposedly inflicted on the poor nun of Faenza have obscured a much more interesting question, which is, exactly why did Hawkwood sack the place at all? Was there really a revolt, or merely a conspiracy, and what part did the Florentines play in the affair? It is very difficult to find the answer. It seems to be agreed that the town was governed for the Papacy by a French bishop, and, according to some reports, he feared that the population were 'planning' to cast off papal rule. Others paint a picture of open rebellion. Some chroniclers tell us that Hawkwood was simply ordered to 'garrison' Faenza. However, it appears from the records of a lawsuit investigated by the American historian Gene Brucker that the town of Faenza – or at least the citadel (*rocca*) – may actually have been besieged by a Florentine army at the time, and that Hawkwood and his men were called on to raise the siege. If this is right, his mission was not just to put down (or prevent) rebellion, it involved a full-scale military operation. If a siege were in progress, doubts about the loyalty of the Faentini would still have had some foundation. The chronicles of the great war in France often mention sieges where the inhabitants give in to the temptation to surrender their city prematurely, and in this case it is likely that some Faentini were sympathetic to the Florentine cause, while others are known to have favoured the restoration of the town's former lords, the Manfredi. Both factions were, at least potentially, hostile to the Papacy.

What happened when the papal troops entered the town is less contentious. Having taken up their positions, Hawkwood's men disarmed the populace, and he gave orders that every male inhabitant should deliver up his arms, on pain of a fine and some form of corporal punishment ('pena l'avere e la persona'). Then it would seem that his men did indeed drive the men, old women and children out of the town, keeping the young women and girls for themselves. Lastly, they helped themselves to the moveables left behind. These events make for unpleasant reading, by any standards, and if we simply read the chronicles, we would conclude that Hawkwood and his men went berserk, to satisfy their own lusts. But the record of Brucker's lawsuit (preserved in the merchants' court in Florence), suggests that they may have had to do battle with Florentine troops before they occupied the city, and then found that some of the townsmen had been engaged in treasonable correspondence with the *Signoria* all along. If so, they may have been out of their minds with rage and fear, even before the drinking started.[9]

We learn from the same lawsuit that Sir John's men killed several merchants in Faenza, including a factor working for the two defendant Florentines, Petribuoni and Bernardetti, but we should recall that, on the outbreak of the War of the Eight Saints, Pope Gregory had laid Florence under an interdict and decreed that it was lawful to expropriate her merchants, wherever they might be. In that light the actions of Hawkwood's men look less like rapine than the execution of the Pope's lawful commands. Moreover, though Petribuoni was accused of spying for Florence, he was not executed. Instead, Hawkwood ordered that he be transferred to Bologna for trial. In the event, he escaped (as did Bernardetti), though he later claimed that his house in Faenza had been ransacked. He lamented 'that there remained neither garden nor stable, nor orchard, nor cistern, nor wardrobe in the house or its environs, which was not dug up or broken into', but what may appear to be wanton violence to a suspect may be no more than a thorough search, so far as the authorities are concerned.

What is not usually related, when the story of the atrocities in Faenza is told, is the sequel. Two months after the sack, Hawkwood attacked the city again with the help of none other than its former lord Astorre Manfredi, and this time he had Florentine backing. Having entered the town by stealth, this new coalition besieged the *rocca*, defeated the Papal garrison and, after twenty days of fighting, made Manfredi lord of Faenza, a fait accompli which even the Papacy was forced to accept. Moreover, by all accounts, it was now that Faenza enjoyed its 'peak of splendour'.

In some histories of Faenza, not a word appears about the sack of 1376, let alone about the mass rape of virgins, or of nuns being cut in half. Yet others did not forget, or forgive, so easily. In 1410, some thirty-four years after the events we have related, those who drew up the *Statutes* of Faenza still thought fit to include a 'rubric' (no. 109), which provided that anyone found guilty of collaboration with the English when they sacked the town should be hanged by the neck until dead and have his property confiscated by the state. Despite the passage of time, the draftsman of this legislation still thought it appropriate to refer to the men under Hawkwood's command as 'the accursed English'.

The Massacre at Cesena, 1377

The inhabitants of Cesena remained loyal to Pope Gregory when nearly all the key cities in the Papal States – Città di Castello, Perugia, Viterbo and Bologna – declared for the league, and despite the fact that the Florentines were busily inciting further rebellion. Fifty English troops had been killed during the troubles in Città di Castello, so the blood was up, but what led directly to the tragedy at Cesena was a mundane dispute about food, between the citizens and the supposedly friendly papal army encamped outside the town. Many of these troops were Bretons who (like the English) had gained a reputation as skilful and ruthless fighters. They had travelled to Italy in some numbers in 1375, at the request of the Pope.

Disputes about food for the military were commonplace. It was the Great Company's behaviour in taking what it needed from the local people in the upper Val di Lamone, without paying for it, which had led to its defeat at Marradi. Even in England, where the monarchy was strong, the system of purveyance (which allowed supplies to be commandeered at fixed prices) was extremely unpopular and was the subject of many protests. Alastair Dunn, recent historian of the English Peasants' Revolt, cites it as an underlying cause of that rebellion. In *Piers the Ploughman* a character called 'Peace' petitions Parliament, complaining vociferously about the wrongs done to him by 'Crime', who is thought to have been a royal purveyor:

> He has run away with my wife … and assaulted Rosy, Reg's girl, and had his way with Margaret too, for all her struggling. And besides that, his ruffians have seized my pigs and geese, and I'm too scared of him to argue, or put up a fight. He has borrowed my horse and never brought it back, and refused to pay a farthing for it, though I begged him for the money. He stands by and eggs his men on to murder my servants, and forestalls my goods and starts a brawl over them at the market. He breaks down my barn doors and carries off my corn, and all I get is a tally-stick for two hundredweights or more of oats. And on top of all this, he beats me up and goes to bed with my daughter, and I live in such terror of him, I daren't lift a finger.[10]

In the winter of 1377–8 the leaders of the Bretons who were stationed outside Cesena complained that their victuals were too dear. As a result the Pope's vicar-general, Robert of Geneva, gave them permission to enter the town and requisition what they needed, rather than pay the rate previously fixed. This was interpreted as an order to help themselves and the Bretons plundered the butchers' shops for meat. Given the fighting spirit of the men of Romagna, demonstrated at Marradi and elsewhere, it comes as no surprise to learn that the inhabitants of Cesena rose against their oppressors, under the loyal cry of 'Death to the Bretons! Long live the Church!' ('Moriantur Bretones et vivat Ecclesia!').[11] They took reprisals, despite the gross inequality of arms. In the course of the fighting, they killed a number of Breton mercenaries.

The Cardinal's reaction was so extreme that he has been vilified ever since. Temple-Leader and Marcotti, often so proportionate in their comments, wrote that Robert of Geneva was:

> ugly and deformed of body, whilst in character he could rank first among those Avignonese bishops, who scandalised the world with injustice, simony, avarice, gluttony, lust, luxury, pride, and all the cardinal vices. Added to these, as an especial characteristic, was bestial ferocity.

This does seem a little exaggerated, when one considers that this same Cardinal of Geneva was later elected Pope – admittedly by a group of French cardinals – and gained an international reputation as a patron of the arts and humanist writing, and a collector of books and manuscripts. However, according to the conventional account, the Cardinal was guilty of appalling duplicity and cruelty, in that he disarmed the Cesenati by trickery and then arranged for Hawkwood to put the city to the sword. He promised a pardon to any who expressed remorse for what had been done to the Bretons, provided the offenders surrendered their arms and provided fifty hostages. He released these hostages to allay suspicion, but then sent for Hawkwood, who was in nearby Faenza. Sir John arrived secretly and the Cardinal ordered him to 'descend' on Cesena and 'do justice'.

The Sienese chronicler, who had carefully recorded his depredations around Siena and had no reason to make excuses for him, nevertheless tells us that Hawkwood attempted to qualify this order, by saying that he would indeed make the Cesenati give up their arms, but the Cardinal pointed out that he had already achieved disarmament and what he wanted now was retribution: 'blood, blood and justice!' ('sangue, sangue e justizia!'). Hawkwood tried to tell the Cardinal that he ought to consider the consequences if the men were turned loose on unarmed civilians, but, faced with a clear and repeated order, he did as he was told.

The Bretons and the English now went to work with a will. Indeed they ran riot, for three days and nights. The results were as Hawkwood had predicted: the town was sacked and several thousand people were killed. The Reggio chronicler recorded that more than 2,000 died, though he wrote that the soldiers saved the women they desired, as they had done at Faenza. Sozomeno thought the number of dead was about 3,000, though he mentions that others thought it as high as 5,000. That is as many people as were killed in the World Trade Center in New York in 2001.

The chronicler of Rimini told of heart-rending scenes:

As many men, women and nurselings as they found, they slaughtered, so that all the squares were full of dead, of both sexes. A thousand drowned in trying to cross the moats – some fled by the gates with the Bretons pursuing, who murdered and robbed and raped, and would not let the handsomest women escape, but kept them for themselves.

The Sienese chronicler wrote of bodies being left in the streets to be eaten by dogs and others thrown down wells in the city, though the Estense chronicler entered a plea in mitigation: 'Sir Hawkwood, not to be held entirely infamous, sent about a thousand of the Cesenese women to Rimini.'[12]

Sir John's Defence

Hawkwood's career did not end in ruins after the shocking events at Cesena. In the short run, what happened in Romagna did not even damage his prospects of employment – indeed, it may have enhanced them. The massacre may have been a contributory factor in leading to the breakdown in his relations with the Papacy, but the situation was always volatile, and the end would have come soon enough, when Pope Gregory XI died in March 1378. It was only in the long run that the massacre injured his reputation – so much so that, for many, it is the only well-known event of his career. Yet, while the chroniclers speak with one voice about the horror of what was done, there are some factors which need to be weighed in the balance.

The worst atrocities may not have been committed by Hawkwood's brigade of English, since it was the Bretons whose comrades had been murdered and who most felt the need for revenge. The Florentine Leonardo Bruni's account revolves entirely around the Bretons, and he does not even mention Hawkwood, though he does refer to a contingent of English soldiers. The chronicler of Reggio states that Hawkwood was the commander but that his army consisted of Bretons. The anonymous Milanese blames Hawkwood fairly and squarely for the sack of Faenza, but says that at Cesena the English merely assisted the Bretons,[13] and even today that atrocity is known locally as 'the sack of the Bretons'. As we have seen, Hawkwood is supposed to have intervened to spare the lives of at least some of the women and girls, and he was certainly not the only commander at Cesena. Alberigo da Barbiano, who later won fame among nationalists as the founder of a new 'school' of Italian mercenaries, was also there and so too were Galeotto Malatesta and other local lords who took the Pope's side. It was Malatesta who even helped the inhabitants of Cesena to lay down their arms. The sack was not the work of foreign barbarians alone.

The Papal commanders were acting under orders from the Cardinal, if not the Pope himself, and Hawkwood would not have been at Cesena if he had not been summoned by Robert of Geneva – a senior member of the Papal bureaucracy. Sir John's orders came from the top, even if they were (by modern standards) disproportionate. Acting under orders would not amount to a defence before a modern war-crimes tribunal, but at the time Francesco Sacchetti condemned the master rather than the servant. He reserved his sharpest invective for Pope Gregory, whom he called 'papa Guastamondo' – 'Pope Ruination' – though it is true that he had little time for Hawkwood.[14]

It may be questioned whether Hawkwood could have hoped to preserve the allegiance of his men if he had denied them the chance to supplement their wages through plunder, and the lower ranks were known to go to extreme lengths to obtain what they thought was their due. (At Savigliano in Piedmont in 1360 followers of Konrad von Landau and Hanneckin von Baumgarten were said to have perpetrated acts of great cruelty to find out where valuables were hidden.) The difference was that the atrocities at Cesena were widely publicized. Coluccio Salutati made sure of that: he excoriated the Cardinal and his minions in dozens of elegant letters addressed to the chancelleries of Europe.[15]

Why did the Cardinal give that terrible order? For many he is quite simply an evil man, twisted in body as well as in mind, like Shakespeare's Richard III. This accords with a medieval English tradition of seeing the papal legates as villains. The citizens of London are known to have staged a procession in January 1377 which showed the Pope's creatures wearing horrible masks, but it is no good blaming Robert of Geneva for the secular ambitions of the Papacy, which had lasted for centuries before the fourteenth began, and which were to last right down to 1870. In faraway England, where the Pope had no territorial objectives, William Langland could write, 'He's a poor sort of Pope who sends armies to kill the very folk he's meant to save', but in Italy, the Pope ruled a large swathe of territory, and shared the attitudes of other rulers towards his domains. Robert of Geneva had the ebullience of relative youth – he was thirty-five – and the pride of his class – he was a close relative of the King of France, and from his point of view he was doing no more than pursue his master's policies, as Cardinal Albornoz had done during the reign of Innocent VI.

Successive popes in Avignon needed to pacify their Italian domains to pave the way for their return to Rome, but the difference was that in the late 1370s the project met fierce resistance locally. By 1377 the revolt in the Papal States had spread and the Church had lost control of the most important towns. The princes of the Church must have been deeply worried about whether she could hold on to her Italian possessions at all. In this light, the Cardinal's order to Hawkwood can be seen as an act of desperation. Cesena was not in open rebellion in 1377, but the town had thrown off papal rule in the late 1350s, when the Ordelaffi had stubbornly resisted Albornoz, just as the Manfredi had resisted him at Faenza. In fact we do not have to speculate as to what Pope Gregory's policy was. He was a lawyer by training and he was quite capable of mounting his own defence. This was his reply to the Florentine ambassadors sent to him in Avignon after the sack of Faenza:

> We are not tyrants, nor do we wish to be. But we believe that citadels are relevant to the safety and utility of peoples, to control them and keep them quiet, and so that unstable and reckless men, of which cities are full, do not dare incite revolutions contrary to the will of the good. With respect to your blaming the governors for these revolts, it is quite obvious to us that none of these peoples defected until they were driven to defect by your urgings and promises, so that you, not our governors, are the cause of the revolts. At the end of your speech you lament piteously the calamity of the people of Faenza – but as though the origin of that calamity were not the rebellion of Bologna! For the English would never have invaded Faenza if Bologna had remained loyal. Thus, those who were the cause of the Bolognese rebellion are also the cause of the wretched destruction of Faenza.[16]

What had happened at Cesena was only a reprise of what had happened at Faenza, and the Pope's defence would have been the same, if he had ever had to make one. His views would nowadays be regarded as extreme, but they were conventional in his day. The assumptions and priorities of a late medieval ruler were not the same as those of a modern, democratically elected politician.

The Cardinal of Geneva had told Hawkwood that he wanted justice, and it is important to realize that his was a medieval idea of justice. We can see what this was in Cardinal Albornoz's *Egidian Constitutions* of 1357 and John of Legnano's *Treatise on War* of 1360. In the *Constitutions*, rebels, and anyone supporting or assisting them, receive short shrift. There is an almost endless list of sanctions, the nub of which is that, if a person is associated with rebellion, he places himself outside the law. This means that he cannot sue or gain a good title to property, he cannot make a valid will, his relatives cannot administer his estate when he dies and his subjects and servants are released from their obligations to him. One is reminded of the draconian terms of the papal interdict against Florence, except that Albornoz was making law here for the Pope's own subjects. As for John of Legnano, he dedicates his entire treatise to Cardinal Albornoz. He does not question the Pope's right to rule Central Italy, and no medieval lawyer would have questioned a ruler's right to use force to put down unlawful resistance. When Pope Pius II sent mercenaries to lay waste to the rebel city of Aquila in 1461, he regarded the looting and burning which ensued as nothing more or less than 'the rightful vengeance of God'. This attitude helps to explain why Hawkwood used the harpy as a chivalric emblem: the creature was a symbol of divine retribution.[17]

Chandos Herald records that, when the English defeated a French force in a preliminary skirmish prior to the Battle of Poitiers in 1356, the latter 'were all either killed or taken, *as the book says*'. This probably refers to the book of Deuteronomy, for there are passages there which tell how the Israelites killed every inhabitant of the towns which God supposedly gave to them. The same book in the Old Testament contains the following recommendation:

When thou comest near unto a city to fight against it, thou shalt offer it peace ... But if it will make no peace with thee ... thou shalt smite all the males thereof with the edge of the sword.

This was the rule Edward III had applied when he sacked Caen in 1346, and the violence was not merely confined to the male population. A city which rebelled against its rightful lord was quite simply regarded as 'forfeit'. When Crete rebelled against Venetian rule in 1362, the Pope preached the crusade and the revolt was put down with the utmost ferocity. In 1370 the Black Prince sacked Limoges because he considered it was in rebellion against his regime in Aquitaine. In 1472 that epitome of Renaissance man, Lorenzo di Medici, caused Volterra to be sacked by Federigo da Montefeltre of Urbino, the inspiration for Castiglione's *Book of the Courtier*.

In trying to understand the behaviour of the papal authorities, we must also put aside the modern idea that men are born equal. In the late Middle Ages men were expected to accept their lot, and rebels were regarded as little better than rogue animals. The knights who are Froissart's heroes use crude language to describe the French peasants who rebelled in 1358 – they call them 'Jacks': they are short and dark, and they all look the same. Likewise, the chronicler describes the English rebels of 1381 as 'wicked people', 'false and evil traitors', 'stinking boors' and even just as 'shit'. Italian attitudes towards the lower orders were not so different, even in the towns, where one might have expected to find a social melting-pot. The revolt of the labouring classes in Florence (known as the Ciompi) was put down with great ferocity, though the Florentines had fomented rebellion in Romagna.

There is a strong case for saying that there was nothing unusual or even – by the standards of the day – unlawful, about what happened at Faenza and Cesena. In this respect the author of Hawkwood's eighteenth-century *Memoirs* had a better understanding of the position than many modern writers. Without a trace of irony, he wrote:

Compared with the excesses authorised by the Italian generals and even the Pope's legates ... all the ravages committed by Hawkwood will be the pure though unhappy effects of lawful war.

If Sir John had ever had to defend himself in a court of law in relation to what he did in Romagna in 1376–7, he would have argued that he had merely done what he had been ordered to do by the Pope, who was the legitimate ruler of the area. The main objective, of subduing rebellion, was not unlawful in the eyes of either English or Roman law, and proportionality in the use of force was an idea which had occurred to philosophers but had not yet been translated into the real world.

Conclusion

Hero or Villain? The Reputation of Giovanni Acuto

The farmer's wife knew that she was living in the castle of Giovanni Acuto, but who he was, she neither knew nor cared.

H V Morton, *A Traveller in Italy* (1964)

'An Unsung Villain'?

Despite Caxton's plea that Englishmen should remember him (see p. 175 below), Hawkwood was neglected for many centuries after his death. In Elizabethan times the antiquary William Camden wrote: 'this renowned knight, thus celebrated abroad, was forgotten at home.' Only one full-length biography was published in the nineteenth century, whereas the French devoted twenty-one to their hero Bertrand du Guesclin. Temple-Leader and Marcotti's biography of 1889 remained without a rival for over 100 years, though Hawkwood did feature in Baedeker's *Guide to Northern Italy* of 1930 and H V Morton's *Traveller in Italy* in 1964. When historians did mention him, some elementary mistakes were made: Desmond Seward's otherwise excellent *Hundred Years War* refers to him twice as Nicholas Hawkwood. In the 1990s a former Chichele Professor at Oxford wrote that Hawkwood was 'a great unsung villain'. Why was this so?

It is partly a question of evidence. Unlike Caesar and Xenophon, Sir John did not record his own campaigns, nor did any of his heralds or knights, so we have no campaign diaries as we have for some episodes of the Hundred Years' War. Hawkwood is mentioned only twice in Sacchetti's *Trecentonovelle*. He appears only fleetingly in Froissart's chronicles and no humanistic life exists, as it does for the Italian *condottieri*: Castruccio Castracani, 'Sforza' and 'Braccio'. He was never the subject of a chivalric biography, as were the Black Prince and several French heroes, including Bertrand du Guesclin. We do not have the private account books, which enabled Iris Origo to bring her merchant of Prato back to life, and allowed Ian Mortimer to tell us what Henry Bolingbroke used for toilet paper. Hawkwood appears frequently in Italian chronicles, but these were not printed until the eighteenth century, while the administrative sources had to wait until the nineteenth.

Villain or no, Hawkwood is no longer 'unsung'. In 2001 he appeared as a minor character in Kenneth Fowler's *Medieval Mercenaries*, and the same historian contributed the definitive article to the new *Oxford Dictionary of National Biography* in 2004, the year when Frances Stonor Saunders's *Hawkwood: Diabolical Englishman* was published in England. Temple-Leader and Marcotti's *Sir John Hawkwood* (1889) was republished in the United States in 2005, and in 2006 the American William Caferro's meticulously researched *John Hawkwood* set a new standard for books about Hawkwood in English. The knight has also featured on British television in an episode of Terry Jones's *Medieval Lives*. People re-create Hawkwood at pageants and tournaments, both in England and in Italy. Yet he is referred to only once in the *Cambridge History of Warfare* (2005) and is not even mentioned in John Keegan's *History of Warfare* (2004), or in the relevant volumes of *The New Oxford History of Modern England*.

The neglect was relative in Italy, since Hawkwood had a parallel life, and he was always better known as Giovanni Acuto, but even in Italy, nationalism meant that his importance was downplayed. When Ercole Ricotti published his *Storia delle Compagnie di Ventura in Italia* in 1844 he devoted only thirty pages to Hawkwood and the English companies, and effectively used them to prepare his readers for the arrival on the scene of Alberigo da Barbiano and his so-called 'pupils' Sforza and Braccio. In addition, Hawkwood's 'particular enemy' Gian Galeazzo Visconti, and his generals Facino Cane and Jacopo dal Verme, were popular with some Italians for the part they played in defeating the French at Alessandria (1391) and the Germans at Brescia (1401). Hawkwood played no part in any of this. In the 1930s twelve cruisers were built for the Condottieri class in Mussolini's navy. One of these was named *Alberico da Barbiano*, another *Muzio Attendolo* (after the first of the Sforza) and a third *Bartolomeo Colleoni*. No ship was named for Giovanni Acuto.

Even so, the Hawkwood revival of the last few years seems to have started earlier in Italy. Mario Tabanelli's *Giovanni Acuto: capitano di ventura* provided a very good summary as early as 1975. Santino Gallorini's *Montecchio Vesponi: un territorio, un castello e una comunita* (Calosci-Cortona, 1993) is still *the* book about Hawkwood's castle, while *Echi e memoria di un condottiero, Giovanni Acuto* was published in Castiglion Fiorentino in 1994, to mark the 600th anniversary of Sir John's death. Duccio Balestracci's *Le armi, i cavalli, l'oro: Giovanni Acuto e i condottieri nell'Italia del Trecento* followed in 2003. This is probably the best account written in the last ten years in any language, though it takes a bleak view of Hawkwood.

The Black Legend

'Mercenary' has become a dirty word. In Hawkwood's own day Sacchetti referred to 'the wicked race of armed men'. De Mézières called mercenaries 'leeches' in his

Dream of the Old Pilgrim (1389) and 'locusts' in the *Letter to King Richard II* (1395), and modern writers have been no kinder. Sir William Blackstone, professor of English law at Oxford in the eighteenth century, thought there was something noble about the feudal system and something 'wretched' about using it to raise money to pay for 'occasional mercenaries'. Twentieth-century English historians wrote extensively about what they called the 'bastard feudalism' of the later Middle Ages – a feudalism supposedly debased by the introduction of money into a relationship originally based on land. In 1989 the United Nations opened an International Convention against 'the Recruitment, Use, Financing and Training of Mercenaries'. When Anglo-American forces invaded Iraq in 2003, Saddam Hussein's Foreign Minister Tariq Aziz excoriated them as 'mercenaries'. No further condemnation was thought necessary.

Hawkwood has always been heartily disliked in some quarters. Towns which he had sacked or preyed on had no reason to think highly of him. The English were so unpopular in Pont-Saint-Esprit after the sack of 1360 that there was a riot there two years later, when seven German or Flemish pilgrims were mistakenly thought to have come from England. Filippo Villani, who wrote in Florence in the 1360s, called the English who sacked Figline 'cruel and bestial men who enriched themselves at our expense'. Sacchetti, who wrote at a time when Sir John had became a favourite son of Florence, nevertheless criticized him bitterly in poetry and short stories. Men and women in holy orders looked at the world in biblical terms and, in the letter she wrote to him, St Catherine of Siena accused Hawkwood of doing the Devil's work. It is easy to see why later generations concluded that Sir John was the origin of the Italian proverb, 'Inglese italianiato, diavolo incarnato' – 'an Italianized Englishman is the Devil incarnate'.

Popes Innocent VI and Urban V used very harsh language about the Free Companies who harried their territories in France and Italy. Innocent referred to them as 'sons of iniquity' and preached the crusade against them after their attack on Pont-Saint-Esprit. Urban issued no fewer than three bulls in 1364–5, invoking terrifying penalties against the *routiers* and all who associated with them, though he hoped that they might be persuaded to depart for the Holy Land. He castigated

> That multitude of villains of divers nations, associated in arms by avidity in appropriating to themselves the fruit of the labours of innocent and defenceless people; unbridled in every kind of cruelty, extorting money; methodically devastating the country, and the open towns, burning houses and barns, destroying trees and vines, obliging poor peasants to fly; assaulting, besieging, invading, spoiling and ruining even fortresses and walled cities; torturing and maiming those from whom they expected to obtain ransom, without regard to

ecclesiastical dignity, or sex, or age; violating wives, virgins and nuns, and constraining even gentlewomen to follow their camp, to do their pleasure and carry arms and baggage.

The Holy Roman Emperor Charles IV joined the chorus. In 1369 he described Sir John as 'the captain of the Satanic congregation known as the English company'. John Bromyard, the English Dominican friar who wrote a handbook for preachers, regarded Italy as a land of incessant warfare, where mercenaries deliberately nourished wars for their own ends, and made them last as long as they could.[1]

Even the Florentines, who employed Hawkwood for most of the 1380s, distrusted him. A letter written by their Chancellor Salutati in 1385 still refers to him cursorily as one of five robber chieftains who married the daughters of Bernabò Visconti,[2] and, in letters sent to their emissaries Vettori and Jacobi in June 1389, the Florentines advised that he be approached with caution: the envoys were told over and over again how to avoid trickery and fraud. Even as late as 1390, when the republic was at war and money was not so important as victory, Sir John's motives were still suspect. The Florentines told their ambassadors in Bologna that, if their embassy was not successful, the *condottiere* was capable of anything. They admitted that 'he has our entire State in his hands.' This warning was issued at a time when Hawkwood was their commander-in-chief.

Uccello's majestic portrait of Hawkwood displays the pride the Florentines came to feel in him, but there is another painting which is equally relevant. *The Legend of the Wolf of Gubbio*, by the Sienese artist known as Sassetta, was painted for an altarpiece in San Sepolcro between 1437 and 1444, and depicts a miraculous episode in the life of St Francis. The story it tells is of a wolf who has been preying on the people of Gubbio, eating animals and human beings alike, but the Saint negotiates a deal with it. As a result 'Brother Wolf' agrees to leave the Eugubines in peace provided he is fed at public expense for the rest of his life. Sassetta shows us the trunk and limbs of the wolf's last victims in the background, but the most striking figure is the notary in the foreground, who is poised to record the terms of the transaction. The parallels between this wolf and Hawkwood are striking. To some, he must always have been a predator of foreign extraction, who fought his way to the negotiating table.

Hawkwood earned a mention in Conan Doyle's *The White Company* of 1891 but it is scarcely an honourable one. This novel and the 'prequel' of 1906 (*Sir Nigel*) are actually about Sir Nigel Loring, a real soldier who fought in the first division at Crécy and was a founder knight of the Garter, but in Chapter 32 (How the Company Took Counsel Round the Fallen Tree) the men debate, in remarkably democratic fashion, whether they should stay in Aquitaine, go with the Black Prince to Spain, or try their luck in Italy. An unpleasant French knight asks:

What do we not hear of our comrades who have gone with Sir Hawkwood ... In one night they have held to ransom six hundred of the richest noblemen of Mantua. They camp before a great city, and the base burghers come forth with the keys, and then they make great spoil; or, if it please them better, they take so many horse-loads of silver as a composition and so they journey on from state to state, rich and free and feared by all. Now, is not that the proper life for a soldier?'

At which point, a stout English yeoman roars out:

The proper life for a robber!

It is clear what Conan Doyle thought of Hawkwood. Marcel Gouran and Guy Dupré, the historians of Pont-Saint-Esprit, took much the same view – Hawkwood was but one of many brigands who preyed on their town.

The Noble Tradition
There is another side to the story. Many writers praised Hawkwood as a military genius. Filippo Villani called him 'grand master of war' and by the 1390s he was a legend in his own lifetime. In his *Europe during the Middle Ages* (1818) the Whig historian Henry Hallam claimed Sir John as 'the first real general of modern times'.

There was more to admire than military skill. Sir John has often been presented as a 'Worthy'. The starting point here is Froissart. In his Prologue the great chronicler explains that he wants to preserve the memory of 'the honourable enterprises, noble adventures and deeds of arms which took place during the wars waged by France and England', and it is Froissart's Bascot of Mauléon – speaking in the late 1380s – who first describes Hawkwood as 'a fine English knight'. What distinguishes a knight in Froissart's eyes is prowess – a combination of courage, strength and artistry. A man is well thought of if he performs fine feats of arms and is true to his friends. If he does that, it does not much matter whom he serves, and whether he does so as a result of feudal obligation, an English indenture of war, or an Italian *condotta*.

The author of *The Vows of the Heron* revered nine 'Worthies', or champions of chivalry: Joshua, David and Judas Maccabaeus (from Biblical times), Hector, Alexander and Julius Caesar (from classical history), and Arthur, Charlemagne and Godfrey de Bouillon (from the Christian era). The French author Eustace

Deschamps added a tenth, who was Bertrand du Guesclin, while the Scots preferred to add Robert the Bruce.[3] Other candidates included Sir Hugh Calvely of Cheshire, who made his reputation with du Guesclin in Spain in the mid-1360s. Hawkwood was never in quite the same league, but thirty years later the Marquis of Saluzzo wrote about him in glowing terms in his *Chevalier Errant* – 'there was no captain more valiant and wise than he in Italy in the last hundred years'.

The Florentines had once been harsh critics, but many of them changed their tune when Hawkwood became their captain. The shift in opinion was slow at first – and the chronicler Stefani remained unimpressed, even by Hawkwood's military skills, in 1381[4] – but in 1393 the governing body of the city agreed, by 177 votes to 8, to reward him with an elaborate tomb in their cathedral, and they addressed him as 'the great and brave knight Sir Hawkwood'. The tomb was never built, but the city did pay for a lavish funeral and it also paid tribute by commissioning a portrait by the Gaddi, later replaced by Uccello's masterpiece. The Florentines' opinion of their late commander was demonstrated again when Richard II sent Nicholas Clifton to Florence, suggesting that he take over as captain-general. The Florentines were embarrassed and politely declined this offer. They explained that they were now at peace and had no need of assistance, but they flattered Richard by saying there was no nation on earth more glorious in arms than the English, and added that, if they should change their minds, they would undoubtedly choose Sir Nicholas as their new champion. This handsome compliment must have owed more to Hawkwood's achievements than to the reputation of English arms, which had declined considerably since the 1360s.

Hawkwood's fame was not confined to Florence. Even the Venetians and the inhabitants of Treviso in the North-East of the Italian states (whom he had never served but, perhaps more significantly, never harmed) came to regard him as the leading general of his day.[5] The Paduans had more reason to be grateful, since Hawkwood had helped them in their struggles with the Veronese in 1387 and with the Milanese in 1391, but it was Gattamelata, the 'Honeycat', who had a statue erected outside the basilica of St Anthony, when the Venetians crushed the Carrara and took over the Paduan state.

It is not clear how people came to hear of Hawkwood's Italian exploits in England, though several English chroniclers mention him. Englishmen who fought with him may have returned home and brought their memories with them; Italian merchants trading in England may have brought news; Professor Goodman has written of a 'vast lost corpus of ballads' sung in the late Middle Ages; and Sir John's tomb in Sible Hedingham – doubtless far more impressive in the fifteenth century than it is today – may have attracted visitors. Memories were doubtless kept alive by the priests who sang masses for him and his military companions, in the chantries founded in Sible Hedingham and Castle Hedingham. So far as is known, they continued in being until the wholesale abolition of chantries in the reign of Edward VI.[6]

There was a reading public in England and, although Englishmen would not have had ready access to Italian chronicles, the work of the greatest chronicler of all was available to them in French. Caxton, father of English printing, exhorted his readers to read Jean Froissart's work and was himself a great advocate of the chivalric way of life. He regarded Hawkwood as a champion of a lost golden age. In 1485 he printed Malory's *Morte d'Arthur*, referring in the preface to the nine 'Worthies', while the text contains fantastic stories of Arthur and his knights in Italy. In his translation of Ramon Lull's *Book of the Order of Chivalry*, Caxton also bracketed Hawkwood's name with those of Sir John Chandos, Sir Robert Knollys and Sir Walter Manny. This was august company indeed, since these were all knights who had achieved fame or fortune by long years of military service in France, and been closely associated with Edward III and the Black Prince. Chandos and Manny both belonged to the exclusive Order of the Garter and Manny was a close friend of the King. Looking back from the twenty-first century, there seems to be a marked contrast between their lives and Hawkwood's. One has to ask why Caxton chose Sir John as his comparator.

The answer is that he wanted to remind his readers of the good old days, and persuade them to mend their ways. By the 1470s, when he started his printing business in London, it was over fifty years since Henry V's victory at Agincourt, and over 100 years since Crécy and Poitiers. England's armies had recently suffered crushing defeats at the hands of the French, at Formigny (1450) and Castillon (1453), involving the loss of both Normandy and Gascony, long regarded as the 'barbicans' of England. The ancient French connection had been damaged irretrievably. In its place had come civil strife in England and a disgraceful vulnerability to French invasion. In Normandy it was an almost post-colonial situation, involving the expulsion of settlers, the return of soldiers to a life of unemployment and crime, and a deep wound to the nation's pride. Hence Caxton's passionate appeal to Hawkwood's example: he may not have served the royal and national cause in quite the same way as Chandos, Knollys and Manny, but his name could still be used as a rallying cry.

The noble tradition survived and Sir John remained of perennial interest to antiquarians, including Leland and Stow in the sixteenth century. A woodcut of Sir John *de* Hawkwood, based on Uccello's portrait but showing a rejuvenated and idealized figure in profile, was made by the Swiss artist Tobias Stimmer in 1582, with a verse in German – eloquent testimony to an international reputation.[7] Back in England, Richard Johnson parochialized medieval ideas about 'Worthies' in a book entitled *Nine Worthies of London*, of whom Hawkwood was one.

Thomas Fuller included him in his *Worthies of England*. Travellers continued to visit the Duomo, see his portrait and bring back travellers' tales. In 1680 the Merchant Tailors put him at the centre of the Lord Mayor's Show and in 1687 William Winstanley published what was in effect a short novel, with a very long title, which tells us all we need to know about the contents. This was *The Honour of the Taylors, or the famous and renowned History of Sir John Hawkwood knight, containing His many rare and singular Adventures, witty exploits, heroick Achievements, and noble Performances relating to Love and Arms in many lands.*

There was renewed interest in the eighteenth century, when there was a revival of enthusiasm for the idea of chivalry. Some of the Fellows of the Society of Antiquaries (which received its Royal Charter in 1751) considered Hawkwood fit to rank with the heroes commemorated in the *Temple of British Worthies* at Stowe in Buckinghamshire. In 1765 Thomas Hollis – Dr Johnson's 'strenuous Whig' – attempted to buy a gold medal of Hawkwood, said to be 'of ancient and finest Italian workmanship'. Hollis consoled himself for losing out at the sale to a mere 'toyman', by writing about Sir John in his diary.[8] In 1768 Philip Morant published his *History and Antiquities of the County of Essex*, highlighting Hawkwood's achievement by claiming that he was still 'the poorest knight in the army' when he left France for Italy. In 1771 Thomas Patch, an English expatriate in Florence, made an engraving based on Uccello's portrait but showing Hawkwood with a much younger face. This drawing was presented to the Society of Antiquaries by the judge, Lord Hailes, and prints were offered to the public. In 1775 another Fellow of the Society made an engraving of Sir John's tomb in Essex. In the following year a paper entitled *Memoirs of Sir Hawkwood* was read to the Society by its printer John Nichols. Written at the time of the American Revolution, these lay claim to Hawkwood as one of the greatest soldiers of his age, a man of irreproachable fidelity, a man against whom there could be no charges of cruelty, oppression or injustice, indeed a gentleman who was 'no mere mercenary soldier'. The atrocities in Romagna are passed over very quickly indeed.

In 1840 a three-volume Gothic novel was published, entitled *Hawkwood: A Romance of Italy* (1840). This celebrated the hero's adventures and featured Gian Galeazzo Visconti as the villain. The curiously anonymous author wrote both an introductory and a concluding essay, in which he claimed that Sir John was 'no vulgar adventurer who sold his sword indifferently to the highest bidder', but rather 'the main founder of the great school of modern warfare', a precursor of Napoleon and Wellington. This novel has remained obscure, in marked contrast to Samuel Smiles's *Self-Help* (1859), which also gave a favourable view of Hawkwood and which became an international 'bestseller'. In Smiles's view, Hawkwood deserved praise because he had risen from humble beginnings and achieved high office. He describes the knight in a section dealing with tailors, calling him 'the brave Sir John who so greatly distinguished himself at Poictiers [sic] and was knighted by Edward III for valour' – both dubious statements.[9] *Self-Help* can still be bought in paperback today.

In 1889 Temple-Leader and Marcotti published *Sir Hawkwood (L'Acuto): Story of a Condottiere*. They wrote in the heyday of Victorian self-confidence in Britain and of national self-assertion in the new Kingdom of Italy. Sir John Temple-Leader was part of a group of expatriates living in Florence, having taken refuge there after abandoning a promising career as a Whig MP for Westminster. He saw Hawkwood as a symbol of Anglo-Italian friendship, and one of the strengths of the book is its strong Italian flavour, contributed in part by his friend Giuseppe Marcotti. They both liked Hawkwood, and Temple-Leader was wealthy enough to buy and restore the ruined castle of Vincigliata near Fiesole, which had reputedly been sacked by the English in 1364. Their book was described in the first edition of the *Oxford Dictionary of National Biography* as 'marred by diffuseness of style and strange inaccuracy in the citation of authorities' but it became an essential work of reference and is still a mine of information. It was undoubtedly the source for many later accounts, including Fortescue's in his jingoistic *History of the British Army* (1899).

Several novels were written about Hawkwood in the twentieth century, though none with the impact of Conan Doyle's. William Beck's of 1911 was 'the boy's book', written at a time when J M Henty was writing his ripping yarns, and *The Boy's Own* newspaper enjoyed a wide circulation. It was unashamedly entitled *Hawkwood the Brave*. Over fifty years later, Hubert Cole published a trilogy: *Hawkwood* (1967), *Hawkwood in Paris* (1969) and *Hawkwood and the Towers of Pisa* (1973). By now, the British Empire had more or less ceased to exist and these novels no longer contained a simple patriotic message. They contain large elements of pure fiction: the second of the three relates entirely to adventures in Paris, for which there is no evidence at all. The hero is portrayed as a bold but likeable rogue, in the mould of George MacDonald Fraser's *Flashman*. Sir John's boldness is likewise celebrated in Fairport Convention's song 'Hawkwood's Army', one of the tracks on *Sense of Occasion* (2007).

Hawkwood is also a local hero. In the City, the Merchant Tailors still claim him as one of their first Liverymen, though there are no guild records from before 1400 to confirm this. In Sible Hedingham in Essex he is hailed, at least by some, as 'our famous fighting son'. In addition to the Hawkwood memorial chapel in the parish church, there is a sixteenth-century Hawkwood Manor and a modern Hawkwood Road. The village sign in Church Street sports a small effigy of him which is modelled on Uccello's masterpiece and displays his coat of arms and his Florentine cap.

Modern Verdicts

In his TV series and book *Medieval Lives* (2004) Terry Jones did the full hatchet job on Hawkwood. He argued that Sir John 'turned war into a business' and that his career represented the end of chivalry. Both propositions are highly dubious, though the book as a whole was designed to rehabilitate the Middle Ages.

The professional mercenary was not a new phenomenon in the late fourteenth century. The Norman and Plantagenet kings of England made regular use of them, as did the Crusaders in Palestine, at a time when the Papacy was already complaining loudly about their activities.[10] So far as Italy is concerned, we have seen that German mercenaries were a regular feature of warfare some decades before Hawkwood. The Catalan William della Torre was in Sienese service in 1277, while in the early fourteenth century another Spaniard, Diego de Rat, earned himself notoriety in Boccaccio's *Decameron*. Roger di Flor and his Catalan Company, which overran the Duke of Athens's principality in Greece in 1311, would have been surprised to learn that it was Hawkwood who 'turned war into a business', as would Castruccio Castracani, who constructed a short-lived empire on the River Arno in the 1320s.

The view that Hawkwood's career in some way represents a decline from the high standards of a previous age – that he was 'mercenary' by trade, mercenary by nature – presupposes that there was ever an 'age of chivalry', but it is difficult to identify when this is supposed to have been, and Jones himself has his doubts. Indeed, he has now changed his mind. In a foreword to William Urban's *Medieval Mercenaries* (2006), he confesses he was wrong to blame men like Hawkwood for the incessant warfare of medieval times, but he now blames the barons, like the Duke of Gloucester. Finding someone to blame is not the most illuminating way to approach history, though it can be amusing.

The Italians have long nationalist traditions, despite the fact that the country was only unified in modern times, but they come in different forms. One celebrates the achievements of those who fought against foreign invaders and looked towards the reconstruction of the nation. Writers of this ilk tend to deprecate the Papacy's pursuit of secular power, since this is regarded as anti-nationalist. In relation to the events in the Papal States in the 1370s, there is a natural sympathy for those who rebelled against a regime subsequently labelled as 'foreign'. For Italian nationalists, Hawkwood was on the 'wrong' side when he fought for the Pope: he was the Pope's lackey, employed to crush courageous and noble Italians.

There is another nationalist tradition, which specifically celebrates the achievements of Gian Galeazzo Visconti of Milan. On this view, the Visconti were the true patriots. In pursuing the traditional Milanese policy of expansion, he served the nationalist cause, even though the nation state was only brought into being 500 years later. From this perspective, Florence was in the wrong, since she invited the foreigner into Italy, while Milan hired the greatest of the Italian *condottieri* – Alberigo da Barbiano, Lucchino dal Verme and his sons Jacopo and Taddeo, and Facino Cane. The victories these men won were deemed to be 'Italian' victories. Unfortunately for Hawkwood, he is no hero of this tradition either, since his relationship with the Visconti was very complicated. Often at odds with Bernabò, he never worked for Gian Galeazzo.

If we must sit in judgement on Hawkwood, we should judge him as a soldier, and as a medieval soldier. In the 1950s Professor Southern pointed out the chasm that existed between the high and low theory of knighthood. The high theory, propounded by theologians and philosophers, thought that it was ordained:

to protect the Church, attack infidelity, reverence the priesthood, protect the poor, keep the peace, shed one's blood and, if necessary, lay down one's life for one's brethren.

If this was the ideal, Sir John was a miserable failure, but so were most of his contemporaries. By contrast, most 'working' knights thought it was enough:

to defend one's rights, see justice done, keep one's inferiors and superiors in their place, be a wise counsellor and a bold fighter, a loyal vassal and a respected lord, and make the exercise of arms profitable.

If this was the code to live by, Hawkwood was a success. He lived a long life and did not suffer a decline in later years, as Edward III did. He was a commoner and a younger son who left home and became a knight, whereas his elder brother and namesake – who stayed at home in Essex – always remained 'Hawkwood the elder'.[11] He served the King of England as well as his Italian masters and he lived to see his daughters married, though his son was only made a knight after his death. He progressed from being captain of an English brigade to holding the highest office in the Florentine army and, like Little Meschin before him, defeated some of the greatest noblemen in Europe. Unlike Knollys in 1370 he was never criticized for being promoted beyond his station.

Hawkwood's successes in Italy filled many Englishmen with deep pride – even monks, servants of God who looked at the world through the prism of religion. News of his adventures had filtered back home as early as 1369, when the continuation of Murimuth's chronicle records that:

In that time, the Englishman Sir Hawkwood rose to prominence [*floruit*]. He had the White Company with him, and fought now against the Church, now against the lords of Milan, and he did many extraordinary things, really marvellous things, the like of which no one had heard of before [*mirabilia inaudita*].

News of Sir John's death in 1394 was soon received in Pistoia, Milan, and elsewhere in Italy, and within a few weeks it filtered back to England. The Milanese annalist recorded simply that Hawkwood was 'British', an 'excellent captain', indeed, 'very famous', but Thomas Walsingham of St Albans wrote, 'in this year died Sir Hawkwood. He was the most famous soldier in the whole world and his deeds need a history of their own.' The monk of Westminster, who had recently taken great pride in telling how Henry Bolingbroke had crusaded in the Baltic, recorded Hawkwood's death in similar vein:

At this time the death occurred ... of the celebrated knight Sir Hawkwood who, having started life as the poor apprentice of a London hosier, made his way to Lombardy, where his exploits, both in foreign wars and in internal conflicts, were so marvellous that his like had never been found there.

These verdicts, delivered by Englishmen who might have been expected to share the diabolical view of Hawkwood, should be weighed in the balance against the criticisms of his modern detractors.[12]

Francesco Sacchetti's View

In Novella 181 Sacchetti records an amusing tale about Hawkwood, just as Machiavelli later recorded a number of witticisms attributed to Castruccio Castracani of Lucca. It is frequently cited as evidence of the Englishman's sense of humour, although it is clear from the rest of the Novella that Sacchetti strongly disapproved of all mercenaries. On the other hand, Novella 36 tells us that the average Florentine was a complete innocent when it came to military matters. Looking at the two tales side by side, one might well conclude that professional soldiers were a necessary evil in the chaotic conditions of fourteenth-century Italy. Even in 181, Sacchetti blames the Italian states who did the hiring as much as he blames the mercenaries, for the incessant warfare that Italians had to endure. Rhyme 92 is a *caccia* (a free-verse poem) which describes an unnamed battle fought in about 1363 when Hawkwood was fighting for Pisa. I have included the Italian version of some of the battle-cries, because no English translation gives the full flavour of the original.

Novella 181
Where Sir Hawkwood gives two Franciscan friars a swift and pleasing reply, when they wish him 'God grant you peace.'

The reply Sir Hawkwood gave to two Franciscan friars was a nice one. These friars were in some need and had gone to visit him at one of his castles called Montecchio, about a mile from Cortona. Arriving in his presence, they greeted him in their usual way – Sire, God grant you peace –

And he gives them this reply – May God take away your alms –

The friars, who were quite frightened, said – Sir, why do you speak to us in that way?

And Sir John said – Well, I could ask you, why do you speak to me in that way?

And the friars said – We thought we were wishing you well –

And Sir John replied – How do you think to wish me well, when you come to me and wish that God should make me die of hunger? Don't you know that I live by war, and that peace would be my undoing? And so just as I live by war, so you live by alms, so that the reply which I gave you was similar to the greeting you gave me.

The friars shrugged their shoulders and said – Sir, you are right. Forgive us. We have been stupid.

And once they had attended to some other business which they had with him, they left and returned to their monastery at Castiglion Aretino,[1] where they told this anecdote, which was pleasing and ingenious, especially for Hawkwood, but not for those who would have preferred to live in peace. And it is certain that this man's military career in Italy lasted longer than anyone else's, in fact for about sixty years,[2] and that almost every part of the country paid him tribute money; and his achievement was that there was little peace in his day. And woe to any man or people which places too much faith in people like him, because people, communes and cities live and grow by living in peace, and people like him live and thrive on war, which is the undoing of the cities, as they destroy themselves and waste away. In those men,[3] there is neither love nor faith. And it often happens that those people do more harm to those who give them money than to the soldiers on the other side; because, although they pretend to be willing to attack and fight each other, they usually hold each other in greater esteem than those who have hired them, and it appears to me that they say to each other 'You rob that side, and I'll rob this.' People are like lost sheep, who don't see that, every day, it is the cunning of these mercenaries which leads to war, and forces people to act in a totally irrational way. And what is the reason so many of the cities of Italy are under the rule of the *signori*, when they were once free? Why is Apulia in the state she is in, and for that matter Sicily? And where did the war between Padua and Verona get them, as so many other cities which are now in such a sorry state?

Oh you poor few, and you are few, who still live in freedom: don't be taken in by the wily men at arms. Stay at peace, even if you have to put up with two or three humiliating experiences at the hands of your enemies, which might otherwise lead to war; because a war may begin slowly, but it soon escalates at an unbelievable rate; and the evil that comes of it cannot be put right quickly.

Novella 36

Three Florentines rush before the Priors, one after the other with strange news about the war with the Pisans, saying that they have seen things, none of which were remotely true; and moreover, they tell what they have done but they could not explain a thing.

In comparison with the priest of the last tale, the three Florentines in this episode knew much less about what they were saying. At the time the Florentines last had a war with the Pisans, and when the English, who were on the side of the Pisans, were riding towards Florentine territory, there was a certain Geppo Canigiani, who was at his place at San Casciano. He was frightened out of his wits by a sound, either of water or of wind, as those that herald bad weather, but he convinced himself that it could be nothing other than the enemy army, and he brought news of this to the *Signoria* in Florence, so as to keep in favour with them. And so he got on his horse and spurring the animal on he arrived at the Palace of the Priors;[4] and he dismounted; and going in front of the *signori*, he told them he was coming from San Casciano and that the enemy were approaching Florence from there, making a great din as they did so.

The *signori* ask him if he has seen the enemy. He tells them no, but that he has heard them.

What have you heard?

And he says he has heard a great din.

The Priors say – But are you sure that that din was made by the enemies? –

He answers – They were either horsemen or perhaps it was only water –

They shrug their shoulders and thank him, and wish him godspeed.

There was a second man called Giovanni da Pirano, who being outside the San Niccolo gate[5] on one of his old nags, and seeing some oxen fleeing towards the gate, he thought he had the enemy at his coat-tails, spurred on his mare and, getting in ahead of the oxen, did not stop till he got before the Priors, and said – God have mercy, all the oxen have unyoked themselves and are fleeing into the city by the San Niccolo gate –

And the Priors took note of this, together with the previous report, and said he should stay on the alert and bring them any further news.

There was a third man, named Piero Fastelli, who, although he was in commerce, habitually armed himself with a crossbow and a small breastplate in time of war, and went about like that on foot, for a mile or two. It happened that, when the English were in the Pisan camp on the plain at Ripoli, about two miles from Florence, there was a spell of really bad weather – it was raining and misty for several days. Well, when this Piero was outside the city gate, about the distance a crossbow can shoot, he shot a bolt towards the narrows of the Arno; and then he returned to Florence and he went to see the Priors and said – My lords, I got very close to the enemy camp, and I fired a great bolt at them, and I succeeded in doing them much harm; but I wasn't able to see exactly what, because of the mist.

The *signori* look at one another and say – Piero, if only we had enough men like you, we could defeat the enemy with less than fifty bolts; go now and do your best to shoot more arrows, and continue to bring us news.

This was how the *signori* were informed, in only a few days, by three valiant men of war, of three different things which even the great Dabuda (derived from

Dabbudà) would have avoided.⁶ And yet those who are used to commerce cannot know what war is; and this is indeed how communities are ruined, when we are not at peace. Men who should stick to the arts and crafts they know say: 'We have beaten the enemy'; but this is like the fly, who sat on the neck of an ox and, when asked: 'What are you doing, fly?' replied '*We* are ploughing.'

Rhyme 92

> Join battle right there in the plain,
> fiery people, everyone at once to arms, to arms! [*a l'arme, a l'arme!*]
> let each one be brave and proud.
> Down, bugles and trumpets,
> you who sound reveille and you who sound castanets,
> towards the enemy, horns and tambourines!
> Advance, good shieldmen!
> Follow on, infantrymen, over there, and you crossbowmen.
> O marshal, arrange your cavalry.
> O you with the regal coat of arms,
> dismount, dismount, dismount;
> go down, go down.
> You, who bear the banner of the light cavalry,
> forward, forward! [*avanti! avanti!*]
> lead that line of men
> Come up, come up,
> 'Go get them, Go get them', [*Alloro, Alloro!*]
> keep your good name in mind! –
> Spur on your mounts with lance on thigh,
> wielding your swords,
> horses whinnying,
> cutting and battering,
> so that helms and helmets fall
> and crossbows shoot,
> men leave the saddle with a crash of the lance
> and the clash of bascinets,
> – Unto death! Unto death! – [*A la morte, a la morte!*]
> the enemy were forced back;
> When the good captain,
> calls out – Turn back, turn back,
> and gathered in his men, valuing their manhood.

Hawkwood's English Letters
(with thanks to Valerie Nicholson)

These letters were discovered in the Guildhall in London in the 1920s by Dr A H Thomas. They were written in Florence and addressed to Thomas Coggeshall, the first on 7 November 1392, the second in 1393. They were enrolled by the chancery of the Mayor and Aldermen of London on 15 June 1411, when produced by Robert Rykedon of Essex, referred to in the second letter as 'Hopky'. Dr Thomas considered that they were the earliest surviving private letters written in the English language.[7] There is no way of knowing if they were originally written by Hawkwood himself, since the handwriting on the plea roll is clearly that of a copyist.

> Dere S I grete you wel and do you to wytyn [know] that at the making of this letter I was in god point [health] thank god … I send Johan Sampson bryngere of this letter to you enformed of certeyn things quiche he schall tellyn you be mouthe therefore I preye you that ye levyn [treat] hym as my persone Wrytn at Florence the vii day Novembre
>
> John Haukwode Chivaler

> Dere trusty & welbiloved frend hertliche I grete you wel desirying to heren god tidynges of youre welfare & preying you that ye be helping & counseillyng to my welbiloved squyer Jankyn Sampson touching that he hath to purseu for me atte this tyme will & nameliche for my sauf condutes [safe conducts] & touching my will & purpose I praye you that ye wele yeve [give] fei [faith?] & credence to the forsaid Jankyn Sampson of al that he wele seyen you by mouthe & also I preye you that ye wele speke to Hopky Rikyngdon & to Jankyn Serjaunt, Robert Lyndeseye & alle myn other frendes that thei don as the forsaid Jankyn Sampson seth to you touchyng my will. Tristy frend ye holy gost have you in his kepyng written at Florence the xx day of Feverer the yer of oure lord mccclxxxxiii

Notes

Abbreviations used in the Notes

CCR   Calendar of Close Rolls
Condottieri   Zucchini, Stefania (ed.), *Condottieri, War and Society in Central Italy in the Fourteenth Century*, Working Papers of the Uggucione Ranieri di Sorbello Foundation, no. 11 (Perugia, 2006)
CPR   Calendar of Patent Rolls
CSP   Calendar of State Papers
T&M   John Temple-Leader and Giuseppe Marcotti, *Sir Hawkwood (L'Acuto): Story of a Condottiere* (London, T Fisher Unwin, 1889); republished by Martino Publishing, 2005

Introduction: The Battle near Marradi, 1358

1. Muratori, vol. 14, 508–12 (Matteo Villani).
2. Larner, *Crossing the Romagnol Apennines*.

Chapter 1: 'A Fine English Knight': France, 1360–2

1. Muratori, vol. 14, 746 (Filippo Villani); vol. 16, 176 (Sozomeno).
2. Green, p. xiii. Bruce's ransom was only 100,000 marks.
3. *ODNB*, Robert Knollys. A 'mouton' was a French coin, worth 4s. 10d. in 1355: Green, p. xiii.
4. *Thalamus Parvus*, 356–7; Muratori, vol. 14, 642–3 (Matteo Villani); Jean le Bel, vol. 2, 322; Denifle, vol. 2, 391(n.); Gouran. The evidence for Hawkwood's presence is based on the Bascot of Mauléon's narrative to Froissart, and there is a letter from Pope Innocent VI addressed to 'Johanni Scakaik'. This may be a reference to Hawkwood: it is a strange spelling, but some of the Italian spellings are also very odd.
5. Froissart, edition of Thomas Johnes (2 vols, London 1857), vol. 1, 298.
6. Muratori, vol. 14, 642–3.
7. Jean le Bel, vol. 2, 324: 'le Pape leur pardonna tous leurs meffais et les assout de paine et de coulpe.'
8. *Thalamus Parvus*, 360; Muratori, vol. 14, 680–2 (Matteo Villani); Denifle; Fowler, *Medieval Mercenaries*, vol. 1. Caferro, 57, 361, accepts that Hawkwood was at Pont-Saint-Esprit, but thinks it unlikely he was at Brignais.

9. Froissart, ed. Johnes, vol. 1, 296.

10. Keen, *Laws of War*, 98.

Chapter 2: From Captain to Captain-General: Italy, 1361–77

1. Philip Morgan, *War and Society in Medieval Cheshire* (Manchester, Chetham Society, 1987), 161. I owe this reference to Maurice Keen.

2. Green, p. xiii; CCR 1381–5, 367; Prestwich, *Plantagenet England*, 497.

3. *Memoirs of a Renaissance Pope*, 32–6; Sacchetti, Rhyme 197, line 80 and n.

4. Bruni, vol. 2, 433.

5. Mortimer, *Fears of Henry IV*, 55.

6. Muratori, vol. 16, 731–2.

7. Though the birth of an illegitimate child, who was made a priest in England in 1373, would seem to throw some doubt on this: see p. 39 below.

8. Boccaccio, *Decameron*, 2, 8.

9. Bruni, vol. 2, 449.

10. Ibid., vol. 2, 409, 449; Tigler, 8; Muratori, vol. 16, 1075 (Sozomeno); vol. 14, 734 (Filippo Villani); Sercambi, 124.

11. Muratori, vol. 14, 738 (Filippo Villani).

12. Sacchetti, Rhymes 94, 119a, 119b (n.).

13. Compare the bodyguard of 750 men recruited by Richard II in England in 1397: Harriss, 483.

14. Bruni, vol. 2, 455.

15. Ibid., vol. 2, 417; Ricotti; Walsingham, 145; Muratori, vol. 16, 1076 (Matteo Villani); Machiavelli, *Life of Castruccio Castracani*, 21.

16. Bruni, vol. 2, 461.

17. Muratori, vol. 14, 761 (Filippo Villani); vol. 15, 185 (Siena), 1045 (Pisa).

18. Boccaccio, *Decameron*, 4, 5, 7, 9.

19. Muratori, vol. 15, 187–9 (Siena).

20. Pearsall, 53.

21. *Memoirs of a Renaissance Pope*, 162–3.

22. Baluzus, *Lives of the Avignon Popes* (Paris 1914), 391.

23. Stefani, 272.

24. Sacchetti, Rhyme 137.

25. Keen, *Grey v Hastings* in *Nobles, Knights and Men-at-Arms*.

26. Muratori, vol. 16, 514 (Piacenza). The author of the Milanese annals uses the same phrase: vol. 16, 750.

27. *ODNB* 2004 (Fowler).

28. Cited by Chambers. The exact remark was, 'Oho! The Pope? How many divisions has he got?'

29. Petrarch, *Canzoniere*, 136; *Letter to Posterity*, 4, 6.

30. Bruni, vol. 2, 483–7.
31. Sacchetti, Rhyme 189, lines 58–64.
32. Papal Letters, 28, 105, 114, 116, 118, 191; Caferro, 159.
33. Muratori, vol. 15, 245 (Siena); Sercambi, 212; Stefani, 292.
34. Noffke, letter 30, 105–7.
35. Muratori, vol. 18, 496 (Chronicle of Bologna). To be fair to St Catherine, one of the MSS of her letter to Hawkwood contains an introduction, which makes it clear that she did not expect him to leave for the Holy Land unless there was an expedition for him to join.
36. Muratori, vol. 16, 763 (Milan); Murimuth, vol. 2, 141.
37. Balestracci in *Condottieri*, 26.
38. CSP Venice (1).

Chapter 3: 'The Best Commander': Italy, 1377–94

1. Muratori, vol. 17, 236, 239, 270 (A Gataro).
2. Sacchetti, Rhyme 197, lines 79–84.
3. Walsingham, 83; Stefani, 421.
4. Keen, *Nobles, Knights and Men-at-Arms*, 12, 124.
5. Russell, 249–50; Green, 185.
6. It is curious that in the winter of 1381–2 Richard II also ordered all Englishmen owing him allegiance in the different 'parts of Italy' to support a projected invasion by his brother-in-law, the Holy Roman Emperor Wenceslas, and to put themselves under Hawkwood's orders. Richard seems to have expected Sir John to command the English, despite the fact that they were under contract to various Italian states, and he offered them no remuneration, simply referring to the fact that Hawkwood had been retained in some way by Wenceslas: Rymer, *Foedera*, vol. 4, 140; Perroy, 290 n. 2, 280 n. 7, 159.
7. Rolls of Parliament, 2, 372, items 76 and 77.
8. The change in Hawkwood's relations with the Crown explains a curious order given to him by Richard II on 4 March 1388. The King wrote ordering Hawkwood to ensure the security of the inhabitants of Provence and Forcalquier, because they were 'threatened by incursions of Louis [II] of Anjou and those lands were near Aquitaine.' The order makes some kind of sense when we look at the full context. Provence had belonged to Queen Joanna of Naples until it fell to Louis of Anjou at the end of her reign. By 1388 the County had passed to Louis II, but his supporters experienced some difficulty in obtaining the submission of the County, in the face of opposition from Durazzo-Angevins based in Aix-en-Provence. Edward III had often profited from civil wars in the French provinces, and Hawkwood signed a fresh contract with the Durazzo-Angevins in November 1388: Perroy, 295, citing Rymer's *Foedera*, vol. 7, 569; *Dictionnaire de Biographie Française*, vol. 2 (Paris 1936) for Louis of Anjou.

9. Gian Galeazzo had been given the County of Virtù in France in 1360, when he married Isabella of Valois.

10. A fortress in Milan which contained Bernabò's treasury: Muir, 86.

11. *La Politica Finanziaria dei Visconti*, Caterina Santoro (Arti Grafiche, Colombo, Gessate, 1979) vol. 2, 1385–1412, 2; CSP Milan (1) no 1.

12. Muratori, vol. 17, 539.

13. Russell, 62.

14. Muratori, vol. 17, 555 (A Gataro).

15. Ibid., vol. 16, 815–18 (Milan).

16. Ibid., vol. 17, 806 (A Gataro).

17. Ibid., vol. 18, 544 (Bologna).

18. Ibid., vol. 15, 522 (Este).

19. Ibid., vol. 18, 807.

20. *Westminster Chronicle*, 477.

21. Muratori, vol. 15, 524 (Este).

22. *Thalamus Parvus*, 419. The language is that spoken in the Langue d'Oc.

23. 'Dopo molti abbracciamenti e offerte': Muratori, vol. 17, 809 (A Gataro).

24. *Westminster Chronicle*, 465–7.

25. Lewis, 11.

26. *La Morte di Giovanni Acuto*, by A Medin, *Archivio Storico Italiano* (Florence, 1886).

27. Caferro, 317–18.

28. *In re Holy Trinity, Bosham* [2004] 2 Weekly Law Reports, 833.

29. Harriss, 470. For Dalyngrigge, see *ODNB* 2004. For Clifton, see Mortimer, *Fears of Henry IV*, 123–4, 400. T&M, 147 mention a man of this name at Bagnacavallo in 1378, who subsequently served Florence.

30. For the boar see Green, 185. The harpy could be a griffin – it appears to have a tail. There are some medieval tiles in a drawer in Sible church (2006), one showing a hawk, another the coat of arms of Robert de Vere, Duke of Ireland. In the eighteenth century William Holman wrote of a wall painting, showing Sir John and *two* wives at prayer, and the words – 'True Son of God, remember me' (Vere Filie Dei memento mei). The de Vere coat of arms has the motto 'Vero nihil verius' (Truly nothing is more true): Majendie.

Chapter 4: Mercenaries, *Condottieri* and Women

1. Daniel Waley, 'The Army of the Florentine Republic' in Rubinstein, 72; Prestwich, *Plantagenet England*, 329.

2. Fowler, *The Kings' Lieutenant*, Appendix 4.

3. Bruni, vol. 2, 447; Muratori, vol. 14, 722 (Villani); Blackstone, vol. 2, 444–5; Spufford; Kohl, 28–9.

4. T&M, Document 24.

5. Ibid., Document 65; Canestrini, 52.
6. Gouran, 41.
7. Stefani, 371.
8. Ibid., 300.
9. Keen, *Nobles, Knights and Men-at-Arms*, 121.
10. CCR 1381–5, 367; Caferro, 215–16.
11. Muratori, vol. 15, 1047 (Pisa); Sercambi, 135.
12. Stefani, 403.
13. Balestracci, *Le Armi, i Cavalli, l'Oro*, 153, 160–1.
14. Larner, 203.
15. Novelle 36, 181; Rhymes 189, 194, 215, lines 53–6.
16. Muratori, vol. 14, 739 (Filippo Villani).
17. Keen, *Nobles, Knights and Men-at-Arms*, 34.
18. CSP Venice (1), Nos 67–74.

Chapter 5: English Tactics and the Notion of Italian Cowardice

1. Muratori, vol. 16, 380.
2. Russell, 7–8.
3. Muratori, vol. 14, 748.
4. Caferro, citing Harleian MS 6148, folio 143r; Majendie, 18.
5. Muratori, vol. 16, 380 (Azario); vol. 14, 748 (Filippo Villani).
6. Jones, *Chaucer's Knight*, 273.
7. Bruni, vol. 2, 475; Muratori, vol. 15, 524 (Este); vol. 16, 554, 754 (Piacenza); *Westminster Chronicle*, 477.
8. Russell, 447.
9. T&M, 292n.
10. Muratori, vol. 16, 380.
11. Stefani, 300.
12. Rymer, *Foedera*, vol. 4, 140.
13. Christine de Pisan, 33.
14. T F Tout, *Chapters in Medieval Administrative History* (Manchester, 1928), vol. 4, 470–1.
15. Muratori, vol. 17, 558 (A Gataro).
16. Prestwich, *Plantagenet England*, 310.
17. Keen, *Richard II's Ordinances of War*, clauses 9, 10 and 11.
18. Muratori, vol. 14, 748.
19. T&M, 193 n.

Chapter 6: Booty, Ransoms and Rewards

1. Russell, 109.
2. Harriss, 87.

3. Prestwich, *Plantagenet England*, 345.
4. Keen, *Richard II's Ordinances of War*, clause 16.
5. Muratori, vol. 16, 380.
6. Balestracci, in *Condottieri*, 22.
7. Sacchetti, Novella 135.
8. Legnano, 250; contrast chapter 69, p. 274.
9. T&M, Document 19.
10. *Archivio Storico Italiano*, 186, 166–72.
11. Calendar of Select Pleas, 257.
12. Papal Letters, 124, 143, 154, 160, 206.
13. Larner, 6–7, 81.
14. Sacchetti, Rhyme 194, lines 35–40; Novella 222.
15. Fabio Giovannini, 'Montecchio Vesponi: Storia di un Castello Attraverso L'Archaeologia dell' Architettura', thesis, 42, 44.
16. Sacchetti, Rhymes 168 n.; Bruni, vol. 2, 481.
17. Sachetti, Novella 24.
18. T&M, 299 and Document 68.
19. A signalling codebook of 1260 tells us that one fire means 'the enemy is near'; two that '200 soldiers are near'; Gallorini, 126; T&M, Document 68; Ghizzi (1874), 9.
20. Giovannini, 'Montecchio Vesponi', 167.

Chapter 7: Leadership and Chivalry

1. Sacchetti, Novella 41.
2. Gough, 34–5, citing British Library Harleian MS 6989, r2, which is also cited by Caferro. The hawk is technically a 'hawk volant' – with wings outspread. In March 2007 a ring with a hawk on it, and thought to be late medieval, was found by an amateur archaeologist in a paddock behind Hawkwood Manor in Sible Hedingham.
3. *Antistoria degli Italiani* (Mondadori, 1997).
4. Prestwich, *Plantagenet England*, 555.
5. Christine de Pisan, 23.
6. T&M, Documents 36–43.
7. CPR 1377–81, 337; CCR 1377–81, 262.
8. Bruni, vol. 2, 455; Muratori, vol. 16, 1076: 'Anglici … coniuges, aut precario aut vi, coitu et adulterio vituperabant.'
9. Sacchetti, Novella 122 (dice); 81 (chess). For dice in England, see Mortimer, *Fears of Henry IV*, 94.
10. A mythical beast.
11. Canestrini, *Documenti della Milizia Italiana*, 58.
12. CSP, Venice (1), nos 57–94.
13. Lewis, 153.

14. Sacchetti, Rhymes, p. 405; Novelle 33, 49, 4.
15. Barber, *The Knight and Chivalry*, 334.
16. Christine de Pisan, 219.
17. Mancini, 139; Machiavelli, *Life of Castruccio Castracani*, 24.
18. Muratori, vol. 15, 186 (Siena); 1046 (Pisa); Balestracci, *La Festa in armi*, 204.
19. Bruni, vol. 2, 523.
20. Geoffrey le Baker's chronicle, 43, in Barber, *Life and Campaigns of the Black Prince*.
21. Sacchetti, Novella 7.
22. Bruni, vol. 2, 455; Ricotti, vol. 2, 104–5, 315–28; Balestracci in *Condottieri*, 35. Chaucer's Miller played the bagpipes in *The Canterbury Tales*.
23. Legnano, 236; Boccaccio, *Decameron*, 10, 7; Sacchetti, Novella 24.
24. Muratori, vol. 18, 544 (Bologna).
25. *Memoirs of a Renaissance Pope*, 109.
26. Sacchetti, Novella 129.
27. Mortimer, *The Perfect King*, 172.
28. Lewis, 89.
29. Barber, *The Knight and Chivalry*, 238.
30. Novella 213.
31. Jager, 178–9.
32. Calendar of Select Pleas, 257, 309.

Chapter 8: *Chevauchée* and Battle

1. Novella 39.
2. 'Guerre sans feu ne valait rien, non plus que andouilles sans moustarde': Prestwich, *Armies and Warfare in the Middle Ages*, 200.
3. Sacchetti, *Il Trecentonovelle*, p. 41.
4. Keen, *Nobles, Knights and Men-at-Arms*, 34.
5. Machiavelli, *Life of Castruccio Castracani*, 27.
6. Muratori, vol. 19, 795.
7. Sacchetti, Rhyme 138, lines 1–4; Muratori, vol. 16, 1087 (Sozomeno).
8. Prestwich, *Plantagenet England*, 333.
9. Muratori, vol. 16, 754.
10. Based on Muratori, vol. 17, starting at 571 (G Gataro); and at 566 (A Gataro, his son).
11. Kohl, 238.
12. Prestwich, *Plantagenet England*, 339.
13. Based on Barlozzetti, in Del Treppo.
14. Smail, ch. 6.
15. Donati, 68.

Chapter 9: Strategy, Spies and Luck

1. Bruni, vol. 2, 439, 461.
2. T&M, 221.
3. Sacchetti, Novelle 38 and 41.
4. T&M refer to two sons. The source is the Chronicle of Bologna – Muratori, vol. 18, 503, which refers to 'figliuoli' – sons, in the plural, and says both that they were young and that they were illegitimate; but Caferro (184,187) thinks this is disproved by Venetian sources.
5. Smail, 138.
6. Legnano, ch. 19; Barber, *Life and Campaigns of the Black Prince*, 70, 77–8.
7. Christine de Pisan, 33.
8. Larner, *Crossing the Romagnol Apennines.*
9. Muratori, vol. 18, 542; *Memoirs of a Renaissance Pope*, 113.
10. Canestrini, 52.
11. Legnano, ch. 62; Christine de Pisan, 163.
12. Bruni, vol. 2, 455.
13. *Westminster Chronicle*, 157.
14. Mézières, *The Dream of the Old Pilgrim*, I, 419–22; Sacchetti, Novella 90.
15. Stefani, 352–4.
16. Papal Letters, 122.
17. T&M, 216.
18. Sacchetti, Rhyme 231; Legnano, 211–16; Keen, *Chivalry.*

Chapter 10: The Atrocities in Romagna, 1376–7

1. *Memoirs of a Renaissance Pope*, 76.
2. Legnano was consulted by Charles V of France about the validity of the Treaty of Brétigny: Keen, *Nobles, Knights and Men-at-Arms*, 225.
3. Legnano, chs 43–8, pp. 265–8.
4. Christine de Pisan, 15.
5. *Epistolario di Coluccio Salutati*, vol. 16, 157.
6. Muratori, vol. 16, 1097 (Sozomeno); vol. 18, 501 (Bologna), 86 (Reggio); Stefani, 296.
7. Muratori, vol. 15, 221–2 (Siena).
8. Bruni, vol. 2, 487.
9. Brucker, 77.
10. The Statute regarding Purveyance, 1362; Langland, 56.
11. Muratori, vol. 15, 500 (Este); 917 (Rimini).
12. Muratori, vol. 15, 252–3 (Siena), 500 (Este), 917–18 (Rimini); vol. 16, 1100 (Sozomeno); vol. 18, 87 (Reggio).
13. Muratori, vol. 18, 87 (Reggio); vol. 16, 762 (Milan).

14. Sacchetti, Rhyme 194, line 102.
15. Balestracci, in *Condottieri*, 10.
16. Bruni, vol. 2, 507.
17. *Memoirs of a Renaissance Pope*, 195.

Conclusion: Hero or Villain? The Reputation of Giovanni Acuto

1. G R Owst, *Literature and Pulpit in Medieval England* (Oxford, 1961), 174.
2. *Epistolario di Coluccio Salutati*, vol. 16 (2), 157.
3. Keen, *Nobles, Knights and Men-at-Arms*, 71–2.
4. Stefani, 398, 403.
5. T&M, Documents 70–1; Muratori, vol. 19, 236 (Life of Carlo Zeno); 788 (Treviso).
6. Morant, vol. 2, 291.
7. There may have been a later woodcut, used in Rossi's *Ritratti* of 1647: T&M, 2.
8. This medal was subsequently sold to the Princess of Wales and then passed into the Royal Collection, but it is not there now, nor is it in the British Museum: Blackburne's *Memoirs of Thomas Hollis*, supplemented by enquiries of the Royal Collection and the Curator of Medals at the BM. See also Edward Hawkins, *Medallic Illustrations of the History of GB and Ireland* (London, 1885), 6.
9. T&M did not accept that Hawkwood was ever a tailor, but Fowler (*ODNB* 2004) – citing the Westminster chronicle – does not exclude the possibility.
10. Smail, 93.
11. CPR Richard II 1377–81, 277; 1381–5, 433; 1391–6, 98; and CCR 1377–81, 367; 1392–6, 465.
12. Murimuth, vol. 2, 122; Muratori, vol. 16, 821; Walsingham, 292; *Westminster Chronicle*, 521; Mortimer, *Fears of Henry IV*, 98.

Appendices

1. Castiglion Fiorentino had a Franciscan church, which still survives. The town was known as Castiglion Aretino when it belonged to the town of Arezzo, but the name was changed when the Florentines took control.
2. An exaggeration.
3. Sacchetti is speaking of mercenaries, especially foreigners.
4. Sacchetti was a Prior himself for a short time.
5. On the Arezzo side of the city.
6. Dabbudà – a nickname for someone who told lies, derived from a musical instrument.
7. Calendar of Select Pleas and Memoranda, 308–9. The original plea roll is in the London Metropolitan Archives.

Bibliography

Primary Sources
Published Documents and Letters
Calendar of Close Rolls [CCR]
Calendar of Patent Rolls [CPR]
Calendar of Select Pleas and Memoranda of the City of London AD 1381–1412, ed. A H Thomas (Cambridge University Press 1926–43)
Calendar of State Papers [CSP] Milan, vol. 1 (HMSO 1912)
Calendar of State Papers [CSP] Venice, vol. 1 (HMSO 1864)
Colliva, Paolo, Cardinal Albernoz, *The States of the Church and the Egidian Constitutions* (Bologna, 1977)
Dean, Trevor (ed.), *The Towns of Italy in the Later Middle Ages* (Manchester University Press 2000)
Egidian Constitutions, 1357: *Costituzioni Egidiane dell'anno MCCCLVII*, ed. Pietro Sella (1912)
Epistolario di Santa Caterina da Siena, 1, *Fonti per la Storia d'Italia*, Historical Institute of Italy (Rome, 1940)
Epistolario di Pier Paolo Vergerio, Fonti 74 (Rome, 1934)
Epistolario di Coluccio Salutati, Fonti 15–18 (Rome, 1891)
Feet of Fines for Essex, vol. 3, 1327–1422, Essex Archaeological Society (Colchester, 1949)
Mézières, Philippe de, *Letter to King Richard II: A plea made in 1395 for peace between England and France*, trans. G W Coopland (Liverpool, 1975)
Noffke, Suzanne (ed.), *The Letters of St Catherine of Siena*, Medieval and Renaissance Texts and Studies (New York, 1988)
Papal Letters: *Calendar of Entries in the Papal Registers of Great Britain and Ireland*, Papal Letters vol. 4, 1362–1404 (London, 1902)
Perroy, Edouard (ed.), *The Diplomatic Correspondence of Richard II*, Camden Third Series, vol. 48 (London, 1933)
Rolls of Parliament (*Rotuli Parliamentorum*), vol. 2, 1326–77
Rymer, *Foedera* (London, 1869)

Statutes of Faenza (*Statuta Faventiae*), vol. 1 in *Rerum Italicarum Scriptores*, ed. L A Muratori (Bologna, 1929)

Willement, Thomas (ed.), *A Roll of Arms of the Reign of Richard the Second* (1834)

Chronicles, Annals, Treatises and Literature

Anon., *Sir Gawain and the Green Knight*, trans. Brian Stone (Penguin, 1974)

Barber, Richard, *Life and Campaigns of the Black Prince* (The Boydell Press, 1979)

Boccaccio, Giovanni, *The Decameron* (Oxford World's Classics, 1993)

Bruni, Leonardo, *History of the Florentine People*, ed. and trans. James Hankins (I Tatti Renaissance Library, Harvard, 2001)

Castiglione, Baldessare, *The Book of the Courtier*, trans. George Bull (Penguin, 1976)

Charny, Geoffroi de, *The Book of Chivalry*, ed. and trans. Richard W Kaeuper and Elspeth Kennedy (University of Pennsylvania Press, 1996)

Chaucer, Geoffrey, *The Canterbury Tales* (Oxford World's Classics, 1998)

Christine de Pisan, *The Book of Deeds of Arms and of Chivalry* ed. and trans. C C Willard (Penn State Press, 2003)

Cronaca Fiorentina di Marchionne di Coppo di Stefani (Città di Castello, 1903)

Dante, *The Divine Comedy of Dante Alighieri*, trans. John D Sinclair, vol. 1, *Inferno* (Oxford University Press with The Bodley Head, 1961)

Dati, *L' Istoria di Firenze dal 1380 al 1405* (Norcia, 1902)

Fortescue, Sir John, *De Laudibus Legum Angliae*, ed. and trans. S B Chrimes (Cambridge University Press, 1942)

Froissart, *Froissart's Chronicles*, ed. and trans. Geoffrey Brereton (Penguin Classics, 1968)

Jean le Bel, *Chronique*, ed. Jules Viard and Eugène Déprez (Paris, 1905)

Langland, Willam, *Piers the Ploughman*, trans. J F Goodridge (Penguin Classics, 1966)

Legnano, John of, *Tractatus De Bello, De Represaliis et De Duello* ed. T E Holland (Oxford University Press, 1917)

Lull, Ramon, *Book of Knighthood and Chivalry*, Caxton's edition, trans. Brian R Price (London: Greenhill, 2001)

Machiavelli, Niccolò, *The Prince* trans. George Bull (Penguin Classics, 1964); *Il Principe* (Einaudi Tascabili, 1995)

——, *Life of Castruccio Castracani* (London: Hesperus Press, 2003)

Malory, Sir Thomas, *Le Morte d'Arthur* (Everyman, 1961)

Memoirs of a Renaissance Pope: The Commentaries of Pius II, trans. Florence A Gragg, ed. Leona Gabel (George Allen & Unwin, 1960)

Mézières, Philippe de, *The Dream of the Old Pilgrim (Le Songe du Vieil Pèlerin)* [1389], trans. G W Coopland (Cambridge University Press, 1969)

Muratori, L A, *Rerum Italicarum Scriptores* (Milan, 1723–51)

Murimuth, *The Continuation of Trivet and Murimuth's Chronicle*, 2 vols (Oxford, 1719–22)

Petrarch, *Selections from the Canzoniere and Other Works* (Oxford World's Classics, 1999)

Sacchetti, Francesco, *Il Libro delle Rime*, ed. Franca Brambilla Ageno and Leo S Olschki, Italian Medieval and Renaissance Studies 1 (University of Western Australia Press, 1990)

——, *Il Trecentonovelle*, ed. Davide Puccini, Classici Italiani, (Turin, 2004)

Sercambi, *Cronache di Giovanni Sercambi Lucchese*, vol. 19 (1), *Fonti per la Storia d'Italia* (Rome, 1892)

Stefani: see *Cronaca Fiorentina*

Thalamus Parvus, or *Le Petit Thalamus de Montpellier* (Montpellier, 1840)

Vegetius, *Epitome of Military Science*, trans. with notes and introduction N P Milner (Liverpool, 2001)

Walsingham, *Chronicle of Thomas Walsingham 1376–1422* (The Boydell Press, 2005)

Westminster Chronicle 1381–1394 (Oxford: Clarendon Press, 1982)

Secondary Sources

Allmand, C T (ed.), *War, Literature and Politics in the late Middle Ages* (New York: Barnes & Noble, 1976)

Allmand, Christopher, *Lancastrian Normandy, 1415–1450* (Oxford: Clarendon Press, 1983)

——, 'The De Re Militari of Vegetius', *History Today* (June 2004)

Balestracci, Duccio, *Le Armi, i Cavalli, l'Oro* (Rome, 2003)

——, *La Festa in armi* (Rome and Bari: Economica Laterza, 2003)

Barber, Richard, *The Knight and Chivalry* (The Boydell Press, 2000)

Barker, Juliet, *Agincourt* (Abacus, 2006)

Baron, Hans, *The Crisis of the Early Italian Renaissance* (Princeton, 1966)

Barzini, Luigi, *The Italians* (Penguin, 1968)

Bellamy, J G, *The Law of Treason in the Later Middle Ages* (Cambridge University Press, 1970)

Bennett, Matthew, Jim Bradbury, Kelly Devries, Iain Dickie and Phyllis Jestice, *Fighting Techniques of the Medieval World AD 500–AD 1500* (Amber Books, 2005)

Biggs, Douglas, *Three Armies in Britain* (Leiden and Boston: Brill, 2006)

Blackstone, William, *Commentaries on the Laws of England* (Oxford: Clarendon Press, 1765–9)

Brucker, Gene A, *Renaissance Florence* (University of California Press, 1969)

Burckhardt, Jacob, *The Civilisation of the Renaissance in Italy* (Penguin, 1990)

Burke's General Armory of England, Scotland, Ireland and Wales (1884)

Caferro, William, *John Hawkwood: An English Mercenary in Fourteenth-Century Italy* (Johns Hopkins University Press, 2006)

Canestrini, Giuseppe, *Documenti della Milizia italiana dal secolo XIII al XVI* (1860)

Chambers D S, *Popes, Cardinals and War* (London and New York: I B Tauris, 2006)

Conti, Giordano, *La Rocca Malatestiana di Cesena* (Milan: Fabbri Editori, 1990)

Curry, Anne, *Sex and the Soldier in Lancastrian Normandy, 1415–1450*, Reading Medieval Studies, 14 (1988)

Dean, Trevor, 'Marriage and mutilation: vendetta in late medieval Italy', *Past & Present* (November 1997)

Deiss, Joseph Jay, *Captains of Fortune: Profiles of Six Italian Condottieri* (London: Victor Gollancz, 1966)

Del Treppo, Mario (ed.), *Condottieri e uomini d'arme* (Naples: Liguori Editore, 2001)

Denifle, Henri, *La Desolation des eglises pendant la Guerre de Cent Ans* (Paris, 1899)

Donati, Ignazio, *Memorie e Documenti per la Storia di Montopoli* (Montopoli Val d'Arno, 1903)

Dunn, Alastair, *The Peasants' Revolt: England's Failed Revolution of 1381* (Tempus, 2004)

Dupré, Guy, *Le Pont de Pont-Saint-Esprit* (Nimes: Lacour, 2002)

Echi e Memoria di un Condottiero, Giovanni Acuto (Castiglion Fiorentino, 1994)

English Historical Documents, vol. IV: *1327–1485* (Eyre & Spottiswoode, 1969)

Fortescue, the Rt Hon. J W, *A History of the British Army*, vol. 1 (The Naval & Military Press, 2004)

Fowler, Kenneth, *Plantagenet and Valois* (London: Elek Books, 1967)

——, *The King's Lieutenant: Henry of Grosmont, First Duke of Lancaster 1310–1361* (London: Elek Books, 1969)

——, *Medieval Mercenaries*, vol. 1 (Blackwell, 2001)

Gallorini, Santino, *Montecchio Vesponi* (Calosci and Cortina, 1993)

Ghizzi, Giuseppe, *Cenni Storici sopra Il Castello di Montecchio Vesponi* (Castiglion Fiorentino, 1874)

Girard, Alain (ed.), *Images du Pont-Saint-Esprit* (Pont-Saint-Esprit, 2003)

Goodman, Anthony, *The Wars of the Roses* (Tempus, 2005)

Gough, Richard, *Memoirs of Sir Hawkwood* in J Nichols FSA, *Bibliotheca Topographica Britannica*, vol. 6 (1780)

Gouran, Marcel, *Histoire de la Ville de Pont-Saint-Esprit* (Paris: Le Livre d'Histoire-Lorisse, 2006)

Grant, R G, *Battle: A Visual Journey Through 5,000 Years of Combat* (Dorling Kindersley, 2005)

Gravett, Christopher, *Medieval Siege Warfare* (Osprey, 1990)

Green, David, *Edward the Black Prince: Power in Medieval Europe* (Pearson Longman, 2007)

Harriss, Gerald, *Shaping the Nation: England 1360–1461*, The New Oxford History of England (Oxford, 2005)

Hewitt, H J, *The Horse in Medieval England* (London: J A Allen & Co., 1983)

——, *The Black Prince's Expedition* (Pen & Sword Military, 2004)

——, *The Organisation of War Under Edward III* (Pen & Sword Military, 2004)

Holmes, George, 'Florence and the Great Schism', in G Holmes (ed.), *Art and Politics in Renaissance Italy* (British Academy Lectures, Oxford University Press, 1995)

—— (ed.), *The Oxford Illustrated History of Italy* (Oxford University Press, 2001)

Howard, Michael, *War in European History* (Oxford University Press, 1976)

Jager, Eric, *The Last Duel* (Arrow Books, 2006)

Jones, Michael (ed.), *The New Cambridge Medieval History*, VI: *c.1300–c.1415*, (Cambridge, 2000)

Jones, Terry, *Chaucer's Knight*, (Methuen, 1994)

——, *Medieval Lives* (BBC Books, 2005)

—— (with Robert Yeager, Terry Dolan, Alan Fletcher and Juliette Dor), *Who Murdered Chaucer?* (Methuen, 2004)

Keegan, John, *The Mask of Command* (Pimlico, 2004)

——, *Intelligence in War* (Pimlico, 2004)

Keen, Maurice, *The Laws of War in the late Middle Ages* (Routledge and Kegan Paul, 1965)

——, *Chivalry* (Yale University Press, 1984)

——, 'Richard II's Ordinances of War of 1385', in R E Archer and S Walker (eds), *Rulers and Ruled in Late Medieval England* (Hambledon Press, 1995)

——, *Nobles, Knights and Men-at-Arms in the Middle Ages* (Hambledon Press, 1996)

—— (ed.), *Medieval Warfare: A History* (Oxford, 1999)

——, *Origins of the English Gentleman* (Tempus, 2002)

Kekewich, Margaret L and Susan Rose, *Britain, France and the Empire 1350–1500* (Macmillan, 2005)

Kohl, Benjamin G, *Padua under the Carrara, 1318–1405* (Johns Hopkins University Press, 1998)

Larner, John, *The Lords of Romagna* (Macmillan, 1964)

——, 'Crossing the Romagnol Apennines in the Renaissance', in Trevor Dean and Chris Wickham (eds), *City and Countryside in Late Medieval and Renaissance Italy* (Hambledon Press, 1990)

Lewis, R W B, *Dante* (Weidenfeld & Nicolson, 2001)

McFarlane, K B, *The Nobility of Later Medieval England* (Oxford, 1973)

McKisack, May, *The Fourteenth Century: 1307–1399* (Oxford, 1959)

Majendie, the Rev. Severne, *Some Account of the Family of De Vere* (Castle Hedingham and London, 1904)

Mallett, Michael, *Mercenaries and Their Masters* (The Bodley Head, 1974)

Mancini, Augusto, *Storia di Lucca* (Maria Pacini Fazzi Editore, 1999)

Matilli, Giuseppe, *La Via del Grano e de Sale* (Grafiche di Marradi, 1988)

Morant, Philip, *The History and Antiquities of the County of Essex* (London, 1768)

Mortimer, Ian, *The Fears of Henry IV* (Jonathan Cape, 2007)

——, *The Perfect King: The Life of Edward III* (Pimlico, 2007)

Morton, H V, *A Traveller in Italy* (Methuen, 2006)

Muir, Dorothy, *A History of Milan under the Visconti* (Methuen, 1924)

ODNB: Oxford Dictionary of National Biography, 1st edn 1917; 2nd edn 2004 (Oxford University Press)

Oman, Sir Charles, *A History of the Art of War in the Middle Ages*, vol. 2: *1278–1485* (Greenhill Books, 1998)

Origo, Iris, *The Merchant of Prato* (Penguin, 1992)

Ormrod, W M, *The Reign of Edward III* (Tempus, 2000)

Pearsall, Derek, *The Life of Geoffrey Chaucer* (Blackwell, 1994)

Perroy, Edouard, *L'Angleterre et le Grand Schisme* (Paris, 1933)

Pollard, A J, *John Talbot and the War in France 1417–1453* (Pen & Sword, 2005)

Prestwich, Michael, *Armies and Warfare in the Middle Ages: The English Experience* (Yale, 1996)

——, *Plantagenet England 1225–1360* (Oxford University Press, 2007)

Price, Brian R, *Ramon Lull's Book of Knighthood and Chivalry* (Chivalry Bookshelf, 2001)

Procacci, Giuliano, *History of the Italian People* (Penguin, 1991)

Rendina, Claudio, *I capitani di ventura* (Rome: Newton & Compton, 2004)

Renouard, Yves, *The Avignon Papacy* (Barnes & Noble Books, 1994)

Ricotti, Ercole, *Storia delle Compagnie di Ventura in Italia* (Turin, 1844)

Rubinstein, N (ed.), *Florentine Studies: Politics and Society in Renaissance Florence* (Faber & Faber, 1968)

Russell, P E, *The English Intervention in Spain and Portugal in the Reign of Edward III and Richard II* (Oxford, 1955)

Saul, Nigel, *Richard II* (Yale University Press, 1997)

Saunders, Frances Stonor, *Hawkwood: Diabolical Englishman* (Faber & Faber, 2004)

Scattergood, V J and J W Sherborne (eds), *English Court Culture in the Later Middle Ages* (New York: St Martin's Press, 1983)

Schevill, Ferdinand, *History of Florence* (London: G Bell & Sons, 1937)

Seward, Desmond, *The Hundred Years War* (Constable, 1996)

Slater, Stephen, *The Illustrated Book of Heraldry* (Hermes House, 2006)

Smail, R C, *Crusading Warfare, 1097–1193* (Cambridge, 1956)

Southern, R W, *The Making of the Middle Ages* (Hutchinson, 1967)

Spufford, Peter, *Power and Profit* (Thames & Hudson, 2002)

Squibb, G D, *The High Court of Chivalry* (Oxford, 1959)

Staffa, Stefano, *Cotignola Ricorda* (Walberti Edizioni, 2003)

Strickland, Matthew (ed.), *Anglo-Norman Warfare* (The Boydell Press, 1992)

—— and Robert Hardy, *The Great Warbow* (Sutton Publishing, 2005)

Sumption, Jonathan, *The Hundred Years War*, vol. 1: *Trial by Battle*; vol. 2: *Trial by Fire* (Faber & Faber, 1990, 1999)

Temple-Leader, John and Giuseppe Marcotti, *Sir Hawkwood (L'Acuto): Story of a Condottiere* (London: T Fisher Unwin, 1889) [T&M]; republished Martino Publishing, 2005

Tigler, Guido, *Figline e il Valdarno* (Florence: Opus Libri, 1990)

Trease, Geoffrey, *The Condottieri: Soldiers of Fortune* (Holt, Rinehart and Winston, 1971)

Tuchman, Barbara, *A Distant Mirror: The Calamitous Fourteenth Century* (Papermac, Macmillan, 1978)

Urban, William, *Medieval Mercenaries: The Business of War* (Greenhill Books, 2006)

Vale, M G A, *English Gascony 1399–1453* (Oxford University Press, 1970)

Vasari, Giorgio, *The Lives of the Artists* (Oxford World's Classics, 1998)

Vernier, Richard, *The Flower of Chivalry: Bertrand du Guesclin and the Hundred Years War* (The Boydell Press, 2003)

Waley, Daniel, *The Italian-City Republics* (Longman, 1988)

Walker, Simon, 'Profit and loss in the Hundred Years' War', *Bulletin of the Institute of Historical Studies* 58 (1985)

——, *The Lancastrian Affinity* (Oxford, 1990)

Weever, John, *Ancient Funeral Monuments* (1631)

West, Richard, *Chaucer 1340–1400: The Life and Times of the First English Poet* (Constable, 2000)

Zucchini, Stefania (ed.), *Condottieri, War and Society in Central Italy in the Fourteenth Century*, Working Papers of the Uggucione Ranieri di Sorbello Foundation, no. 11 (Perugia, 2006)

I have also benefited from reading two theses submitted to the University of Siena in 2005–6, and from discussion with the authors: *Il Castello di Montecchio Vesponi: Il sistema defensivo nel contesto territoriale della Valdichiana* by Paola Orecchioni; and *Montecchio Vesponi: Storia di un Castello attraverso l'archaeologia dell'architettura* by Fabio Giovannini.

Websites

www.castellodimontecchiovesponi.it
www.castellitoscani.com
www.comune.bagnacavallo.ra.it
www.comune.cotignola.ra.it
www.condottieridiventura.it
www.cronologia.it
www.deremilitari.org
www.fiore.the-exiles.org
www.historytoday.com
www.h-net.org/reviews
www.nipissing.ca/department/history/muhlberger/froissart
http://users.skynet.be/antoine.mechelynck/chroniq/froissart
www.wikipedia.org

Index

Bold type indicates the fullest entry.